GOAL IN PROGRESS

The Detours and Diversions *of a* Spiritual Journey

Bhikkhu Nyanadhammika

GOAL IN PROGRESS
The Detours and Diversions of a Spiritual Journey
Copyright © 2024 by Bhikkhu Nyanadhammika

All rights reserved. This book or any portion thereof may not be reproduced or used in any manner whatsoever without the express written permission of the publisher, except for the use of brief quotations in a book review.

Printed in the United States of America

Luminare Press
442 Charnelton St.
Eugene, OR 97401
www.luminarepress.com

LCCN: 2024905335
ISBN: 979-8-88679-527-1

To spiritual travelers of all religious traditions

Praise for GOAL IN PROGRESS

"This memoir of awakening caught me like a fly in a web. The author's personal story is finely woven, and a call to the reader to contemplate our place in the world with renewed seriousness."

—JON M. SWEENEY, coauthor,
Meister Eckhart's Book of the Heart; author,
*Sit in the Sun: And Other Lessons in the
Spiritual Wisdom of Cats*

"This book is particularly helpful because it traces the story of a man who was always convinced of having some kind of contemplative calling, and was willing to engage with a number of traditions over many years to find the best expression of that calling. What comes across is a growing sense of assurance that the best guide in the journey is the inner voice that points out where to go, when to move on, and what has been learned—as in St John of the Cross's great poem, On A Dark Night, it is the inner light that alone offers reliable guidance. We know that this conviction is not always appreciated by religious institutions, and yet in these unbalanced times, perhaps it is time to appreciate anew that inner voice, the inner light. Gurus, abbots, rinpoches, close friends, and even opponents have much to offer, but in the end, it is the voice of conscience that transforms the seeking heart in ways that have to be lived to be truly known. This is a book to be read with pen and notebook at hand."

—(THE REV. CANON) FRANCIS V. TISO, author of
*Liberation in One Lifetime: Biographies and Teachings of
Milarepa*, and: *Rainbow Body and Resurrection: The Dissolution
of the Material Body and the Case of Khenpo A Chö*

"The author's narrative presence is warm and very human; he writes about his various spiritual adventures with an unflagging energy and specificity....[T]he earnest nature of Nyanadhammika's spiritual walkabout will make this an involving read for all of his fellow seekers. A vividly personal story of a spiritual odyssey across faiths."

—*Kirkus Reviews*

"In this engrossing and courageous memoir, Bhikkhu Nyanadhammika recounts his fifty-year spiritual quest, a journey marked by what he refers to as "detours" through various spiritual traditions. These detours brought him, as they can bring all sincere spiritual seekers, to an enlightened understanding of human fulfillment, the goal of every spiritual endeavor."

—Fr. William Skudlarek, OSB, Secretary General of Monastic Interreligious Dialogue (DIM-MID)

"The author writes with candor in detailing his spiritual journey initially motivated by a search for meaning in life, as he takes the reader through his explorations in the Hindu, Tibetan and Theravada Buddhist, Benedictine and Orthodox Christian monastic traditions. He comes to acknowledge and reclaim his own Jewish roots, and subsequently returns to monastic life in the Theravada Buddhist tradition, enriched by the experiences and discoveries of his decades-long sojourn in the different religions he traversed. A refreshing resource for spiritual seekers in our multireligious global society."

—Ruben L.F. Habito, Professor of World Religions and Spirituality, Perkins School of Theology, Southern Methodist University; author of *Living Zen, Loving God; Zen and the Spiritual Exercises; Be Still and Know: Zen and the Bible,* and other titles

CONTENTS

Introduction 1

Negotiating Ways of Life

1. Initial Awakening 7
2. A Cross-Country Spiritual Odyssey 20
3. In the City by the Bay 49
4. Protracted Distractions in Berlin 64

The Heart of the Journey

5. Academic Diversion and
   Re-Discovery of Buddhism 105
6. A Turn to Tibet 127
7. Buddhist Monastic Life:
   Two Colors, Two Traditions 180
8. An Unexpected Detour 226
9. Journey Eastwards:
   The Call of the Jesus Prayer 260
10. Awakening to My Jewish Roots 297
11. Lay-Life Interlude 312
12. A Buddhist Monk (Again) 324

Afterword 339

INTRODUCTION

I put off writing a narrative account of my spiritual journey because I thought it would not be helpful to dwell on the past. For I was seeking freedom from thoughts, regrets, and musings on perceived mistakes. But friends, acquaintances, and family members who had witnessed my ongoing journey from their perspectives often remarked that I should put it down in writing and that my experiences would be of interest, and maybe even beneficial, for others to read. Thus, as I approach my 70th birthday and am in an environment conducive for devoting many hours to this task, I thought I would finally write it.

This is not a full account of my life. I am narrating the story of my spiritual journey towards attaining a vaguely defined goal—a goal that over time I would understand to be reaching a level of awakened awareness by which I perceive all external and internal phenomena, and especially the convention of "I" and "me," as they truly are. I have left out most of the personal and intimate encounters I had over the years, particularly in the early decades, as narrating them would have taken me away from the main subject of the narrative. Also, my spiritual journey has been travelled by me alone, as any spiritual journey must. Even if one treads a path together with a partner or any other individual, the essence of the journey is experienced and travelled internally by each person individually.

As will become evident, my path has not been linear and my goal, fuzzy in the beginning, has been a work in progress. During the course of nearly fifty years, my awareness of what it was exactly that I was seeking began gradually to become more focused as I let notions and ideals that I had outgrown—or no longer found relevant—slip away, though each has left a mark on my consciousness.

Many spiritual journeys can be likened to traveling along an interstate. It may at some point go through a tunnel, maybe even a very long one, but it then comes out into daylight and one is aware that it is the same road as it was before the darkness descended. My journey, however, has been like a country road, for example Rt. 29 East. Periodically it goes through a small town and the road turns right, then left, and right again, maybe joining with other routes, and then continues again in the open countryside, having left behind the other routes. But then sometimes there is road construction. One sees the sign, Rt. 29 East Detour. As the driver follows along the detour route, Rt. 29 East may hook up with one or more routes, each perhaps having a different direction marker, yet the road upon which one is driving is going in only one direction and the sign indicating Rt. 29 East appears now and then, as if to remind the driver that this is still the same route. Eventually the detour ends and Rt. 29 East continues without any further obstacle.

There have been detours and diversions on my journey that may at first seem to be mistakes or misguided movements. All of them were voluntary, yet I felt compelled to make each one—a major change in direction when I felt I had encountered an obstruction to progress. My entry into Tibetan Buddhism was my first major detour and after a temporary return to the Early Buddhist road I had been following previously, I made an even greater, prolonged detour into Christianity. But I hope it will become clear to readers that these changes in direction or emphasis are actually part of the journey. For a detour is not a dead-end. It merely takes drivers on a different route but then leads them back to the road they had been travelling on. The landscape might have changed but the road is the same one. And so it has been with my spiritual journey. I was led for different reasons in a direction I had not anticipated but I never felt I made a wrong turn, and thus on no occasion was I inclined to turn back and return to the point from which I seemingly diverted from the main path. While my departure from Buddhism to continue in a Christian tradition shocked many people, it was not a tangential aberration, not an unfortunate waste of time, but a necessary segment of the journey. Admittedly, I did not and could not have this complete picture at the time the event occurred. From the perspective of hindsight, everything seems clearer. But after each detour in my journey, I gained greater clarity of what my goal was by determining clearly what it was not. Thus, the change in direction was not extraneous to my ongoing path.

I do not attempt to explain or give teachings about any of the religious traditions I have experienced. I am not qualified to do so and there are many resources available for those wishing to learn about a particular religious or spiritual tradition. This is first and foremost a personal narrative of my journey—a journey motivated by a search for meaning in life. Once I had caught a glimpse of seeing the world, and my life, otherwise, I was prompted to begin the search to live in that transcendent state of awareness. I was propelled by an inner force that I could not articulate even to myself, and certainly not to my friends or family. But I listened to that voice and became more astute in discerning it.

It is my heartfelt wish that readers will find inspiration in this autobiographical account of an indefatigable quest for enlightened awareness and clarity of vision regarding the subtle layers of self-identification.

In order to keep the narrative focused mainly on my spiritual journey, I have left out scores of people who in some way played a part as I traveled my path. I thank them in silence.

Negotiating Ways of Life

CHAPTER 1

Initial Awakening

I identify the beginning of my spiritual journey to have occurred on a late afternoon in early October 1974. I was sitting with my good friend and housemate, Bonnie, on the steps of the wrap-around front porch of a late Victorian house on a hill in the upstate college town of Oneonta, New York. We were afforded a spectacular view of the northern Catskill hills across the valley ablaze in autumnal color. The late-day sun was soft yet at the same time of brilliant quality as it shone on the wooded hillside. I had already experienced a few upstate autumns as this was my senior year at SUNY Oneonta but this autumnal scene was different, for my vision, or better, my perception of the scene was enhanced by the hit of mescaline I had dropped about a half-hour before. This was my first "trip" and Bonnie had suggested that we sit outside on the porch and view the foliage as we "got off."

I consider my spiritual journey to have begun on that day but I did not realize I was on a spiritual journey until sometime later. Yet in a momentary flash that occurred while gazing at the brilliant scene, I understood that there was a level of reality beyond what I normally experienced.

The drug prompted me to have an inkling of a transcendent mode of being—one that was not dependent on the drug itself. Mescaline was merely the catalyst. While this initial glimpse of unbiased reality would fade after I returned to "normalcy," the practical, material aspect of that momentary cognizance made an indelible mark on my consciousness. I would like to think that I had the epiphany which would redirect my life during that initial mescaline trip but it was probably on a subsequent "trip" in the weeks that followed. On that occasion, I had the unmistakable realization that my professional goal to pursue a career in dentistry was the wrong one to follow. I clearly recall that while tripping with my friends and housemates, deeply listening to a piece of music, probably Mozart, but possibly early Jazz or modern jazz guitar, in a flash I knew that I had to abandon the road to becoming a dentist. I understood at that moment that what had prompted me in my senior year in high school to embark on that career goal was a romanticized image of being a country dentist in a beautiful upstate New York town—the polar opposite of the Queens neighborhood in New York City where I had grown up. In a split second, which in "tripping" time felt a lot longer, I knew that I did not want to spend my life looking and puttering around in people's mouths.

That moment of realization, however, did not provide any indication of the direction I should follow. No idea of a new profession to pursue or a way to utilize a degree in Biology manifested. Later that year, I considered careers in forest management, horticulture, and finally crop science (strangely each career idea leading me downwards to the soil), but ultimately I would pursue none of them. Nevertheless, the third choice led me to move to Ithaca, New York, and enroll in a few agriculture courses at Cornell University as a non-matriculated student and subsequently apply to the master's program in crop science. None of this actually *directly* relates to embarking on a spiritual journey. Yet, it created the conditions, the causes, for the initial embarkation on that path of no return.

Leaving Oneonta and my close friends was traumatic. I lingered on there for a semester after graduating as they were all one year behind me. This was 1975 and we were influenced by the popularity in that post-hippie era of living on communes in rural areas. We had often talked about setting up a communal life together in the country, living simply, "close to the land." I actually believed that this was a real possibility. But, when I saw that my three friends were not planning to transform those idyllic musings into real action, I decided to move to Ithaca and pursue graduate work in crop science, eventually establishing a life somewhere in upstate New York. My tripping/pot-smoking companion, Michael, gave me a book to take with me for the journey into my new life in Ithaca: Hermann Hesse's *Demian*. I believe that after reading this book I *knowingly* began my spiritual journey in that I understood that there was a way of living one's life as an unfolding of some sort of ongoing spiritual awakening.

I rented a small furnished room in a run-down old house in the Collegetown neighborhood adjacent to Cornell University. In late March I recall sitting on the front porch eagerly opening a letter from graduate admissions at Cornell University. When I read the terse statement that I was not accepted into the graduate program in crop science, I felt the ground give way beneath my feet. But a few minutes later, I felt a sense of relief. I was free from career plans. I could now follow a path of life unconstrained by academic and professional goals. Yet I still did not have a clear idea of what that path was nor did I actually understand what ultimate knowledge I was hoping to gain.

Ithaca was a very progressive town at that time and there were a number of very good bookstores with books on eastern philosophy and spirituality. Some of the books I read then were Alan Watt's *This is It* and *The Way of Zen*, *The Awakening of Intelligence* by Krishnamurti, Suzuki's *Zen Mind, Beginner's Mind* and many others, including all of the works by Hermann Hesse. I had seen someone in a park down by Cayuga Lake doing yoga poses and I decided to copy some of them. I also sat in the chair in my little room a few times a day and attempted to quiet my chattering mind. Occasionally, I attended a small group meditation sit in a house in town. Most sat on high round cushions and kept their eyes open. I realized they were probably practicing Zen meditation. I attempted to copy them but had difficulty concentrating with my eyes open. I felt shy to ask anyone there for meditation instructions and so I just carried on by myself, trying to glean from books what kind of meditation practice I should do. Meanwhile, I had stopped eating meat (I just lost my taste for it). I also no longer felt the need to smoke pot. However, I still had a few hits of LSD which I was saving for the right occasion.

My motivation to have an intense spiritual experience that would perhaps prompt an epiphany or at least some realization that would surpass that which I had had in Oneonta on mescaline led me to embark on a LSD trip alone (which I had never done before). I was in fact so enthusiastic about this that I decided to drop two hits of blotter acid—a recklessness regarding hallucinogens that was uncharacteristic of me. So, on a beautiful Saturday in early spring, I took two hits of LSD and proceeded to walk to the gorge on the Cornell campus. I went down the steep path so that I was actually nestled within the gorge, looking up at the suspension bridge (popularly known as "suicide bridge" as it was, sadly, used by one or two students each year as a site for ending their life by plunging down several hundred feet into the gorge). On that sunny mild afternoon I was not thinking about the suicides at that site but rather just sitting and waiting to "get off." When I felt that familiar rising of exhilaration, I decided to walk up out of the gorge since I was feeling closed in there. I walked around the lake; a path I often took because it was surrounded by stately trees. Today, however, the tall majestic trees did not usher in feelings of serenity, but instead seemed menacing. As fear and anxiety set in, I opted to head back to my room. As luck would have it, just as I was making my way across the campus, a football game had just let out and crowds of people suddenly appeared. I walked in their midst seemingly carried along by them. After what felt like an extremely long journey, I reached Collegetown and nearly ran the rest of the way to my abode. I had the urgent need for being in a secluded and safe place.

With great relief I entered my tiny room, closed the door and pulled down the shades as the sunlight streaming in assaulted my eyes. I plopped down on my bed and just lay there as the walls shimmered and "breathed" in and out. Nothing in the room seemed to stand still. Even my bed was not stable on the floor. I held on to the sides of the bed hoping it would settle down. I then thought maybe some music would help quiet down my growing alarm. I chose a Mozart piano sonata, music that I always found ethereal and soothing in its simple beauty. But the sounds of the piano were now abrasive and jarring in my ears. I turned off the stereo and chose to read the *Tao de Ching*, in the edition that contained calligraphy of the verses accompanied by black and white photographs. However, I couldn't focus on the words, my mind just jumped all over the page. So, I traced the words with my finger, moving slowly from page to page. And, gradually, I calmed down. Despite this inner upheaval, somewhere deep in my mind was a stable presence that was determined to maintain control and not go off the deep end.

The hours were interminable but I then felt that I had passed the "peak" and had begun the long, but calm, journey of "coming down." I ate an orange despite not remembering if it was supposed to help one get off or come down on acid. It seemed, at least on this occasion, to have helped me come down. About ten hours after dropping the acid, I felt mentally exhausted, yet peaceful. The spiritual experience I had hoped for certainly turned out otherwise. I gained no new insights other than experiencing the survival instinct of my mind. I decided that this was my last trip. However, a few weeks later, Michael came for a visit from Oneonta. As I still had two hits of blotter acid left, I reconsidered my decision and opted to trip one last time with Michael, with whom I felt safe tripping as I had spent countless hours with him in Oneonta stoned on pot and each time I had taken mescaline or LSD it was with him. As he and I sat in my little room listening to music for hours, my mind returned to the previous year, where every evening Michael would come up to my room (even smaller than the one in Ithaca), and we would get stoned and listen to music for hours on the same stereo that was in my present room. We were then as now strongly bonded in silence as each of us, fueled with a drug, engaged in his individual imaginative flight. It turned out to be an enjoyable, undramatic trip. No spiritual epiphany occurred but I had the unmistakable realization that this was my final trip. I was very happy that Michael had come for a visit so that we could have one more drug-inspired bonding experience. But I was also glad because his visit allowed me to break with my past in Oneonta. I had changed and grown in the past months and had no further use for hallucinogens. If I wanted to understand reality I knew that it was going to be through meditation and pondering the teachings of Eastern religion, primarily Buddhism.

The spring semester of 1976 ended and I needed to find a job. I luckily found one in a local donut shop as a "fryer," a hot and greasy job, and I soon learned that my mind had to be fully focused on the task at hand. I realized that this type of directed attention would be helpful for me when attempting to meditate. I was content with my new life in Ithaca. I walked down into town every late afternoon, following the beautiful path through the Cascadilla Gorge at the edge of the Cornell Campus. I had a favorite spot along the cascading stream where I would sit and meditate for some time. Sitting beside the flowing water brought to my mind Hermann Hesse's classic work, *Siddhartha*. I tried to cultivate the quality of inner quietness in order to merge with the sound of the stream. Although I managed to quiet the ever-present mental chattering only for brief moments, I nearly always felt refreshed and at peace when I stood up to continue my long walk to the donut shop. Those daily walks allowed me to experience the changing of the seasons. I particularly loved how late summer gradually gave way to early autumn. The first chilly evening in late August, the subtle alteration of light, the beginning of color that would get more vibrant in the coming weeks. And then, suddenly, it was winter. My daily routine was regular and my mind was generally peaceful. I developed casual friendships with the few other young people who worked at the donut shop. But none of them was interested in following a Buddhist spiritual path. I was basically on my own, trying to find my way through reading books, mostly on Zen, and just sitting daily in rather unfocused meditation.

In late spring 1977, I decided to buy a car. I don't know how I scraped together the $1100 needed to purchase a 1971 VW Beetle but I did. The fact that I had never driven with a stick shift did not dissuade me. I simply learned as I drove. During the summer, I decided it was time to look for another place to live. I was tired of living in Collegetown and now with my car I had more options. During one of my frequent visits to the Somadhara natural bakery downtown, where the workers and customers were of a new-age/spiritual type (The young woman behind the counter called herself "Rain"), a hand-written note on the notice board caught my attention. Someone named Ananda was looking for a suitable person to share an apartment just outside of Ithaca. I assumed he was male, but wasn't absolutely sure. I also wondered if he might be from India. I phoned and an American male with a slight New York accent answered. He told me of the garden apartment a few miles from the Cornell campus he had found. I was happy to hear that he was likewise on a spiritual journey, although not Buddhist. He was involved with a neo-Hindu group, Ananda Marga (the Path of Bliss). I had never heard of it and learning more about it did not make it particularly appealing to me. For there was a guru in India, simply called "Baba" by his devotees. He didn't live in an ashram, but rather in prison. Apparently, Indira Gandhi didn't like him nor his group. (His spiritual name was Shrii Shrii Anandamurti, but referred to by his devotees as simply "Baba"). Those who had been initiated into Ananda Marga engaged in directed meditation, following the instructions given by an authorized teacher. In addition, there was a great deal of *kirtan* or devotional song addressed to the photo of the guru, in a white business shirt and wearing black-framed glasses, who looked expressionlessly at the devotees singing to him with their arms above their head, palms facing outwards.

Although I was hesitant about getting involved with this group, I liked Ananda. He was a year older than me, from the Westchester suburbs of NYC, and had attended the State University of NY at Buffalo. He had seemingly large bulging eyes that were not menacing but rather kind and bright. In fact, he was often smiling. A very pleasant and warm person, I thought, and I knew he and I would get along sharing an apartment. I was happy to finally have a friend in Ithaca.

The meditation method practiced in Ananda Marga emphasized the chakras, with the goal of directly realizing infinite, eternal consciousness. There were a series of six lessons that initiates would receive. The sixth one, reportedly was a tantric practice. But only very advanced practitioners would receive instructions in that. While I was not particularly drawn to the spiritual practice of this sect, I did appreciate and slowly became involved in the social aspects. The group ran a pre-school in town which also served as the meeting place on Sunday mornings for group *kirtan* followed by a communal breakfast and socializing. The members who came regularly on Sunday, around twelve, were young, very warm and friendly. Although it was essentially a lay organization, there were some ordained members, *acariyas* (sort of monastic teachers) who had the title of *dadas* and *didis* (male and female, respectively). They wore bright orange garb and had shaven heads.

An important moment that led me deeper into this sect was meeting a charismatic *dada* from Germany, Dada Lokesh. He was probably around 30 years old, was deeply committed to Ananda Marga and, from my very limited understanding, seemed to be spiritually advanced. He had a genuinely calm demeanor and very clear, blue eyes that looked directly at the person with whom he was engaged in spiritual conversation. I had the chance to speak with him one-on-one while he was staying at the pre-school for a few days. Whatever apprehensions I had about this Hindu group that was devoted to a guru sitting in prison dissipated while speaking with him. And at the end of that conversation, I decided that when the opportunity presented itself, I would become initiated into the group.

During this time that their guru was kept in prison, Margis (that was how they referred to themselves) around the world protested against the unjust imprisonment of Baba. Some even resorted to violence despite Baba's repeated rejections of any violence on his behalf. Thus, I was stunned to learn that on February 8, 1978, two German *acariyas*, Didi Uma and Dada Lokesh, self-immolated in front of the iconic ruin of the Memorial Church in West Berlin. I could not believe that Dada Lokesh, this seemingly calm and gentle spiritual practitioner and teacher would undertake such an extreme act that would certainly have no effect on freeing his guru. I very nearly abandoned the group as I feared that there was an underlying extremism in the members. However, having been reassured by Ananda and other Margis whom I really liked and trusted, I realized that these suicides were the acts of misguided extremists in the group and certainly not the majority. I desisted from accusing myself of being blind to the potential irrational behavior of someone who had had such a positive influence on me. For I realized that he was, after all, human, and thus subject to delusions.

During the spring of 1978, I became increasingly close with Ananda. In his company, I even warmed up to Babaji (although perhaps with a less intense, natural devotion than that felt by him and the other Margis). We decided to study tai chi and, after a few months, learned the fifteen-minute short form. I had, since my early days in Ithaca, been very attracted to Taoism, particularly as presented in the *Tao de Ching*. I hoped one day to meet the famed Tai Chi master, Gia Fu-Feng, who had translated and done the calligraphy of the edition that I had treasured. Ananda and I would daily practice the moves in the grassy area behind the garden apartment. There was a growing affectionate, brotherly bond between us. I had never before had such a spiritual friend and soul-mate. I no longer felt alone on what I increasingly considered to be a spiritual journey—despite not really comprehending the goal I was seeking. I felt I was merely being carried along by some force or energy beyond my comprehension and trusted that I would eventually, with diligent effort, attain some state of everlasting peace.

During the summer, we both became restless. I had become interested in spiritual communes that had sprung up around Ithaca. I tried to stimulate Ananda's interest in exploring them, but he was not really interested in communal living, especially if it meant not having the basic comforts of plumbing, heating, and electricity. In this regard, we were actually quite different. I felt a strong calling to live some type of ascetic, monastic life. I had an idealized and hazy image of a Christian monastery that I thought must have a counterpart in an Eastern religion—a Hindu ashram or a Buddhist temple. I felt that in such a secluded and intentional environment, I would find the necessary supportive conditions for leading a spiritual life of peace and contentment. Ananda, however, was committed to following his spiritual path while living in society. He had a cousin, Marty, an artist, who had recently moved with his girlfriend to Oakland, California. And so, one day he suggested that we drive across the country and stay with his cousin while checking out the possibility of remaining in the Bay Area. As I was becoming tired of working in the donut shop and didn't want to explore the communes around Ithaca by myself, I welcomed the adventure. I brought up the possibility of making the trip into a spiritual odyssey, taking our time, travelling across the country, stopping at various spiritual communes along the way. I wanted to experience all kinds of communities, of various religious affiliations. Ananda enthusiastically agreed with my suggestion. We both looked forward to a life-changing experience, one that would enrich our spiritual journey.

Since both of us had very little money, we would try to stay for free at whatever communes we could find and occasionally sleep at campgrounds, if necessary. In order to help with the expense of gas, we decided to advertise for an additional traveler to accompany us on what would turn out to be a six-week journey. Kevin, who had recently returned from a year in Paris, responded to the notice we put up in the Somadhara Bakery in town. He was around our age, quiet, and although he was not really spiritually oriented, he was up for an adventure of leisurely traveling across the country at minimal expense. As he was the only one to reply to our notice, we accepted him as a traveling companion. We were going to drive out in Ananda's roomy 1964 Buick. A Margi friend was going to drive my VW Beetle out to Oakland (taking a direct route). Ananda and I packed all our worldly belongings into a large luggage rack which we fixed on the roof. Kevin was travelling light and had just a backpack. The three of us then prepared for the departure on September 1.

CHAPTER 2

A Cross-Country Spiritual Odyssey

Our odyssey began in the afternoon of September 1, 1978. It seemed to take us a long time to get ourselves organized for departure. Our first stop was going to be a Margi friend who was living in Morgantown, West Virginia. During that long drive down I-81, which ran into the evening darkness, the three of us sat in the front seat because the back seat had a lot of things rather haphazardly piled on it. I was in the dangerous middle seat and maintained silence as Ananda and Kevin engaged in conversation that was decidedly worldly and not spiritual. I was not participating in the topic which was becoming increasingly coarse, but was nevertheless forced to listen to them as their words literally passed over me. I longed for them to be quiet and reflect on the adventure that we had just begun. I was surprised and disappointed that Ananda seemed to have forgotten the purpose of our trip and to develop so quickly a chumminess with Kevin. Instead of encouraging Kevin to join us in our pursuit, he adopted Kevin's attitude of simply enjoying the open road, taking a more Beat-like approach. Kevin was a cigarette smoker and after asking if we minded if he smoked in the car, before I could raise my objection, Ananda not only said it was fine but asked him for a cigarette. I couldn't believe what I had just heard. I had never seen Ananda smoke cigarettes and suddenly felt a sickly feeling in my stomach as I made the hasty conclusion that Kevin was going to be a liability and not only "ruin" the trip, but also cause irreparable damage to the brotherly friendship between Ananda and me. This latter fear surfaced later that evening in our friend's house when I expressed my dismay at Ananda's speech and actions during the drive down. He responded in anger and seemed to resent me for calling it to his attention. However, our Margi friend, Greg, had a sobering effect on Ananda and he returned to his more usual demeanor during the few days of our visit. Nevertheless, I felt unease, wondering how the trip would play out.

We had planned to continue driving south to the famous commune, "the Farm," in Tennessee. But Greg suggested we first check out a large Hare Krishna commune in West Virginia, not too far from Morgantown. We drove along the quintessential back roads of West Virginia, past sorry looking farms and houses in varying states of decrepitude. It was a rugged and beautiful countryside of rolling hills. Miraculously, we stumbled upon a small sign that read "New Vrindaban," and saw in the distance a large farmhouse and a few other buildings spread out over a plateau on top of a steep hill. There seemed to be some construction taking place on a cliff in the distance. We would learn later that it was the site of the future "Prabhupada's Palace of Gold"—what would become the largest Hare Krishna temple in the U.S. We had arrived at the first stop of our spiritual odyssey.

The three of us had all had some experience with followers of Hare Krishna. A few young men with shaven heads and the distinctive tuft of hair hanging down in back and wearing white or pale pink robes could often be seen at the Port Authority Bus Terminal in New York as well as at some airports. They held copies of a book by the founder of the International Society for Krishna Consciousness (the official name), Swami Prabhupada, which they offered for free to anyone who seemed even remotely interested in learning more about the movement. As we got out of the car, we feared we would be attacked by zealous devotees who might aggressively try to convert us. Much to our surprise, a male devotee greeted us warmly, welcomed us and asked if we were hungry. Even though it was late in the day and the community had already eaten, he said he could find something for us to eat. He interpreted our hesitation to mean that we were hungry and said he would be right back. He returned in just a few minutes with an armful of fruit which he passed to us, saying we could eat in the male dorm where we would also be sleeping. I was impressed by his calm, peaceful demeanor. He did not have the vacant look of someone who was part of a cult. He actually was rather normal, except for his appearance.

We brought our sleeping bags into the dorm with a few bare essentials and happily ate the fruit. I speculated that the dorm might have been a very large barn at one time. Our welcomer told us that a bell would be rung at 4am and that the morning service began at 4:30. I expected an early rise, but this was far earlier than I had imagined. My companions were likewise in shock but we merely nodded as if it was quite normal to arise at that hour. He showed us the bathroom facilities which, not surprising, were basic. I noticed that there were many bedrolls on the floor along the walls of the spacious dorm neatly folded up. It appeared that we would have lots of company on the floor. I wondered where the rest of the men were. No sooner had I thought that, male devotees started coming in and unrolling their sleeping mats. There must have been at least 50, maybe more. None of us were ready for bed, as it was only about 8. Ananda took out a book to read and Kevin and I did the same. At nine o'clock the overhead light was turned off. None of us had a flashlight handy and so there was no choice but to go to sleep.

It seemed that I had just fallen asleep when a very loud bell rang several times. The men jumped up at the same time and went to the common bathroom or outside. I thought I would have a shower to help me wake up. I waited outside the shower stalls and noticed that the residents took very brief showers. I soon understood why. The water was ice cold. In early September, the mornings were already a bit chilly in this rural area and so I did not find a cold shower refreshing. Nevertheless, it did wake me up. We all then headed over to the temple where the morning service took place.

The temple was a square building that had a large balcony. The smell of incense was at first overpowering. It wafted in clouds suspended over the open floorspace where the male Hare Krishnas assembled. And then the familiar chanting began: "Hare Krishna, Hare Krishna, Krishna Krishna, Hare Hare, Hare Rama, Hare Rama, Rama Rama, Hare Hare." At first the chanting was slow and deliberate, the men gently swaying with their arms raised up, palms facing outwards. It was similar to how Margis performed *kirtan*. I realized that Ananda Marga and the Hare Krishnas were somewhat related, at least in some practices, including the lacto-vegetarian diet. The chanting became increasingly animated and the clouds of incense thicker. The pace got faster and louder, and the dancing devotees emitted an ecstatic happiness that was contagious. The three of us were swept up in the energy, joyously chanting along with the devotees. Some particularly animated chanters would twirl around in circular movements, expressing with their bodies the sheer devotional joy and love they were experiencing in their hearts. I looked up at the balcony, crowded with female sari-clad devotees with scarfs on their heads, which reminded me of an ultra-orthodox synagogue, except for the saris and the fact that the women were likewise dancing with arms raised. Their chanting was muted by the sheer volume of the men below and their movements were restricted by the space. Nevertheless, they displayed as much enthusiastic joy as the men. Time did not have a place in this daily ritual. I couldn't judge how long the chanting went on. Nor did I become restless, waiting for it to end. I was carried along on this blissful sea of devotion. There was no variation in the chanting, but it would ebb and flow according to the energy of the devotees who were completely in-sync with one another. The chanting lasted several hours and then gradually wound down and finally stopped. I was tired from the exhilarating hours of chanting but also felt very peaceful. The energy of the Hari Krishnas seemed to have permeated me with joy and optimism. While chanting the mantra, I didn't feel that I was actually addressing the god, Krishna, but rather celebrating a transcendent energy that I didn't attempt to analyze or even articulate to myself.

It was then time for breakfast. The three of us were hungry and ready for the expected tasty treats. Afterwards, we volunteered to help with whatever work needed to be done. I was assigned to help with lunch preparation. I was given two huge buckets of peapods that needed to be opened, placing the peas in one bucket, the pods in another. This task, which I performed alone, occupied me for most of the morning work period. I felt relaxed and peaceful after the vigorous chanting service and the delicious and healthy breakfast. I marveled that we were allowed to integrate into the community and noted that we seemed to be the only visitors. I wondered how many outsiders actually came there. I thought I would ask one of the residents when given the chance. Meanwhile, I quietly opened the peapods, enjoying the serene rural environment.

After finishing the task, I stood and waited for someone to indicate what I should do next. A female resident came over and thanked me for all my work. She and another resident carried the buckets into the kitchen. I stood for a while waiting for another task to be assigned to me, and as no one asked me to do anything, I just meandered around. A male devotee around my age walked up to me and asked how I was doing and if I was enjoying my stay. We engaged in some general conversation and I learned that he, like me, was a native New Yorker. He most recently lived in Greenwich Village. I couldn't get over how "normal" he seemed. In fact, I suspected that, also like me, he was of Jewish background. I felt very comfortable speaking with him, realizing that I had never actually spoken at length with a Hare Krishna devotee. I asked him how long he had been there and if he still maintained contact with his parents. He said he had been living there for nearly a year and although his parents did not understand his new life, they accepted it and he corresponded with them occasionally by letter. He had no plans to visit them nor did they plan to visit him. He said it was best to keep their worlds separate. I was struck by his genuinely friendly demeanor and that he seemed content with his chosen life. I thought I could be friends with him. He offered no criticism or dissatisfaction with the community. Nor did he make any effort to convert me or urge me to consider becoming a Hare Krishna devotee, even after learning that I was connected with Ananda Marga (with which he was not familiar) and considered myself to be a spiritual seeker.

We stayed three days and no one requested that we make a donation. It was an enjoyable and uplifting experience. Although I felt no temptation to join them, I carried away within me some traces of the optimistic joy of the residents that I had experienced. In fact, the three days spent there would remain one of the highpoints of the cross-country trip. These people seemed to have found a means of living a communal spiritual life of devotion to higher ideals. I hoped that one day I would find my own spiritual niche among like-minded people.

Our next stop was going to be the famous commune, the Farm, in Tennessee. In the 1970s, the Farm was probably the largest and most well-known commune in the U.S. I was very much attracted to experiencing what I anticipated to be a utopian monastic-like community. After driving south all day it was already dusk when we arrived. Although it was early September, it felt like mid-summer in Tennessee. It was an enormous place, with many large tents, a few old school buses, and shack-like structures scattered across the area. I guessed that there were several hundred residents.

We walked around trying to find someone who might be in charge of welcoming visitors. We found a tent that had a hand-written sign outside that said "Office." We couldn't knock and so we simply walked inside. There was a woman in a long hippie-like dress who was sorting through some papers on a shabby desk. We introduced ourselves and expressed our wish to stay there for a few days. She looked up, unsmilingly, and said it wouldn't be possible. They didn't have any room for visitors. She said we could camp out at a nearby campground and come there to help work during the day. I was very disappointed, not only because we couldn't stay there but also because I felt we were less than welcomed. The fact that we had just spent three days basking in the warmth of the Hare Krishna community made the contrast in the two communes all the more pronounced. Only later, I would reflect that maybe the community was under stress at that time, perhaps there were too many residents, not enough money to run the place. And freeloading visitors were not appreciated, except to be put to work. In any case, we had no choice but to ask her to direct us to the campground.

    The next day, we showed up in the morning. As it was clear that there would be no offering of breakfast for us, we approached a male resident and said we would like to volunteer for whatever helpful work we could do. He thought a bit and said we could weed the vegetable garden and he would try to find some gardening tools for us. He then pointed to a large plot of rows of greens and said we could start there. Although it was still morning, it felt hot and the sun was strong. I hoped I would manage without passing out. My mind was anything but peaceful as anxiety and worry took over. I had no gardening experience and wasn't sure I would be able to tell the difference between weeds and the planted crops. The resident who gave us the work task never returned. I guessed there weren't any spare gardening tools. The three of us stayed together, and I periodically asked Ananda and Kevin if what I was about to pull out was a weed. They had a much keener sense about it than I.

After what seemed to be hours, but probably was only one hour, I took a break, searching for water. I couldn't find any and so returned to my friends. We managed to work our way through several rows when we noticed that there appeared to be movement towards a large tent. We decided to follow. It was lunch time apparently, although there was no signal to indicate it. No bell, no one calling out "lunch"—just a gathering of the community to the lunch tent. We helped ourselves to a generous portion of the assorted vegetarian items. No one spoke to us. In fact, it seemed that we weren't even noticed. After finishing lunch, we decided we had had enough of the Farm hospitality and drove off. I was very disappointed, having built up in my mind an idyllic view of the Farm. I made an effort to remain optimistic about communes in America and that perhaps I might even find a spiritually oriented one in the future.

As the sun was setting on the Nashville skyline, we drove into the city. We decided to seek out a natural food store to purchase some food and also inquire if there were a place where we could spend the night. We thought there might be one near Vanderbilt University. We parked the car and sure enough stumbled upon a natural food store. After choosing a few healthy sandwiches, we asked the young man behind the counter if he knew of a place where we could crash for the night. He indicated the notice board, telling us there may be something listed there. In the midst of an assortment of handwritten notices by people looking for a room or an apartment or a ride somewhere, there was a typed card that said "House of Peace and Equality." The man saw us looking at the notice and volunteered the information that it was a Marxist communal house and the residents usually welcomed visitors to stay there overnight. Since it was just a few blocks away, we left the car where we had parked, and following the store clerk's directions we easily found it. As we were walking there, I reflected on what I knew about Marxist socialism. One of my apartment mates in Collegetown, an Ethiopian graduate student at Cornell, was an avowed socialist. I even joined him in attending a socialist event on campus, where one of the speakers was a woman running for Vice-President of the U.S. in the 1976 election on the Socialist party ticket. Having grown up in the Cold War, and remembering the Cuban missile crisis of the early 1960s, I had a biased and mistrustful view of communism, and I thought of socialism as being inextricably linked with communism. But I recalled feeling that the socialists I met at Cornell that day seemed quite nice and not at all like what George Orwell portrayed in *1984*, nor what the media portrayed about the Soviet Union and its satellites behind the "Iron Curtain." And the residents of this utopian-sounding commune in Nashville, though probably not "spiritual" in the way that is understood in Eastern religions, were undoubtedly friendly if they welcomed strangers into their dwelling.

The House of Peace and Equality was located on a quiet street of unattached but closely packed row houses. We rang the bell and a young African-American woman opened the door. After mentioning the store where we saw the card, as well as the recommendation of the store clerk, we said we were traveling across the country and were wondering if we could spend the night there. She smiled and said that we were welcome to stay there. There was a dorm in the attic and we could bring our sleeping bags and whatever we needed up there. While there was some artwork on the walls, I guessed by some of the residents themselves, I didn't see any political posters or any signs that this was specifically a "socialist" house. The woman seemed to have read my mind, because she volunteered information about the occupants of the house. She said there were currently seventeen people residing there. It was an egalitarian commune, with no one in charge. There was gender and racial equality and the residents contributed half of what they earned to the expenses of operating the house, including food, as well as funding the various social and humanitarian projects they operated in Nashville.

The residents rose early and we did likewise. We were invited to join them for breakfast in the large bare room downstairs. I was able then to have a better look at the occupants. All were young, probably in their 20s, about an equal number of men and women, mostly white, but there were two African-Americans, an Asian, and two who were probably Hispanic. They were warm and friendly, asked us about our journey and showed some interest when I indicated that we were on a spiritually motivated trip, visiting various communes when possible.

Having been well fueled by breakfast and some strong coffee, we took leave of our friendly hosts and proceeded to the car, which was parked near the natural food store several blocks away. It was now time to head west.

Driving west along Interstate 70, we finally came to the great Mississippi River. None of us had ever crossed it, and we were going to do so at St. Louis with a view of the famous arch. The river was fairly wide and so we had the opportunity to relish the significance of crossing from "east of the Mississippi" to "west of the Mississippi." After skirting around the city, we were again in open flat country. As the daylight was waning, we opted to stop at a large campground just off of the interstate. There were a great many large recreation vehicles. But we parked at an area where we could sleep out under the stars, away from the house-like trailers. I was feeling restless from sitting in the car so many hours and also increasingly frustrated with Ananda. He and I sat in the front seat, alternating driving, while Keven carved out a space for himself in the backseat amongst the assorted items strewn about on the seat and the floor. Despite our close proximity, Ananda and I didn't speak much to each other. He often engaged Kevin in conversation about a great variety of topics, none of them particularly spiritual. And, in addition, he occasionally bummed a cigarette from Kevin and seemed to relish smoking while driving on the open road.

 I indicated to Ananda that I was going to take a walk around the campground, hoping he would join me as I thought it was important to talk about our deteriorating friendship without Kevin around. I was pleased that he suggested coming along with me and surprised when a few minutes later, he initiated conversation. He stopped and looked at me. I waited. He then accused me of having no control over my emotions and that I was attempting to direct how he was to experience this trip. He said I was creating tension by being unfriendly to Kevin and that I needed to pull myself together and not expect people to be as I wanted them to be. I was unprepared for what I took to be an insensitive attack on his part. But then he softened and said quietly that I really needed to consider what I was looking for on this trip. We continued walking slowly, in silence. I pondered what he had said and realized that there was some truth in it. I had a fixed sense of being on a spiritual odyssey across America which entailed closing off anything that I felt was not in line with that, whether raunchy conversation, interest in banality—and this was most difficult of all—I refused to recognize that Ananda and I were perhaps not as closely connected as I had thought. We did not, after all, view "spirituality" in the same way, and we were thus looking for very different things. I had a monastic bent that he apparently did not have. I resisted accepting the disintegration of the ideal spiritual brotherly relationship I had thought we had but perhaps never did. I was, however, not convinced that we never had it. In fact, I was quite sure we were closely bonded in Ithaca, but somehow this trip—and Kevin's presence—unglued our relationship. And, thus, I resented Kevin, was disappointed with Ananda, and, perhaps, most painful was feeling that I was powerless to simply allow things to run their course.

I thought back to the intense disappointment I experienced in Oneonta when I realized that my close friends were not going to follow through on our plans to live a communal life together in the country after graduating. It was enormously painful for me to admit and accept the veracity of this. I had been left alone with the disappointment and emotional pain that gnawed at me relentlessly.

At that time I was not equipped with the right psychological tools for processing and eventually dispersing this heavy brick of frustration that weighed on me. And here again, I felt powerless to "pull myself together" and rationally observe how I, myself, was causing this pain. I blamed Ananda for making me feel miserable and frustrated, when I was actually doing it to myself. Despite my early interest in Buddhism, I was unacquainted with the four noble truths, in particular identifying the cause of my suffering and the recognition that there was a way to end it. And that I had the power to do this if I put my mind to it. But in the campground that evening, I did not have recourse to that wisdom and thus I wallowed in weakness, incomprehension, and frustration.

We spent all day driving across Kansas. It was a seemingly endless flat stretch of brown fields with few trees. The telephone poles along the highway were the only relief in the monotony. This was part of the bread-basket of America. The great prairie in the middle of the country. No doubt there was some cultural life in the cities of Topeka and Wichita, but here in the great rural expanse, life must be rather bland and monotonous. I thought of fictional Dorothy in the *Wizard of Oz* and understood her escapist fantasy trip. Yet, she did, after all, wish to return.

We eventually crossed into Colorado and I expected immediately to see the Rockies. But we still had a few more hours of driving through a flat, boring landscape before they appeared in the distance, with the Denver skyline in the foreground.

Our reason for coming to Denver was to pay a visit to the headquarters of Ananda Marga in North America. I was planning to request formal initiation as I had come to be at ease with this neo-Hindu group, mainly because of the wonderful people I had met in Ithaca. Yet I still had some reservations about the jailed guru—and gurus in general. However, I managed to put those thoughts aside and even wholeheartedly participated in *kirtan* with the other Margis. I think it was the energy of devotional song that somehow captivated me. Although lacking the exuberance of the Hari Krishnas we experienced, there was in the more subdued, yet heartfelt singing of the Margis something that seemed genuine and uplifting. Nevertheless, for me the main spiritual practice was sitting meditation and I hoped finally to receive proper instruction from the *Dada* at the Ananda Marga headquarters.

Towards evening, we arrived in downtown Denver and after asking several people for directions, found the office building where this spiritual organization had its main office. I thought it odd that the Ananda Marga central facility was located in a downtown office building. I mentioned my surprise and disappointment to Ananda who merely shrugged off my veiled criticism and said it was probably a convenient and cost effective location. Maybe so, I thought, but what about atmosphere? Would any Margi or curious visitor find such a sterile environment conducive for generating spiritual zeal? But I kept these thoughts to myself. Once again, I realized, I wanted things to be just as I wished. With this recognition I dropped my dissatisfaction.

We located the ground floor suite where the Ananda Marga organization was situated and knocked on the door. An *acariya*, Dada Ganesh, opened the door. He was good-looking, American and appeared to be in his early 30s. In fact, with his chiseled face and bright blue eyes, he could have been an actor or a model. I mused about the irony of him having the name of a deity normally depicted as an elephant. Perhaps, Babaji was displaying a sense of humor in giving this attractive American male this name. He reminded me of the late Dada Lokesh—though without the German accent—but then again young Caucasian men with shaven heads and wearing the same orange attire do tend to look similar at first glance. As it was rather late, he said we should just settle in for the night in the dorm downstairs.

After breakfast, I asked Dada Ganesh if I could meet privately with him. He led me into his office which contained a typical business desk and chair and a small table in the corner with the familiar framed photograph of Babaji. We sat on the carpeted floor facing one another. He asked me how he could be of service. I indicated that I wished to be formally initiated into Ananda Marga. I told him that I had been actively participating in activities with the group in Ithaca, NY for nearly a year. He nodded upon hearing that I was with the Ithaca group. Without much ado he then gave me a Margi name: Rangit Kumar. I was a bit disappointed with the name, as it didn't sound like the name of a deity but rather an Indian insurance broker or office worker. I tried not to let that dampen my initiation. He proceeded to instruct me in the introductory level of meditation, known as "first lesson." There were six levels, and I had heard from others, not from Dada Ganesh, that the sixth lesson was a tantric practice. That had unnerved me as I, in my limited knowledge of tantra, associated it with sexual intercourse. And thus I was skeptical about it as a practice of higher meditation. However, on that morning in Denver, I didn't think about that for it was a long way off and I somehow doubted that I would ever receive that instruction. On a much more grounded plane, Dada Ganesh proceeded to give me clearly delineated meditation instructions. This basic practice consisted of scanning the body beginning with the feet and moving upward through the body, tracing the energy in each part of the body and limbs. Eventually that energy would move upward into the face and out through the top of my head. He didn't mention the chakras as part of the meditation but obviously the energy travelling upward through the body passed through them. I had known something about chakras from yoga practice. He then informed me that I should avoid eating onions or garlic as they interfered particularly with the lower chakras, stimulating one's "lower" nature and dulling one's sensitivity. He then gave me meditation instruction known as "second lesson." This involved simply observing the breath at the nostrils, and following the breath as it moved through the body, focusing on any area that was prominent. Sitting in close proximity to him, I was struck by the clarity of his eyes. Perhaps even more than Dada Lokesh, he radiated peace and genuinely open friendliness. I thought that it would be beneficial to spend time in his presence and was sorry that he resided in Denver and not the Bay Area. Finally, he gave me several traditional orange loin-cloths and indicated that I needed to wear them from now on instead of Western underwear. I was prepared for this since Ananda wore one. And that was it. I was now a full-fledged member of Ananda Marga with a genuine Indian name.

 Despite not really connecting with my new name, I felt serene and at peace with what had just transpired. I even felt lighter as I walked downstairs to the dorm where Ananda and Kevin were waiting for me. I announced that

I had been initiated and given the name "Rangit Kumar." Ananda walked up to me with a broad smile, his face aglow, and gave me an affectionate embrace. I felt once again the brotherly warmth that we formerly had for one another in Ithaca. He proceeded to show me how to wrap the loin cloth around me. He assured me I would get accustomed to it. I wasn't so sure, but I was motivated to try.

The next day we decided to have a look around Boulder. After parking the car, I suggested we seek out the Naropa Institute. It had been established just four years before, and despite my limited exposure to Tibetan Buddhism, and ambivalence about its controversial founder, Chogyam Trungpa, I was nevertheless interested to see this pioneer Buddhist institution. Ananda was also enthusiastic about visiting Naropa. He mentioned that in its opening year, 1974, some of the faculty who taught the summer sessions included such Beat luminaries as Allen Ginsburg and Gary Snyder, and also Ram Dass. The latter's book, *Be Here Now*, was one of the most popular books on eastern spiritual practice, and I had read it, along with his lesser known, *Grist for the Mill*, and found them both very accessible and useful. Although in my mind I linked Naropa with Tibetan Buddhism, because of its founder, Ananda assured me that it was really non-sectarian, and not geared towards study and practice of any one form of Buddhism.

We found it on Pearl Street downtown. There was a simple sign next to a Chinese Restaurant. Naropa Institute was upstairs. Although the front door was open, we didn't find anyone around. In the corridor there was a large notice board that indicated the courses that would be offered in the next session, which wouldn't begin for a few months. Apparently, it was now a break, and no courses were currently going on. There really wasn't much to see. A few offices and a very small library. I thought it odd that there were no classrooms. But then we saw another notice indicating that the location of where the classes would meet would be posted in December. I was disappointed, expecting to see a thriving Buddhist educational institution, with a diversity of spiritually-seeking students.

It was already late afternoon and we thought we should see about finding a place to sleep that night. We passed a vegetarian café and went inside to inquire. The café wasn't busy, and so we went up to a waiter, asking him if he knew of a place where we could spend the night as we were just travelling through. He directed us to a communal house in town that usually welcomed overnight visitors. We rejoiced in our luck once again in finding a free place to stay, where, like in Nashville, the residents would be friendly and welcoming.

We easily found the house on a quiet residential street, close to the downtown area. It was quite large and though relatively old, it seemed very well maintained. The waiter did not mention that it was a Christian communal house. That was obvious from the artsy sign over the door that read, "Jesus welcomes all to His house." While Kevin, having a Christian background, was unfazed by the sign, Ananda said he wasn't sure he wanted to go inside. He feared that the residents were going to aggressively try to convert him and me, since we were both of Jewish background. I was less worried, for the café did not seem to be an evangelical Christian establishment, and this was, after all, Boulder, a very hip town. There was no doorbell, so we simply knocked.

After knocking a few times, and waiting for someone to come, we tried the door knob and opened the door. We cautiously walked through the foyer into a large sparsely furnished living room. There we found a small group of people sitting around having a conversation. There were two young men, probably in their twenties, and an older woman. They did not seem like conservative Christians, or members of a proselytizing sect, such as the Jehovah Witnesses or Mormons. In fact, they appeared rather new-age-like in their attire—the woman was wearing some interesting-looking jewelry—and I noticed artwork on the walls that confirmed that this was not a traditional Christian house. I didn't see a cross anywhere, nor a religious picture or statue. The three of them looked at us as we entered the room and smiled. I spoke up and mentioned that the waiter at Nature's Garden Café recommended that we come here as we were looking for a place to spend the night. The woman said without hesitation that we were welcome to stay. We should bring in our sleeping bags and whatever else we needed and leave them in the foyer. Later, we would be able to spread them out in the living room which served as a dormitory at night. One of the men informed us that there were currently fifteen residents but usually an additional dozen or so people showed up in the evening, like ourselves, just to spend the night, or several nights.

After exploring Boulder, we returned to the house at around 9pm, and found many more people there. The living room had at least a dozen sleeping bags laid out. I guessed that the residents lived in rooms upstairs but wayfarers, like ourselves, were accommodated in the living room. It was very quiet. Some of our fellow dorm-mates were reading a book or magazine, one seemed to be meditating, another doing yoga. It was an eclectic group, mostly young or youngish, and mostly men. I spotted just two women, who seemed to be traveling together. As we laid out our sleeping bags, one of my neighbors informed me that we would need to be up by 8. For there was a morning ritual that took place in the living room. I was wondering what that would be, but did not feel threatened by it. It was probably some new-age kind of activity, I thought.

All of us in the dorm/living room were up well before 8 and waited for the residents to come down. We were now about 30 people and gathered in a circle holding hands. The residents began by first asking us to bless one another as we start a new day. This involved turning to the person who was on our right and blessing him or her, and then doing the same with the person on our left. The older woman whom we met when we arrived led the group in singing a simple tune acknowledging that God was watching over us, as well as all animal and plant life. The song continued enumerating all aspects of the natural world that was under God's providential care. I particularly liked the mentioning of still lakes and flowing streams. After we had exhausted all of the objects of God's attention and protection, we let go of our partners' hands and stood in silence for about five minutes. Then we each turned to face the person on either side of us, wishing him or her a peaceful day filled with love. I felt elated and uplifted by the simple ritual and noticed that my traveling companions were likewise positively moved by it. How genuinely warm, open, and, in a sense, humbling it was, even if one didn't believe in an almighty God, to acknowledge that someone or some force protected us and all life on the planet indiscriminately. I reflected that this communal household was providing a beautiful service to the visitors who slept there, setting them off into the new day equipped with feelings of peace and love.

Our next stop was going to be the Stillpoint Foundation, a Taoist community in Manitou Springs, not far from Colorado Springs. I was very excited about coming here because a well-known Tai Chi master, Gia-Fu Feng, was the head of this community. His translation of the *Tao de Ching* by Lao Tsu along with his beautiful calligraphy, accompanied by stunning black and white photos by his American wife, Jane English, was a key text for me during my early time in Ithaca. Not only did I want to meet him and possibly receive some further instruction in tai chi, but I wanted to experience a Taoist commune. In the back of my mind was the hope that maybe this would be the right place for me. Ananda and I had studied tai chi together in Ithaca and used to perform the short 15-minute tai chi form together nearly daily. I tried to keep it up during the trip because I was afraid of forgetting it. Ananda's interest in tai chi seemed to have faded during the trip and he made no effort to do it.

According to the address that we had, we located the house in town. Although it was large and had spacious grounds, it was nevertheless in the town and I couldn't imagine that this was the actual commune. I was expecting something more rural. We found only one person in the house, a young American woman who introduced herself as Serena. She invited us to come in and sit in the living room and offered to make some tea for us. When she returned, I asked her if this was, in fact, the Stillpoint commune where Master Gia-Fu Feng resided. She informed us that the actual commune was in the countryside about ten miles away, in the foothills of the mountains. I was relieved to hear that. After learning that we were on a cross-country journey, seeking out spiritual communes to visit, she asked if we would like to have our tarot cards read. Neither Ananda nor Kevin responded, but I said I would. I sat on the floor in front of the coffee table where she was preparing the cards. She held them in her hands for some time with her eyes closed. And then slowly laid them out one at a time. I noticed the tower, which I had once come across in a book. It was a powerful image. In fact, all the images were intense and I nervously anticipated her interpretation of them. She studied them in silence for several minutes. My heart started racing as I waited in suspense. Serena then looked directly at me and smiled. I felt instantly relieved. She then told me that I had drawn very powerful spiritual cards and that I was on a profound journey. After a few seconds, she pointed to the Empress card and indicated that this, however, was my immediate destination. It wasn't clear how long I would remain there. I studied the card. A royal figure in costly attire did not seem at all to symbolize to me where I was headed. She went on to explain that although I was on a search for something transcendent, I was first heading into the mundane world. She was certain about her interpretation of the cards. I was crestfallen, thinking that it couldn't be right. I had no wish or inclination to go into the mundane world. I knew that for the past two years I was dedicated to finding a way to rise above it—for it held no attraction for me. Although I tried to shrug off her reading, I felt an unsettling disturbance within me.

 Serena then asked Ananda if he wanted his cards read. He declined. She didn't ask Kevin. After sitting in an uncomfortable silence for a few minutes, Serena volunteered to take us to the commune. I offered to go in the back seat, letting her ride up front with Ananda. I squeezed in among the piles of clothing and assorted wares; for Kevin had gradually created more space for himself.

The commune was housed in a medium-sized farmhouse, old but well-kept. There was a barn but no animals. We noticed a large vegetable garden where a woman was gathering lettuce. Serena led us into the house where we found a few people sitting around, drinking tea. A tall, blonde woman, around 30 years old, came into the room and casually took off her blouse. She walked around topless for a few minutes as if she were looking for something and then went into another room. A few minutes later she emerged wearing a different blouse. A young blonde man sitting on the worn sofa asked us where we were from. He had a slight accent, German or maybe Scandinavian. We explained our journey and that we wished to spend a few days there. I said that we practiced tai chi and were very interested to meet the famed tai chi master who resided there. The man informed us that he only talked to guests after the morning meditation and teaching. We were instructed not to approach him at any other time of day. We also learned that he sometimes led tai chi in the morning, but not every morning, and that after lunch he took a nap and then usually went for a walk alone. I was unhappy to hear about his inaccessibility since I was the one who had suggested we come there. Ananda wasn't nearly as interested in coming to this Taoist commune and just went along for the ride, so to speak.

As it was still afternoon, we asked if we could help with anything. Hans, the blonde man, who had provided us with the information about Gia-Fu Feng's daily schedule, took us outside and pointed to the vegetable garden. He said we could pull out any weeds we found there. The three of us proceeded to bend over and carefully pull out the weeds without injuring the densely growing greens. Hans meanwhile went back into the house. I was thinking that the residents did not seem to be hard workers. I wondered who did all the work of cooking, cleaning, gardening, etc. A short time later, someone else called out to us, telling us not to bother pulling out the weeds. Instead, we could help move a stack of wood from its present location to one nearer to the house. After showing us the wood and where it was to be stacked, he, too disappeared, leaving us to work by ourselves.

Before settling down to sleep, Serena found us, and passed on the information that the master expected us to be present for the 4am meditation in the meditation hall, which was followed by questions and discussion. She also mentioned that the master often taught *Lung Ch'i*, which was a Chinese term for a teaching method whereby the master "roared" at his students in an attempt to stimulate and awaken them. I was intrigued and looked forward to possibly experiencing this.

We rose very early the next morning so that we would be on time for the group meditation. I particularly looked forward to the discussion session with the master that would follow. We arrived to find only Gia-Fu Feng on a raised seat in the front of the room. None of the other residents were there. We duly took our places towards the rear, thinking that the residents would arrive eventually. Gradually, the residents arrived and by the time the meditation period had ended, there were about eight present. Gia-Fu Feng looked at us and said we were welcome to ask him questions.

Ananda proceeded to ask him about how to integrate the body into meditation practice. His response was very brief as he seemed to consider it not a worthy question to devote much time to. Ananda, clearly dissatisfied with the master's curt response, asked another question. He didn't make any attempt to reply but merely said, with what I interpreted as anger, that Ananda had "psychotic eyes." When Ananda immediately asked him to explain what he meant by that, he led out an enormous fart that lasted some time. No one but us seemed to notice. I reflected that perhaps that was part of the master's "roar." There were a few additional loud farts emitted from Gia-Fu and then more silent meditation.

After breakfast, we were told the master would demonstrate some tai chi moves. We went outside and saw him do a few basic moves that were extremely gracious, but then he stopped and walked away. I grumbled to myself, thinking 'that was it?' After lunch we were informed that Master Gia-Fu Feng wanted us to leave right away because we were disturbing the energy at the commune. We had no choice but to pack up and prepare to depart. The residents ignored us and we couldn't find Serena to whom we wanted to say goodbye. Ananda was anxious to be off as he didn't like the feel of the place at all. I couldn't blame him and likewise felt that the vibes were strange and the commune was not at all the spiritual haven I had hoped it would be.

The last spiritual commune we were planning to visit was the Lama Foundation, in northern New Mexico, near the popular town of Taos. Of all the communes we had planned to stay at, this was the one that I thought was most promising. It was, perhaps, the most well-known spiritual commune in America at that time. I had heard that Ram Dass was very involved in its early days and there was also a strong connection with the Sufi mystical tradition. Already having had some exposure to Hinduism, Buddhism, and Taoism—not to mention our brief experience of the new-age Christian community in Boulder—I was looking forward to perhaps learning a bit about Sufism.

When we arrived, we received a very friendly welcome from a female resident. Upon hearing that we wished to spend a few days there if possible, she responded that we certainly could. Our spirits were raised by this warm invitation, especially after our last experience. She said we could camp out if we liked or there was also a dorm in the main house where we could sleep. Since we were in the high altitude of mountainous northern New Mexico, and the nights were most likely chilly, I opted for the indoor lodging, as did Ananda and Kevin. Our greeter, Melody, then informed us of the community guidelines: Neither drugs nor alcohol consumption was permitted and there was a daily meditation practice that we were encouraged to attend. We were free, however, to do any form of meditation we wished, for there was no prescribed practice.

The three of us did our own thing the rest of the day. We each needed some time to be by ourselves. It was an absolutely beautiful location, spacious with also many tall evergreens. I had never expected New Mexico to be so green. The air was fresh and invigorating. I felt immediately uplifted and optimistic after the previous disappointing experience

About twenty people attended the morning meditation at 5:30. I had no idea who were visitors and who were residents. Everyone seemed so at home there. After breakfast, there was a group gathering outside and we engaged in *sufi* dancing. We were told that this wasn't going to be the active whirling around type but a less intense communal form of dance. It was a new experience for me and I enjoyed it immensely. In some ways, it reminded me of square dancing, which I often did when a student in Oneonta, NY. Interacting with all the others in the group was somewhat similar, but here, we acknowledged one another's inner being, greeting one another heart to heart. It was beautiful. Ananda and I had a truly bonding moment as we warmly greeted one another in this manner. The dance ended with us all standing in a circle joining hands. A leader said that we should try to join also with the spirit of the land we were standing on. We then stood in silence for about ten minutes. It was, I thought, an experience even more potent than that which I had felt with the group in Boulder.

We spent three peaceful and rejuvenating days at Lama Foundation. I noticed one day a small sign on the wall of the dorm that said "Lama Foundation honors the unique role and perspective of each individual." If only the world followed this philosophy, I mused.

It was early October. We had been on the road for more than a month and there was a palpable restlessness among us to finally get to our destination. I was ready to begin a new chapter of my life in San Francisco and offered no resistance to Ananda and Kevin's suggestion that we take a more-or-less direct route to the Bay Area. Our last stop on our cross-country spiritual odyssey was a fine bookend; for it, along with our first stop at the Hare Krishna commune were, in my perspective, highpoints in our journey.

CHAPTER 3

In the City by the Bay

We arrived in San Francisco on October 13, 1978, entering through the back door, so to speak, as we came up from the south on Highway 101. We proceeded to drop Kevin off at the YMCA near the Embarcadero Center, and then Ananda and I drove across the Bay Bridge to where Marty, Ananda's cousin, and his girlfriend, Melanie lived. I had met them during a visit they made to Ithaca and liked them very much. They lived in a garden apartment in the pleasant residential neighborhood of Piedmont, sandwiched in between Berkeley and Oakland.

Marty led us into the small second bedroom which was actually his art studio. There were large canvases on the floor against the wall, lots of eggs in bright colors. That seemed to be his theme. The room had a noticeable smell of oil paint. Melanie informed me that my yellow VW bug had arrived safely. The Margi who had driven it across the country had dropped it off about a month before. Ananda and I settled into the small bedroom, laying out our sleeping bags. He was silent and didn't seem interested in conversing. So I let it be. After a few days, I discerned that after travelling together for six weeks, it was time for us to head out on our own. I was thus determined to find a job and a place to live as soon as possible. I also felt the need to be settled so that I could develop the meditation practice I had been introduced to when in Denver.

The next day I drove across the Bay Bridge by myself for the first time, and seeing the iconic city by the bay raised my spirits. I was optimistic that everything was going to work out. I looked forward to the experience of living in this beautiful city. Although I did not relish having to make donuts again—I summoned up the memory of the smell of grease and sugar—I was resigned to doing it at least initially just to get myself established. I tried several donut shops and with my two years of experience, I was told I would certainly be hired if and when there was an opening. I was both disappointed and relieved at the same time. I returned to the East Bay and was determined to set out again the next day with a new plan.

After some thought, I decided to try natural food stores and expected that there were bound to be quite a few in San Francisco. I compiled a list of half a dozen and the next day, drove again into the city. I made, I thought, a convincing argument that despite never having actually worked in a natural food store before, I had experience volunteering at the food coop in Ithaca which gave me the necessary skills. In addition, I was highly motivated to work in such an environment. Each of the managers was sympathetic and encouraged me to stop by periodically to check if there were an opening. I was now getting desperate for I felt I had to find a job very soon as I was becoming increasingly uncomfortable staying at Marty and Melanie's. While they were still warm and friendly towards me, I knew that my continued presence there was irritating Ananda and probably affected them as well.

There was one place left on my list. I hesitated to go there because it was located on Union Square in the downtown area which didn't appeal to me. I preferred a neighborhood store. Yet, I couldn't afford to be so demanding. I walked into Nature's Own Health Food Store which was, as I had anticipated, void of atmosphere. It obviously catered to those working downtown who weren't looking for a cozy, warm neighborhood store. I indicated to the clerk behind the counter that I wished to apply for a full-time job there. He sent me downstairs where I found the manager sitting at a desk in the back. The front of the room had a long counter where perhaps two dozen boxes of food items were piled up. A price gun lay next to them. The manager was young and seemed rather hyper. He handed me an application form and a pen and asked me to fill it out there. I had a feeling that I was going to be offered a job as I assumed that someone was needed to unpack those boxes and price the items. I handed him the application and after he looked it over he said that they needed someone to work in the basement, receiving deliveries, stacking boxes of food items in the storage area, pricing items with the price gun and then carrying them upstairs and shelving them. It was a nine-to-five job, Monday to Friday, and paid minimum wage. He asked if I was interested. Without hesitating for a moment, I said I was. He then said that if I was ready, I could begin work the next day.

I was actually elated when I walked out into the street. My step was light as I headed for the nearby BART station. I thought to myself, 'OK, this is a beginning. Next will be finding a place to live.' And I wasted no time searching for one. During my lunch hour, I looked at ads in the newspaper for rooms to rent. I wasn't having any luck but did not give up. My peace of mind and spiritual practice depended on getting myself out of Marty and Melanie's apartment and into my own living space. I resolved to keep looking every day until I found a place to live. A handwritten note on a small bulletin board in a café/bakery on Church St. sounded promising. And the rent was very low, just $80 a month. Since I was near the address, I thought I would stop by, hoping someone would be at home. My street map indicated that Landers St. was just off of 16th St, about halfway between Church and Dolores. I managed to walk right past it though and found myself at Dolores St. I turned around and walked back and sure enough saw the small sign that indicated that this was the street I was searching. It was very narrow, more a lane than a street. I soon stood in front of 181 Landers St, but I was looking for 181A. There didn't seem to be a house with that address. I stood for a few minutes and looked around and then spotted a narrow passageway next to the garage of the house. Although it was still daylight, the passageway was nearly dark as I walked through it. I came out into an open area and saw a small carriage house. I figured that must be 181A. I walked up the stairs and knocked. The sign had said to contact Norman, and so I assumed that was who opened the door. He was tall, very thin, wore glasses and had black curly hair. I thought he looked very Jewish. As it turned out, he was and had grown up in the Bronx. I indicated that I, too, was a native New Yorker, born in Brooklyn but had grown up in Queens. He nodded. He seemed very nervous and uncomfortable talking to me. I soon realized he was like that with everyone. Norman said there was one condition about living there I would need to be on board with. He played the saxophone every afternoon for about two hours, seven days a week.

He said his parents were supporting him so that he could devote himself to the saxophone. His goal wasn't to become famous though. Having mentioned that I tried to meditate every day, he said that playing the saxophone was for him a spiritual practice. I soon learned how true that was, having had ample opportunity to hear his at times ecstatic playing. I accepted the conditions.

I was elated. I had managed to find a job and a place to live in the same week! Two days later, on Saturday, I drove into the city with my things and moved in. The room was cozy and suited me well. It had a small entranceway which I could use as a meditation area and a little bathroom (toilet and sink) that was added on to the room and which had a glass roof. It thus felt like I was outside when using the bathroom. The room was very quiet with no street sounds and, I thought, conducive for me to strengthen my meditation practice. There wasn't any furniture in the room but it was carpeted and so I would simply use my sleeping bag as a bed. I kept my clothes in my suitcase and would look for a few empty boxes to use as drawers. I laid out my books on the floor against the wall and felt joyful at having now settled into my new life in San Francisco.

After moving out of the apartment in Piedmont, my relations with Ananda improved. But I discerned that we were no longer "kindred spirits"—and I reflected that maybe we never were. I had been perhaps merely projecting my wishes on someone else. I was happy to be part of the Ananda Marga community although there were only a few Margis in San Francisco. Despite not having a strong devotional relationship with Babaji, I was glad to participate in the weekly *kirtan* that Ananda had organized in the basement of a unitarian church on Dolores St, not far from where I lived. I enjoyed coming together with the few other Margis living in the city on Sunday evenings and we often then ate dinner together at a wonderful vegetarian restaurant on the corner of 19th and Dolores. I liked having a reason to walk down that beautiful street with a middle island of tall, stately palm trees. After being initiated into Ananda Marga, I felt that I had at last some structure in my spiritual path. I tried to follow the meditation instructions I had been given but I wasn't clear about what the goal of my practice was. I didn't let that bother me though, and just plugged along.

About three months later, we received word that Dada Ganesh was making a short visit to San Francisco and needed a place to stay. None of the Margis seemed to have space for him, so I said I would ask my apartment mate if he could stay in our apartment. Thus, I got to host him in my shack-like dwelling. I offered him the use of my room, thinking I would sleep in the living room, but he wouldn't allow that. Norman seemed delighted to host him, and didn't even seem nervous or uncomfortable around him. Dada Ganesh was as warm and friendly as I had found him to be in Denver and I was in awe of his *acarya* status, which I considered made him like a monk. I recognized that there was a part of me that wished to lead that kind of life, although not necessarily in Ananda Marga. During the two days he stayed with us, in the mornings he led *kirtan* in my small entranceway. Ananda joined us, and much to my surprise, so did Norman. He swayed along with us and chanted the simple devotional songs. On one of the evenings Dada Ganesh led a meditation session in the basement of the church. A few additional Margis from the Palo Alto area drove up to participate. It thus felt like a real community. Three months later, however, I was shocked to learn that he had given up his life as an *acarya*, left Ananda Marga, and got married.

Despite this disappointment, I embraced my new life in San Francisco and felt excitement flowing through me as I embarked on a new chapter in my life. Riding the old Church Street tram to Union Square every morning was a novelty that never lost its freshness. I had successfully shaken off the tension and disappointment I had experienced upon arriving in the Bay Area. The air in this special city by the bay felt clean and refreshing and my mind drew on that freshness. I knew that I had crossed a threshold but did not know what direction my life would take. Although I maintained a daily meditation practice, I was not aware of any change in my overall state of being nor in my view of the world. In fact, I felt meditation, following the simple instructions I had been given, was an obligation that I dutifully engaged in. My attention seemed to be directed toward the city in which I was now living. I felt invigorated by the cityscape—the hills, the pastel-colored houses, the cafés, and the daily fog. Every afternoon when it rolled in, I perceived my mind being purified of the clutter that had accumulated during the day.

I was, however, getting tired of working at Nature's Own. It became a drudge, a nine-to-five job in an unaesthetic environment, working mainly by myself. I decided that now with some work experience, I could possibly find a more agreeable situation. I realized that despite being a quiet, somewhat introverted person, I had another side that was sociable; I actually enjoyed and felt comfortable interacting with other people, no matter what their background was. One natural food store caught my interest as I sensed it would fulfill my needs. It was just below Nob Hill, off California Street and a few blocks from Polk Street. The name was Buffalo Whole Food and Grain and it had a rustic décor. It felt like a neighborhood store and the few people who worked there seemed very friendly with each other and with the customers. The store was owned by two gay men, who were not in a relationship, and the one whom I saw each time I stopped by, Dan, was extremely nice. He said they may have an opening in a month or two and I should check back with them. I followed his advice and stopped by every two weeks or so. Finally, my persistence paid off and he said that someone was leaving and they were going to hire a replacement. Fortunately, the other owner was there and so I got to meet him as well. Dan said that he thought I would be a good fit and the other partner, Jerry, had no objections.

After giving my current employer two weeks' notice, I was free to begin my new job. It felt like a family there. I quickly developed friendships with the other employees as well as with the owners, and gradually grew more distant from Ananda Marga. Instead of a spiritual community, I had actually found a community of friends with whom I would be spending many hours every day. When Christmas came around, Jerry invited all the employees to his apartment on Haight Street for a celebration. There was an exchange of presents, and one of my co-workers, Theresa, gave me a writing journal. It was a timely gift because I had recently become interested in writing poetry but had not yet begun to write. This journal seemed to be the push I needed to actually try. Over the coming months, I gradually developed a "poetry persona." I began frequenting a few cafes in North Beach which I had found during my regular trips to the famous City Lights Bookstore. At that time, the owner, Lawrence Ferlinghetti, was often behind the counter. An obvious café choice was the Caffe Trieste across the street, the former hangout of the Beats and other poets. In the evenings, I often sat on the terrace of the Savoy Tivoli, which was very popular, and I thought it was probably similar to cafes in Paris. In many of the poems I wrote, I endeavored to give expression to the ethereal atmosphere of the fog I often experienced. I tried to find new ways of describing its softness, its intangible, evanescent quality. I also tried to capture the quality of light. In poems that took aspects of city life as its subject, I recorded observations as an outsider not a participant in the life I was describing. In fact, that was how I actually viewed myself—as someone not really belonging to any category of San Francisco life.

I don't recall why I decided to have my bushy hair and beard cut, but in spring 1980, I did. I hadn't trimmed either since 1975! I informed my friends at Buffalo that I was about to alter my appearance and they supported my decision. Linda, a kind and ever-optimistic friend who was from Princeton, New Jersey, and daughter of a well-known professor there, said that changing my look would open me up to new adventures. I was ready for that. I headed for a barber shop around the corner from the store and watched as the years of accumulated hair was cut off. I was astonished to see my clean shaven face and my hair, although not completely shaved off, was extremely short. I walked back to the store and there was great jubilation from Dan, Linda and even a few regular customers. A few days later, the Buffalo gang gave me gifts of assorted clothing to go with my new appearance. I had previously worn baggy army pants and khakis and sneakers, but now I would adopt a very different look. I opened the boxes to find a pair of black pants, a black casual jacket, and a few pastel-colored shirts. There was even a pair of soft textured black shoes. I was touched by the generous and supportive gesture by the staff. Jerry said I should get rid of my former attire.

Two of my co-workers had recently been going to clubs to hear live New Wave bands. San Francisco and Berkeley both had a lively punk and New Wave scene. One Friday, they invited me to join. They were going to the Back Door, an intimate-sized club that featured live New Wave music and was unlike the larger, and very well known, Mahubay Gardens, which was more inclined to host punk-rock groups. I would have been hesitant to go there because I had heard that some of the punks who frequented it would sometimes be violent. Both clubs were in the entertainment section of North Beach. I put on my new clothes and set off with Theresa and Paul. They said I was in for a real treat, for the band scheduled to play that night was reported to be excellent. We could hear the music even before we entered the club. My first reaction once inside was how loud it was. There would be no possibility to speak while the band was playing. The place was fairly full and some people were standing up front near the stage, while the majority danced behind them. I stood towards the rear and just took in the scene. The music had a potent rhythm that seemed to pull my legs into motion. It was impossible to stand still and just passively listen. Without consciously deciding to dance, I found myself moving my body in rhythm with the music. I didn't pay attention to anyone else, including Theresa and Paul, whom I had lost sight of soon after entering the club. I let go of self-consciousness about my movements. I didn't think at all. I just danced. When the band took a break, I finally stopped, and discovered that I was wet from perspiration. Paul came over and patted me on the back, telling me that I had been initiated into New Wave dance. He said, I would now be hooked. I smiled, thinking that there certainly were worse things to be hooked on.

Hearing live New Wave groups became a regular activity for me. I even felt comfortable to go alone, if no one else I knew was able to accompany me. I generally went to the Back Door, where I felt at home, but on a few occasions, I drove over to a club in Berkeley to hear and dance to the pulsing forceful rhythms of a group simply known as "X." Unlike most of the groups I heard, this one had a female lead singer. She was intense both in appearance and in sound. Her voice was powerful and pierced right through my body. I found that I danced even more energetically to X, bouncing around the dance floor, bumping gently into other dancers, which was actually a common occurrence in New Wave dancing. In fact, such interactions fueled my energy. I eventually went to the Mahubay Gardens, along with my friends, for the purpose of hearing—and of course dancing to—one of the most acclaimed groups in the Bay Area at that time, with the strange and disconcerting name, "The Dead Kennedys." I didn't pay much attention to the lyrics, some of which were controversial, but the lead singer, Jello Biafra, was a spectacle to behold. He would periodically throw himself off the stage into the audience, who would then toss him back on the stage—and all the while, he was holding a microphone. I let myself go and bounced around the dance floor, and in some moments, I was so caught up in the movements, that I had lost a sense of self. The music and I seemed one. I afterwards reflected that dancing to this extremely compelling music was a form of spiritual practice. It melted away my inhibitions, taking me outside of myself, so to speak, silenced my thinking, and left me in a calm, peaceful state when I finally stopped. I didn't attempt to analyze why I was so attracted to this music, nor was I alarmed to note that I had been meditating less and less in recent time. I simply followed where my heart was leading me. I was conscious of an innate source deep within that periodically sent me in an unexpected direction. I couldn't articulate it but I inherently trusted it. Looking back, I don't recall any instant when it betrayed me, leading me in a direction that I would come to regret later.

Despite these periodic spiritual-like participations in the New Wave scene, I didn't abandon more stationary spiritual practice. But my practice had morphed from sitting cross-legged in my room to moments of being fully present when alone in an environment of natural beauty, or sometimes when just experiencing a certain quality of light in the city. Two of my favorite spots for the former were the long curved pier in the park below Ghirardelli Square and the bluffs and coves of the Marin Headlands nature preserve just across the bay from the city. I never tried to write poetic descriptions of my experiences in these places. I merely sat or stood in silence for a period of time, without thoughts. I seemed to merge into the environment I was observing, without the sense of an observer. And after some time, probably ten minutes or so, the inner silence would be broken and I returned to my usual mode of being. Yet, I would nearly always feel refreshed and tranquil for the next few minutes at least.

One afternoon in March, while sitting on the pier below Ghirardelli Square, I reflected on the time I had spent thus far in San Francisco. It had been more than two years, and

I let my mind pass lightly over the various changes that had occurred. It didn't seem that I was now the same person who arrived in October 1978. I had not only changed my physical appearance but also the environment in which I lived my daily life and the people with whom I associated. Despite being satisfied with my current lifestyle, as I gazed out on the bay, with the island of Alcatraz clearly in view, I sensed a growing restlessness within me. I realized that I longed for an urban life in a larger city. In some ways, San Francisco seemed like a collection of villages, rather than a major city of distinct neighborhoods. I discerned that I needed more grit. Yet, New York didn't appeal to me, because I feared that daily life there would just wear me out. I thought of Boston, a city I had never visited. But realized it was similar to San Francisco in size, and with so many universities there, it would probably feel like a large university town, which did not appeal to me at that time. I just closed my eyes for some minutes and sat still. A thought surfaced suddenly: Why not go to Europe? Immediately, my heart started racing in excitement. Yes, that was the answer. The thought seemed to rise from a place deep within me. I had the palpable intuitive feeling that some inner force was propelling me to make such a major move. Nevertheless, I was going to let the idea just sit and simmer for a while. While I trusted where it was coming from, I continued sitting there for at least an hour, trying to control my mind from engaging in making future plans to follow through on this sudden idea. I did, however, consider where in Europe I might like to live. After considering and dismissing London and Paris, I landed on Berlin. I had recently read Isherwood's *Berlin Stories* with keen interest and had re-watched the film, *Cabaret*. The atmosphere depicted in both the stories and the film had affected me greatly. And just a few days before, I had browsed through a book about the Weimar Republic and the avant-garde in Berlin at that time. I had become fascinated with Berlin of the 1920s, particularly in light of the fact that its eclectic cultural glory was short-lived. I was convinced that some of that wildly creative culture was alive and well in the walled-in city of West Berlin, located in the middle of Communist East Germany. During the days that followed, I rarely kept the thought of possibly going to Berlin out of my mind.

I was conscious of a potent drive within me to rise above the mundane world. Although my spiritual practice had become primarily dancing in New Wave clubs and writing poetry, in both activities I gave expression to my feelings of not fitting into society, of looking beyond and above the constrictions of societal norms in America. It was a search for something that I was unable to articulate to myself. But I was becoming increasingly convinced that I would find it in the historical cities of Europe. I was thus prepared to shape my life in a way that corresponded to an ideal I created in my mind of the "right" way to lead my life with a vaguely defined goal to realize—an activity of life-sculpting that I would continue to do on several occasions in the years to come.

On May 13, 1981, I boarded an Amtrak train in Oakland for the overnight journey to Seattle. After a few days there, I would continue on to Vancouver and then travel for four days on a train across Canada, all the way to Montreal. I decided not to simply fly across the U.S. to New York for two reasons: I wanted to see Canada, as I had already travelled across the States, and I wanted some practice in travelling alone, since I would be doing it once I got to Europe.

During that very long train journey across Canada, I was excitingly anticipating the coming adventure in Europe. It was a major lifestyle move. I reflected that the spiritual journey that had propelled me to make the cross-country trip of 1978 and which I continued to travel during the first half of my life in San Francisco was fading into the recesses of my mind. I had seemingly turned off from the route I had been following and was now going in a different direction. I smiled. The tarot reading in Colorado had proved after all to have been accurate—I was heading more deeply into the world represented by the Empress.

CHAPTER 4

Protracted Distractions in Berlin

After spending two weeks with my family in New York, I was ready to begin my European adventure. On June 15, 1981, my parents drove me to Kennedy Airport for my late evening departure on a KLM flight to Amsterdam. My parents put on a brave face as we waited for the boarding of my flight to begin. (In those days, airport security was minimal and it was quite common for farewells to take place right at the gate). I had purchased a one-way ticket and had no idea how long I would stay in Europe. I was excited, nervous, and apprehensive about what lay ahead. But at 27, I felt young, open, and ready for a radical change in my life. Although I was planning to settle in West Berlin, I thought I would start off in Amsterdam. People had told me that it was a great city with atmosphere and nearly everyone spoke English.

I spent several days there, walking along each of the canals and exploring many of the narrow streets that connected the canals. I drank coffee in the cozy "brown" cafes and was astonished to see in one of them a back room with a small blackboard listing the different types of marijuana and hashish for sale. People openly smoked joints in the café and the acrid smell hung in the air. I thought I might get high just sitting in there. I visited the Van Gogh Museum but was disappointed in the collection. I thought the Metropolitan Museum and the Modern Museum of Art in New York had a far better representation of the well-known masterpieces.

Although I could have stayed longer, just soaking up the atmosphere, I was worried about how much money I was going through, and thus opted to move on to Berlin.

PART ONE

In Search of a New Weimar Berlin

On a Monday evening in early July, I boarded a night train to Berlin. It was going to be a nine-hour journey. I was planning to reread Isherwood's Berlin stories during the ride. I knew that this train, as all trains going to Berlin, had to pass through East Germany and even though we would cross the border in the middle of the night, I expected to be wide awake and ready for the experience. At around 1am we stopped at a grim, deserted station on the West German side of the border. There were incomprehensible announcements from a loud speaker. I heard barking dogs and saw uniformed East German police walking along the train with dogs on leashes. Suddenly, I heard the sound of what seemed like an army of East German police officers boarding the train. We eventually moved and passed through an area lined with barbed wire and bright lights that glowed in the misty night air. I was so engrossed in looking out the window that I literally jumped in my seat when the door of the compartment was forcefully opened and the overhead light flicked on. A uniformed officer stood in the doorway, bellowing out something I did not understand. I noticed the other people in the compartment handing their passports to him and I did the same. My hand was slightly shaking as I handed him my passport, reassuring myself that I had nothing to worry about for I was an American citizen and was not doing anything illegal. He opened it, looked at me, looked at the photo, looked at me again. He then thumbed through the passport and when he found an acceptable page, stamped it with such force I thought he would crush the passport. He then unsmilingly handed it back to me. I was relieved when he shut off the light and left.

Just after dawn, the train stopped and I looked out the window and got very excited because there it was, the infamous Wall. It wasn't nearly as high as I had expected. But it was very solid concrete and I could see beyond it rows of barbed wire. The East German police disembarked and again I saw officers leading dogs along the train. I supposed they were looking for anyone foolish enough to hide under the train, attempting to escape into West Berlin. But then I thought how could someone have possibly gotten on the train since it never stopped at an East German station. I concluded that it was merely a formality. We eventually moved across the border and I breathed an audible sigh of relief to be within the safety of West Berlin.

Disembarking at the shabby and rather dirty Bahnhof Zoo (the main—and only—train station in the western part of the city), I was surprised to see a few scraggly people, who appeared to be drug addicts, sleeping on the floor in the central hall. As the accommodations office in the train station was not yet open, I put my suitcase in a locker and walked outside. I saw the ruin of the Kaiser Wilhelm Memorial Church, the most popular image of West Berlin. Next to the formidable ruin was a modern church building, squat and octagonal. The two structures were irreverently referred to by Berliners as the "lipstick and pillbox." I recalled that it was here that Didi Uma and Dada Lokesh had self-immolated in protest of Babaji's imprisonment. I resisted the attempt to pursue further thought on that act nor to imagine what effect it must have had on passersby here in the center of West Berlin. I then turned and went back into the station and in a few minutes the office opened.

    I procured a reasonably priced room in a *pension*, which was like a small hotel, except that it normally occupied a floor or two in an apartment building, and most of the rooms did not have an attached bathroom. It was on a quiet cobblestoned street in the Charlottenburg neighborhood, not far from the center of the city. This neighborhood, like many I would later discover, had escaped damage from the extensive bombing of the city during the war. Thus, I was able to get a sense of what prewar Berlin was like. I particularly liked to walk the streets at dusk when the gas lamps were lit. Although the five-story buildings that lined the streets had generally gray facades and some were in need of renovation, I found the cobblestoned streets, some containing antique shops, cafes, and corner *kneipe* (a ubiquitous and distinctive Berlin type of pub) to be aesthetically pleasing and my thirst for old world atmosphere was met, at least initially.

    I fortunately obtained a job rather quickly. A young Frenchman I met in my Berlitz German class suggested I try the Schweizerhof Hotel where he worked as a waiter.

After fabricating my work experience, I landed a job in the banquet department, but it didn't take long for my supervisor to see that I had no waiting experience. I was then transferred to the breakfast service which, as it was a buffet, only involved bringing individual cannisters of coffee to the tables. I also had great luck in finding a furnished room to rent in a widow's apartment on Weimarer Strasse in Charlottenburg. I thought how appropriate to be living on that street given my keen interest in Weimar Berlin. While Fr. Knoeppel, my landlady, was not at all like Frl. Schroeder in Isherwood's stories or in *Cabaret*, nor was the one other tenant in any way peculiar or exotic, I, nevertheless, let my imagination fill in the missing details.

After securing the room, I walked down the stairs into the street, marveling at how smoothly my move to Berlin had been. In celebration, I decided to visit Nollendorf Strasse 17, the address where Isherwood resided during his entire stay in Berlin. On the way there, I passed Wittenberg Platz, where West Berlin's premier department store, KaDaWe (Kaufhaus des Westens) stood. In a prominent position on the plaza was a very large monument that I instantly recognized was a list of all the concentration camps. I was able to understand the final sentence, which read "Orte des Schreckens die wir niemals vergessen duerfen" (Places of Horror that we are obligated never to forget). I stood still and felt tears come into my eyes. I could hear my mother's voice when I first told her of my plan to go to Berlin: "Why not London or Paris, why Berlin?" Although our family did not suffer from the Holocaust because my great grandparents had all settled in New York several decades before, I realized I had been—and continued to be—insensitive to my mother's feelings regarding Germany.

I remembered that one of my elementary school friends was the daughter of a Holocaust survivor and I had seen the branded number on both her mother and grandmother's arms. They had been the only ones in their family to make it out alive and they both seemed to have serious emotional problems even twenty years later. For the few moments I remained standing there, oblivious to the bustling activity around me, I speculated that my fascination for the period of the Weimar years was that it was destined to be cut short by Hitler's rise to power. And that the exuberant and decadent cultural expression of those years was fueled by a sense that the present conditions were not going to last. I knew that during those same years there was a great deal of conflict in Berlin between communists and nazis which often erupted in street fighting. The menacing cloud of the nazis must have registered in the minds of some of those avant-garde writers and artists who were sensitive to the environment in which they lived.

It was with such disturbing thoughts in my mind that I continued walking on to Nollendorf Strasse. I found house number 17 that had a plaque on the wall simply stating that the English writer, Christopher Isherwood, lived here from 1929 until early 1933 and that his works, *Farewell to Berlin* and *Mr. Norris Changes Trains* (known collectively as *The Berlin Stories* in its American publication) were based on the experiences he had had here. It also mentioned that these literary works were the basis for the film *Cabaret*. I let the upsetting and unsettling thoughts that had occupied me during my walk drift away, and I summoned up a picture of what Frl. Schroeder's rooming house might have been like. I conjured up images of the eclectic occupants based on the film, but tried to imagine Isherwood, rather than Michael

York, as the writer living there. This flight of imagination lasted for a few minutes and then I was back in West Berlin.

During those first months of my life in Berlin, I was able to smooth over the formidable differences between Weimar Berlin and West Berlin in the early 1980s. The old neighborhoods like Charlottenburg and Schoeneberg lent themselves to my mental manipulations. As chilly autumn days arrived, I noted the acrid smell of coal that permeated the air and guessed it must have been even more pervasive in the prewar days. I found aesthetic and atmospheric beauty in the gray foggy evenings. Although the cafes I frequented did not offer the ambience of what I imagined existed currently on the left bank in Paris in the famed Café de Flores and Café Deux Maggots (the former had been frequented by prewar Anglo-American ex-patriates, the latter by Sartre, Simone de Bouvier, and other postwar existentialist intellectuals), I was nonetheless able to sit in Berlin's modern cafes, disregard the ever-present American or British rock music that played over the speakers, and write.

On one of my explorations after finishing work at the hotel at 3pm, I stumbled upon a true coffee house on the otherwise unexceptional Kurfuersten Strasse, not far from Nollendorf Platz. Café Einstein was located in a stately free-standing large private house, which Germans refer to as a "villa," and seemed to date from the nineteenth century. I walked up the stairs and entered a large entranceway which then led into the coffee house itself. There was an L-shaped bar on one side with a few tables against the wall. The globed ceiling fixtures gave off a soft light in the bar area as well as in the main rooms. I stood in awe at the magnificent gold trimmed mirrors that adorned the walls. There was ornate crown molding above the mirrors and red velvet cushioned sofas against the walls that faced rectangular marble-top tables. In the middle of the spacious room were small round tables of similar style. All the chairs were of dark mahogany wood. The floor, likewise, was of a beautifully stained dark wood. The waiters wore white shirts, vests, and black pants with ankle-length white aprons over them. I took a seat at one of the small tables in the middle of the room and just took in the scene. I ordered a *groesser brauner* (similar to an "Americano") which was served on a small oblong silver platter with a little glass of water. This would be my usual beverage as I adopted the coffee house as my habitual haunt most afternoons after work.

On one October evening, while sitting in my small room, I felt restless and thought I would go to the Café Einstein and perhaps have a glass of red wine. I put on a black turtleneck and black pants and headed for the U-Bahn station. The coffee house was quite busy and as I was about to seek an unoccupied table, I noticed that the front room off of the bar which was always closed in the afternoons was now open. I walked in and immediately liked the feel of it. It was apparently originally the library when the villa was a residence. The mahogany glass enclosed bookcases were empty now and in one corner was a phone booth that blended in so well with the décor that I didn't notice it at first. The small marble-top tables—about a dozen in total—each had a lit candle on them. There were a few empty tables and I sat down at one and just took in the atmosphere. The waiter was an interesting fellow. He was small and thin, clad in a black tuxedo with a white shirt. Unlike the waiters in the main room, he did not wear a long apron. He also had a folded white cloth napkin over his arm. I observed how he took an order from a customer, leaning in a bit, with his head inclined towards the person who was ordering, and then after receiving the order he bowed his head in a slight but noticeable movement. It seemed to me as though he had been dropped off there from the *belle epoque*. He suddenly appeared at my table and asked what I would like to order. I glanced quickly at the menu and ordered a glass of the red wine that was listed first. I had the chance to look more closely at him and noticed he was wearing black eye-liner. I thought he looked like he was from an Eastern European country as there was something exotically foreign about him. When he went to fetch the glass of wine, I realized that his exotic look—especially with the eyeliner—reminded me of the mysterious emcee character played by Joel Grey in *Cabaret*. The waiter was back in a flash and graciously placed the glass of wine on the table with a slight bow of his head. He uttered a phrase in German that I didn't understand but I assumed it meant something like "enjoy."

I began going to Café Einstein a few evenings a week and reduced my afternoon visits to just once or twice per week. I was intrigued by the evening waiter for there was something attractive about his manner. I hoped to have a chance to speak with him but being rather shy and not conversive in German, I didn't initiate a conversation with him other than ordering a glass of red wine. After a few weeks, he anticipated my order and just waited for my concurrence. I began reading Sartre's *Nausea* during my evening visits, dressed in black, and let my mind transform my current environment into the Café Deux Maggots. One evening, as I was musing on the fact that I seemed more drawn to the Self-Taught-Man character than the protagonist, Roquentin—for I was not "nauseated" by the recognition of the bare existence of things nor did I concern myself about that—I was startled by the voice of the waiter who had approached the table. He asked me in German if I knew the English word for "quark." I replied in English that I didn't think there was one for I had never come across that type of dairy product before coming to Germany. A brief conversation ensued whereby he learned that I was American originally from New York but had most recently lived in San Francisco. And I discovered that he wasn't Eastern European but rather from Vienna, as were most of the wait staff, and his name was Georg. That broke the ice and after that he regularly stopped at my table to chat when he wasn't busy.

When winter arrived and the cold acrid fog became much more pervasive, I began to consider whether I might want to live in Vienna. I wasn't motivated by a wish to escape the dreariness of winter in Berlin, for I actually liked the pungent night air and expected that it would be similar in Vienna. But rather, acknowledging my gravitating to Berlin's only Viennese style coffeehouse, and my continued fascination with Georg, prompted me to ponder this move. I figured that a city with many coffeehouses like the Einstein, and undoubtedly many interesting "old world" waiters like Georg, would offer me the romanticized European atmosphere that I sought. My efforts to view West Berlin as a modern version of the avant-garde metropolis of the 1920s were weakening. West Berlin was not cooperating with my endeavors that I was increasingly viewing as unrealistic if not delusional. I did not, however, realize that I was imposing impossible standards on modern day Vienna that would also not be met. When I voiced these musings to Georg, he told me that I would not like Vienna. It was a city that was wallowing in its past and that the nightlife there was uninteresting and certainly no match for Berlin's. He then offered to give me a tour of the

Berlin nightlife, telling me that I would then lose interest in going to Vienna. I was very excited at this prospect and said I would like that very much. However, I requested that we do this on a night when I did not have to work the next day, since I began work at 6am. We then made an appointment to embark on the tour in two days' time. We would begin when he finished work at midnight.

As arranged, we began the tour at midnight. I was impressed by Georg's attire for going out into the night. He wore a long camel-colored coat like a cape, sported a Borsalino hat, used a black umbrella with gold trim as a walking stick, and carried, rather than wore, black leather gloves. The black eyeliner seemed to have been freshly applied. He really looked like he came out of another place and era. I was fascinated and looked forward to seeing how he interacted in the night scene. Our first stop was a nearby intimate bistro with a bold, modern décor called the "Neue Heimat," located on a quiet, dark street along the canal. We entered to find only a few customers at the bar and two tables occupied in the restaurant part. The woman behind the bar seemed to know Georg well and he introduced me to her. She had lived in L.A. for many years and spoke perfect English. Without Georg actually ordering a drink, the bartender warmed a glass and poured a generous amount of cognac into it. I gathered that was Georg's habitual drink. We didn't linger there very long for it seemed this was just a place to get fueled for the night ahead. Georg asked the bartender to call a taxi and soon we were off into the night. Our destination was a medium-sized bar not far from my room in Charlottenburg. I had had no idea that this place existed because I seldom walked around at night. I liked the name of the bar, "Back Stage," as it suggested that hidden activities would occur here. Unlike the Neue Heimat, this bar was crowded and loud music was playing. The smoky air assaulted me and made me cough, but I eventually adjusted to it. Once my foggy lenses cleared, I was able to observe that the occupants were mostly young and quite normal in appearance. Georg really stood out. There was the unmistakable scent of hashish in the air and I noticed that at several tables, people were smoking very large joints. I watched how the Germans used tobacco as a base and then sprinkled a generous dose of hashish on top before rolling the joint. Georg didn't seem particularly interested in smoking at one of the tables and we continued to stand at the bar. He asked me what I wanted to drink and I requested a glass of white wine. I noticed that he continued to drink cognac. Here, too, the bartender, who seemed well acquainted with Georg, heated the glass first using a lit match, burning a small amount of cognac, twirling it around with his hand and then pouring out the burned cognac before filling it again. I would observe this procedure countless times. The bartender was tall with long curly hair that hung down nearly to his shoulders. But what was most striking about his appearance was that he was dressed in women's clothing. Yet, he didn't seem to be interested in cultivating a feminine gait; in fact, he walked behind the bar in a very masculine manner, somewhat like a truck driver. On a later occasion, I asked Georg why he dressed in women's clothing when he obviously wasn't a transvestite. He responded that he simply felt more comfortable in women's clothing.

As the night went on, I had ample opportunity to talk with Georg, although we were often interrupted by various women who seemed to flock to him. I observed how he spoke with the women and although I couldn't follow what he was saying because of his Viennese dialect, the women seemed enchanted. I surmised that he did not express himself in the same manner as German men. His words apparently matched his "old world" appearance. After about two hours, we moved on to what Georg described as the mecca of the Berlin night scene. We took a taxi a short distance to a side street off the famed Kurfuerstendamm and walked down a flight of steps to a bar that was only partly above ground. It was called "Mink." This bar was very different from the last one. The top half of the walls were painted black while the bottom half had black and white tiles, that reminded me of the New York subway. It was a dingy place with a large bar and some worn looking stools, and had neither tables nor chairs. There was, however, an area with three levels, like bleachers, also painted black, where one could sit and observe the scene at the bar. The music was loud and there were only a handful of people at the bar. Georg told me that we were still early. People didn't show up until 4 or 5. I switched to drinking mineral water but Georg continued with cognac. I was impressed by how much he could drink of such potent alcohol—as he must have already had at least five—and not get drunk. Sure enough, the bar started filling up. And within the next hour, it was packed. The crowd here was more diverse than at the Back Stage and included a few in punk attire with pastel colored hair. Some seemed to be high on narcotics. But I was taken aback to see a woman in a full-length mink coat. I thought she might have dressed to harmonize with the name of the bar. As the night wore on, I became tired of standing (which Georg never seemed to be) and sat down at the bleachers. A person sitting to my left offered me a cigarette. I was about to say I didn't smoke, but instead I accepted it. He offered a light and I inhaled my first cigarette. Of course, I had smoked a great deal of pot when in college, but never felt the desire to smoke tobacco. But here in Berlin, everyone seemed to smoke, particularly in the bars and cafes. I felt I might as well join them since I was breathing in the smoke anyway.

When Georg noticed me smoking, he procured a pack for me. And so I became a regular cigarette smoker. I found it useful in giving me something to do in bars since I was not inclined to drink more than a glass of wine. The hours went by and Georg remained standing at the bar, drinking cognacs and engaging in continuous conversation and laughter with a variety of people. I observed that he was truly in his element here. I looked at my watch. It was close to 7. I thought I had had enough for one night and told Georg I was ready to go home. He walked me outside where it was already light and asked if I needed a taxi. I told him it wasn't too far to where I lived and felt I needed some fresh air. I thanked him for the tour, telling him it was an interesting experience. He then walked back into Mink.

As I regularly joined Georg for bar-hopping through the night, I decided to quit my job at the hotel. I was actually less interested in the Berlin night life than I was in Georg, with whom I was developing a close friendship, despite being so very different. I was intrigued and fascinated, for I had never met anyone like him before. He not only represented for me an image of "Old Europe" but was also truly a unique creature of the night. I discovered that he was intelligent and well read. Yet he thrived not in a world of books but in the nightlife of this city, and people, especially women, flocked to him. I soon learned that he often went home with one of them—usually a different one each night. I sometimes witnessed this, but often I left before. I wondered if there had been someone comparable to Georg in Weimar Berlin. There were most likely others who drank as much as Georg, but I doubted that they had, in my view, the singular combination of Viennese charm, art nouveau style, and a touch of decadence that Georg seamlessly brought together.

I was soon offered a job at the Neue Heimat, cleaning the place five afternoons per week, and thus was free to accompany Georg on his circuit of bars through the night. Mink was often among the stops we made, but we never arrived there before 4am. Georg had begun to refer to me as his "private secretary" during our nocturnal outings. I really didn't mind occupying this new role which seemed to be important to Georg. My service was essentially just being present. One late night at Mink, I got to witness a side of Georg I had not yet experienced. I was, as usual, sitting in the bleachers, smoking and sipping a mineral water when suddenly Georg, who was standing at the bar, took his empty cognac glass by the lower rim and smashed it against the edge of the bar. It broke in such a way that he, nor anyone standing nearby, was injured. He then nonchalantly ordered another cognac. The bartender showed no visible sign of being angry and produced another cognac at once. About 15 or 20 minutes later, Georg repeated the same action. This occurred at least two more times. I didn't know what to make of this strange behavior and walked up to the bar and asked him if he was alright. He was very drunk but composed, yet made a grinding noise with his teeth that I found unsettling. He had a strange look in his eyes. He then said quietly to me that he needed to kill something inside of him. I considered it best not to request any explanation of what he meant. He said he was fine and I returned to my former place but with a sense that there was something fragile about Georg. The "Old Europe" façade he wore so naturally had some cracks in it. I thus felt even more propelled to keep a careful watch over him.

After that night of Georg's disturbing behavior, I often reflected on how and why I was "serving" Georg. Especially after becoming aware of his dark side, I concluded that my dedication to watching over him was not completely selfless compassion. I probed into my deeper intentions and surmised that I wanted and needed to be accepted by "Old Europe," and Georg was a living and unique representative. He exuded charm and an aesthetic sensibility that I associated with continental Europe—and Vienna was certainly a city that had cultivated this in the past—and, thus, playing the role of Georg's private secretary even in the modern decadent night world of Berlin, strengthened my self-image as an ex-patriate. For one of my motivations for crossing the Atlantic was that I wished to rise above what I viewed as bland, plastic American consumer-driven culture.

During those nights with Georg, especially at Mink, I tended to be an observer rather than a participant in the night life. We of course spoke with one another at times, but more often than not, I would retreat to the sidelines and just watch. I would focus on small groups of people who appeared to be having a good time, laughing loudly, a drink and cigarette in each hand. But I sensed there was, in some people at least, something forced, something not natural. The night scene was a world of sensual indulgence, and what separated Berlin's night scene from that in other cities was not only that it went on all night and into the early morning hours, but that it was not limited to private clubs; most, if not all the establishments, were just bars open to everyone. It seemed to me that it was all rather pointless. I did not yet know about the Buddhist concept of *samsara*, the endless wheel of moving from life to life due to incessant craving for sensual pleasures, but I must have already had an inkling of this view. I decided I was going to take a short break from Berlin—and Georg—and make a brief excursion to Prague.

In February, 1983, having obtained a tourist visa from the Czechoslovakian Consulate in West Berlin, I boarded a train at the Bahnhof Zoo and began my first journey to a Communist country (other than day visits to East Berlin). Although the carriage I was in was unheated, I didn't really mind. I, like everyone else, stayed bundled up as if we were outside. I was excited and also a bit nervous. I was reading Kafka's *The Trial* even though the nightmarish atmosphere it depicted would not be what I would encounter. I wasn't sure if Kafka's books were permitted to be read there, but thought no one would bother me since I was reading it in English translation. I arrived in Prague after about seven hours, without any unpleasant incidences occurring at the border crossing.

Leaving the train station, I walked toward the main avenue where my hotel was located. I knew that Prague was one of the few central European cities to have escaped bombing during the Second World War. The old gothic inner city was virtually intact. As it was the middle of February, it was not only very cold but there was a significant amount of snow about. The hotel, though in an old building, had a somewhat institutional feel to it. There were bright fluorescent lights in the corridors which reflected into the room through the glass above the door. It was late afternoon and darkness would be descending soon, but I nevertheless headed out for a walk. I meandered through the maze of narrow winding streets of the historic center. Many of the facades of the buildings were coated in black soot from decades of coal burning smoke. However, I did not smell the characteristically acrid smell of coal here as I did in Berlin. At twilight I found myself at the exquisite medieval landmark, the Charles Bridge. One entered it through a stately archway. The bridge was lined on both sides with statues and was now used only by pedestrians. It was quite long since the river it crossed was wide at this point. As I walked slowly across the bridge, I glanced at the statues on either side of the bridge that were laced graciously with clean white snow. Snow also clung to the ornate street lamps. When I reached the half-way point, I turned around and faced the historic quarter I had just walked through. There were some soft shades of pink color yet in the sky over the city and I could make out the eclectic collection of ancient church towers behind the archway of the bridge. People, many of them elderly, were shuffling through the snow, carrying bundles with them. A number of them were speaking to one another in German. I stood still and drank in the entire scene. I had no inclination to take a photo, for the essence of what I was experiencing could not be captured by a camera. My observing mind evaporated into the scene. "I" ceased to observe. There was only a multidimensional scene which seemed to engulf me. I don't know how long I stood there, but I eventually became aware of my feet and hands being very cold. As I walked back into the city, the effect of what I had just experienced remained with me. In fact, I would remember it as one of my special moments in Europe many years later.

    I spent the next day exploring the historic city center. I entered what had been the Jewish quarter and came to a small ancient synagogue. I noted that it was built in 1270 and was reported to be the oldest synagogue in Europe. It appeared to be partially buried into the ground because it had a very small door and windows and a low roof. I entered and stood in the small empty space. The color of the walls was of a light brown clay-like texture giving the interior a primitive ambience. I was the only one in the synagogue and was struck by its simplicity and utter stillness. I remained standing in the center for a few moments, imbibing the sacred silence. I then walked outside and saw a building across the way that looked like a small museum. It documented the history of Jews in Prague and in one room off to the side there were some simple black and white drawings adorning the walls. I looked more closely and saw that they had been drawn by children who had later perished in concentration camps. Instantly tears filled my eyes, as when I had come upon the list of concentration camps during my early days in Berlin. The golden image of old Europe that I still clung to was punctured by the stark, ugly reality of modern history. I left the museum and sought solace in a coffeehouse in the city center.

My short trip to Prague had a revitalizing effect on me, which I would need when I returned to Berlin. The day after my arrival, I went to the Café Einstein to see Georg and discovered that he had been fired over the weekend for failing to show up for work on two consecutive occasions. He had come to depend on me phoning him several times during the afternoon to wake him up. Since I had been away for a few days, he failed to wake up in time for work. His private secretary had let him down.

Georg inquired of his friends at the Neue Heimat bistro if they might be in need of waiter for the restaurant section. As luck would have it, the current waiter was leaving in a few weeks and Georg could fill his position. And so, we both would be working at the same place, but not at the same time. Since my job was cleaning up, I generally worked in the afternoon before the bistro opened. Georg would be working during the restaurant hours in the evening. Feeling a bit guilty about his getting fired from Café Einstein, I thought I would fulfill my role as his private secretary by assisting him in his duties as waiter. It actually helped me as well, as I was able to get started on washing the dishes, thus lessening my work the next day.

As I was riding the bus along Potsdamer Strasse to the Neue Heimat one early afternoon, a thought surfaced from a place deep within. It was a nonverbal flash of recognition that I was, in fact, still on a spiritual journey. At that moment, my immediate environment in the bus and the shabby buildings along the street seemed to be in sharper focus, as if I had been fitted with a new pair of glasses that gave me perfect 20-20 vision. Along with this I felt rapturous joy pass through me, rising from my heart center up to my head. I broke into a broad smile that was not under my control. It then subsided, and my inner and outer world felt as it had before the recognition. By the time I got off the bus, the whole experience had evaporated from my consciousness, as I focused on the mundane duties I was about to perform.

One evening as I was assisting Georg at the Neue Heimat, the woman working the bar, with whom I had a good cordial relationship—the one who had lived in California for many years—informed me that she thought it might be better to have the woman who was cleaning the bistro on the two days I was off, and doing a much better job than I was, switch work schedules with me, thus leaving me with work only two days per week. I was dumbfounded, for I did not see this coming. I attempted to change her mind but it was not possible. The decision had been made. This surprising development spurred my growing restlessness and dissatisfaction with life in Berlin. When I spoke to my English friend, Paul, about this, and mentioned that I thought I needed a change. He suggested I consider enrolling in an intensive course in London that provided training and a certification in teaching English as a foreign language (T.E.F.L.). I had resisted teaching English in Berlin because I had wanted to live as a local, soaking up the culture, and not be the foreign English teacher. Yet, I was tired of cleaning and didn't see any promising prospects for employment. I was also aware that I needed to revitalize my ex-patriate writer identity. I had experienced enough of the Berlin nightlife and while I felt a close bond with Georg—as well as a genuine concern for his welfare—I knew I had to seek new adventures in Europe for my own personal growth.

By the end of July, I decided to go to London and with my parents' offered support to pay the cost of the one month intensive course, I planned my departure from Berlin. Paul had a close friend who lived in London who was very happy to put me up while I stayed in London. Thus, it was settled. What only remained now was to explain my plan to Georg. He did not take it well but I remained undeterred, assuring him that I would be back.

An Interim Period

After leaving Berlin in early August 1983, I spent the next three years living in London, Barcelona, and Stuttgart, where I further developed my persona of ex-patriate writer. After finishing the intensive course in T.E.F.L. (Teaching English as a Foreign Language) at International House in

London, I lingered there for a few months, working part of the time in the kitchen of a restaurant in Covent Garden, before moving on to Barcelona and later Stuttgart, where I would make use of my newly acquired English teaching credentials. I devoted much time in all three cities to writing short stories. I can see now but was not aware then that writing had become my spiritual practice, especially writing stories, not because of the concentrated state I was in when I wrote but because I channeled my spiritual longing through some of the characters I created who were searching for—or inadvertently experiencing—a supramundane mode of being. Except for an occasional flash of recognition, as on the bus in Berlin, my awareness that I was on a spiritual journey had become buried under the distractions of my recent life. Yet, on some level, and unarticulated in my consciousness, I was still motivated by a search towards an impalpable goal, which I expressed in some of these stories. Two that I wrote in London particularly stand out. In one very short piece, set in Green Park amidst the golden autumnal splendor captured in late afternoon light, the male figure, captivated by the ethereal autumnal scene realizes he has lost interest in his female partner who is uncomprehending of the change that has come over him. Although I do not describe precisely what he has experienced, I suggest that he has tapped into a higher consciousness, a transcendent state of being, prompted by his awareness of the impermanent majestic scene before him. For him, material relationships have lost their significance. While this interpretation is perhaps more a reflection of me now than then, I firmly believe that what prompted me to write this brief story was my own inchoate awareness of impermanent beauty—the sad majesty of autumn that captivated me ever since those days in upstate New York. In the other story, a seemingly normal middle-aged office worker in London walks to a former residence from 20 years ago, gets invited in by the present resident and while listening to a Bach sonata is carried into an altered, blissful state of consciousness. A state that stays with him as he walks back home.

In Barcelona, I drafted what would be my most ambitious and lengthy short story. The main protagonist, Miguel, an American ex-patriate from L. A., whose mother was Spanish, is restless, living in the world of cafes and bars, not knowing what he is searching for. He isn't particularly interested in sex or finding a partner, but rather for something intangible. There is an ever-present sense of dissatisfaction gnawing at his heart. He is on a quest for what he can't precisely put his finger on but is hopeful he will find it somehow. I can see now that I was expressing my own relentless search through Miguel. I, too, was suffering from the delusion that I would find profound solace in the external world. The story ends with Miguel still unsatisfied and, in a sense, trapped in a compulsive search he is unable to redirect.

During the time I lived in Stuttgart, an unexpected opportunity arose. One of my students, the state secretary of Baden-Wuerttemberg, invited me to join him and a delegation of business executives and government officials who were making a one-day visit to Oslo. I would not, however, be joining them for their meeting with the President of Norway. Instead, I would be taken around the city by a specially appointed guide. The main attraction for me in Oslo was the Edvard Munch Museum, for his painting "The Scream" was one of my favorites. After my guide, Peter, pointed out some of the city sights, we headed for the museum. I was drawn, as if by a magnet, directly to the famous painting. Although it was smaller than I had imagined, its power was not diminished. I indicated to Peter that I wished to stand here for some time to study and experience the full force of this work. He left me and sat down. I just let my mind take in this striking image. I studied the diminutive androgenous figure in the foreground with his hands covering his ears; how his mouth, nose and eyes were widely open, all screaming in terrifying unison. I could almost *hear* the scream. The sheer force of it, I gathered, was represented by the swirling movement of colors. As I stood both horrified and mesmerized by the inner pain that fueled this outcry, I considered what the source of it might be. My perspective on it was that the figure was expressing the unimaginable pent-up frustration he experienced living within the constraints of late 19th century bourgeois Norwegian society—a society that attempted to crush any innovative, non-conformist view of life. And this figure was suffocating in this oppressively "normal" world. The scream was a primal release of his unbearable inner pain which resonated so strongly within me that I felt for a few seconds that I was in the painting, letting out an inner scream without knowing why. With difficulty, I pulled myself away from the painting and walked on to another one.

In early summer 1986, three years after my departure, I prepared to return to Berlin. Georg, with whom I had had intermittent contact during the years I spent away, requested that I come to Berlin to assist him in running the exclusive night-bar that he had just opened. I couldn't refuse him. And I was, in fact, ready once again to live in the night world of that extraordinary gray, walled-in city. I reflected that I wouldn't be merely an observer of the night life as I had been before but rather an active participant. I thus entered another extended period of distractions leading me further away from discovering a way to attain profound inner peace.

PART TWO

Jazz and Living in the Historical Present

My return trip to Berlin was very different from the one I took there in 1981. Five years later, I was on my way back to a city I was familiar with, and having gone transit through East Germany many times—stamps filled several pages of my passport—I was not at all intimidated by the border police. During the long overnight train journey from Paris, I thought about what lay ahead. I was both excited with anticipation of helping Georg make his bar a success and also felt something rebelling within me at the recognition that time and energy to devote to my own interests, such as writing, would undoubtedly be compromised. Once I arrived, though, and saw Georg and the beautiful and very stylish bar he created, I forgot about any misgivings I might have had about returning to Berlin.

Bar Schriller was small and intimate, located on Pestalozzi Strasse, a quiet and mostly residential street in Charlottenburg, near Weimarer Strasse, where I spent my initial period in Berlin. There were two small restaurants on the block and a few doors down was a typical Berlin *kneipe* (pub). The interior of Schriller was a deep red color and the walls were of a beautiful pattern, hand-painted by a set designer for one of Berlin's main theaters. The surface of the

L-shaped bar as well as the nine round tables in the adjacent area were made of beautiful red mahogany that was highly lacquered. The chairs were of a pleasing modern design that wrapped around the person sitting in them. The room was lit by dimmable sconces of a unique contemporary design. In the corner was a very small platform that served as a stage for the upright piano, and there was also room for a vocalist and an additional musician or two. In the two large front windows were pencil-thin blue neon lights, one read "Bar" the other "Café." I was impressed with this artistically crafted night bar and was excited to make it a success, for I supposed it had cost a great deal of money to create.

Georg intended for the bar to be exclusive, not exactly a club, although the door would not be open to everyone. It was kept locked and Georg would open it only to those who seemed to be appropriate patrons. The prices for drinks were also rather steep, thus catering to a certain clientele. On weekends there was live music performed by two outstanding African American musicians from New York, a pianist and a vocalist. They played three sets between 11pm and 4am and were willing to perform for a very reasonable price, as they wanted to support Georg's efforts. While people came on weekends, during the week there was little action.

Georg occupied the apartment directly above the bar and I moved into the back bedroom. Not having to pay rent was helpful since I was intending to help in the bar, waiting on tables and also cleaning the bar during the day without getting paid. As money was tight, I did my best to help out, primarily by making late night runs to the duty-free stalls located at the Friedrich Strasse station in East Berlin. I was able to ride into East Berlin on the above ground "S-Bahn," get off the train, purchase cartons of cigarettes and a few bottles of cognac at steeply discounted prices, hop back on the train and ride back into West Berlin without going through the border checkpoint. To make it even more of an adventure, I never purchased a ticket for the train, since it was the honor system and no one was likely to check for tickets late in the evening.

Business was not picking up during the next months and I was running out of savings, so I obtained part-time teaching work at the Berlitz School. It was becoming difficult to pay for the musicians on the weekend, but Georg wanted to continue the program. Unfortunately, the singer needed to return to America and we were left only with the pianist. I thought it would be sufficient, but Georg wanted to have a singer as well. We didn't need to search very long, for shortly after the singer's departure, a very tall and voluptuous African-American woman—who was actually a transsexual—visited us, asking if we were in need of a vocalist. She had not had a lot of professional singing experience but Georg and I agreed that she would certainly attract attention. For she augmented her formidable presence by wearing colorful and revealing outfits. She was also willing to work for a percentage of what the bar took in on the nights she performed. Our highly professional and accomplished pianist, Reggie Moore, was apprehensive about working with someone with little experience but he graciously said he would give it a try. She was not a particularly good singer but I thought she was adequate and made up for her lack of skill by her dazzling appearance. The number of patrons on the weekend, however, did not pick up, although the ones who came were intrigued with the singer.

As the months went by, I decided I had to take action to convince Georg to make some changes. I suggested we lower the prices, cutting them in half, and make the place into a jazz bar with nightly live music. Since I was well aware that organizing a nightly program would not be Georg's forte, for he was best at working the bar and socializing with the patrons, I said I would manage the program. I placed announcements in the two cultural magazines in the city, and we began to get a steady flow of musicians and vocalists, both German and American, as well a few from the Philippines and England, who auditioned for us. With Georg's approval, I started booking individual musicians for nightly gigs—a trio of piano, bass and drums for every night of the week and a vocalist, as well as a musician playing a saxophone or other wind instrument, for the weekends. Reggie played on the weekends along with a bassist and drummer of high caliber. The musicians generally played three sets, beginning at 11pm and ending at 4, or sometimes 4:30 am. In a short time, business picked up and on the weekends, not only were the tables and bar stools fully occupied, but there were also people standing in between. The smoke that hung in the poorly ventilated room was so thick that when we opened the door when the musicians took a break, the smoke poured out into the street. One casualty of the success of the new program was the exotic singer, whom Georg, backed by Reggie, insisted had to go. I felt bad for her but I knew that they were right. Her musical skills were not of the same caliber as the other vocalists.

Having quit the teaching job at Berlitz, I was now working in the bar every night except Mondays when we were closed. I usually waited on tables, while Georg's current girlfriend worked the bar, and Georg stayed at the door, welcoming guests and engaging in conversation with different patrons. I also would introduce the musicians (and vocalist on the weekends) for each set, because Georg did not know all of their names. On two weekdays I actually worked both the bar and the tables since it wasn't that busy, and this gave Georg a little more time to rest. On the nights he was there, a new influx of guests came at 4am or later, acquaintances of Georg from the night scene who were not interested in the music, but rather to drink well into the morning hours. Thus, Schriller was both a jazz bar and also part of the late-night scene. I felt obligated to remain into the morning hours because Georg would be drinking heavily with the late night guests, which brought in a lot of extra money into the bar, and I was nervous about leaving all that cash there with Georg being so inebriated. Needless to say, this would wear me out. For I would be there for eight or ten hours, smoking innumerable cigarettes, drinking a lot of ginger ale and mineral water, and often I had to observe some raucous and distressing behavior. I had conflicting emotions: on the one hand, I welcomed the business from patrons in the early morning hours as it was often substantial; on the other hand, I felt sorry for these seemingly happy individuals who had the compulsion to drink excessively.

Overall, I was delighted that the bar had become a success—it was even included in a *Sunday New York Times* article on the Berlin nightlife. Schriller also became a late-night favorite for musicians who had played at other places earlier that night—as most jazz clubs ended their live program at 2am. Thus, occasionally there would be impromptu late night jams. I was thrilled to hear such high quality live jazz and considered myself fortunate to be a part of this exhilarating music scene. There was, however, a dark cloud on the horizon. Someone had moved into the upstairs apartment next door to ours, who began to complain about the late night live music. Georg and his financial backer had cut corners in one crucial matter. They did not fully sound-proof the bar. Thus, music could clearly be heard in the tenant's apartment even though it wasn't directly over the bar. He threatened to call the police if we did not reduce the volume of the music. But there wasn't much we could do. A short time later, the police showed up one night while the musicians were playing and, surprisingly, waited for them to finish before ordering the music to cease. We were informed that we were not to have live music there after 11pm. As our unique role in the Berlin night scene was that the music continued until 4am, this prohibition would prompt the slow and painful death of Bar Schriller.

Initially, people continued to come to the bar but when discovering that there would be no live music, either left shortly after having a drink, or even departing without ordering anything. Since Georg had many acquaintances in the night scene, there were a core group of regulars. We even began circulating a petition to be presented to the cultural ministry of the city, requesting aid in finding another location. Although more than five hundred signatures were collected and submitted in person by Georg to the office, and despite his best efforts to persuade the minister to support our efforts, no support was forthcoming.

Georg insisted that we remain open in the hope that someone would come forward and offer assistance. As the months went by, I became increasingly pessimistic about the future of the bar. The light fixtures stopped working and we had to use candles on the tables for most of the illumination. Because of so little money coming in, we were unable to replenish our stock and thus the few customers that came in had a diminishing selection of drinks to choose from. Georg only worked in the bar three nights per week, because he would have easily consumed all the remaining bottles of cognac. Thus, I was there alone on the other evenings, and often not a single person would enter the bar during the seven hours it was open (10pm-5am). As I had become bored with our music tapes, I would sit in the dimly lit bar in silence. I began making word lists, going systematically through each letter of the alphabet, writing down every word I could think of. Needless to say the nights seemed interminable. I had many hours to consider my present and also my early life in Berlin. I realized that I had never before given so much of myself to another person. I had compassion for Georg that I didn't normally feel even for family. My heart would at times ache when I perceived his suffering. For why else would he drink so excessively? I was unable to know with certainty what burned within his heart but I recognized from long experience that he was truly a narcissist—yet an acutely vulnerable one. It was this almost childlike vulnerability and, of course, his old world charm—in a city that cultivated the opposite—that drew my admiration and protection towards him. While my attention and loyalty were not completely selfless, I was far more selfless with him than I had ever been before. My years in Berlin up to that point were inextricably linked with Georg.

During those increasingly painful and depressing months, I began periodically to experience a type of anxiety attack. Out of nowhere, I would suddenly feel the foundation upon which I based my daily existence, and which I took for granted unthinkingly, had given way. Fear would grasp me as the lights seemed to be getting very bright and there was a pressure on my ears. These physical symptoms would fuel the momentary uneasiness I felt in not knowing where I was nor who I was. I would try to calm down by taking slow deep breaths which generally did the trick.

Although I assumed that these "attacks" were occurring because of the situation with Schriller, I had a vague inkling that there was something else behind them.

One afternoon I felt a spontaneous urge to visit a Buddhist temple that I had heard was located in Frohnau, in the far north of the city. Frohnau seemed more like a village than a district of West Berlin. I didn't know where the temple was and just started walking down a tree-lined street. I finally came to a stately compound of light brown brick buildings on a large landscaped plot. The sign read "Das Buddhistische Haus." As I walked through the open gate, I immediately felt the serenity of this hideaway, so far removed from the city. I stopped into the main house, where I heard a soft, gentle voice speaking in German. In a room off to the side, I saw a monk in dark orange robes speaking to a small group of lay people. I didn't want to intrude so I walked outside to explore the grounds. There was a lovely pond watched over by a standing Buddha statue. I noticed in the distance a Buddhist nun collecting wild flowers. I followed a path and came to a separate building that I assumed was the main temple or meditation hall. I removed my shoes and went inside. There was a large Buddha statue and shrine against the wall and maroon cushions arranged on a raised platform on two sides. The middle section had a few cushions laid out and I sat down on one and just gazed at the statue. The serenity in his face reached gently into my heart, and I experienced a calm I had not known in a long time. I closed my eyes and just let the effect spread though my body. All the frustration and nervousness that I had been experiencing regarding the bar evaporated. I sat for a long time, feeling no urge to stand up and leave. Leg cramps eventually punctured my serenity and I slowly stood up and with a lingering gaze towards the Buddha statue, made my way to the exit. I didn't want to return to the city and Schriller. A flash went through my mind urging me to stay there and not return. I felt drawn to this oasis and promised myself I would return.

The inevitable course of events played out and in early July 1989, Bar Schriller closed its door for good. On that last night, as we prepared to leave, I couldn't stop the tears from streaming down. Georg was much more composed. I was sure that he was keeping his inner pain bottled up inside. The last few months had left me completely exhausted—mentally and physically. I neglected to follow up on my promise to return to the Buddhist temple. I didn't have the inner drive or energy to go on that long journey. After a few weeks, I returned to teaching at the Berlitz school and picked up a weekend job at a bar situated in a large live music club on Potsdamer Strasse.

Autumn of that year had a big surprise in store which would change the course of modern history in Europe. On a Thursday evening, November 9th, Georg and I were sitting in a café in Charlottenburg when a young French-woman, whom we knew slightly, came up to us and said that she had heard that the Berlin Wall had opened and people were pouring out of East Berlin into West Berlin. We both thought she had misunderstood what she heard. I didn't give it any further thought at that moment. After midnight, I headed back to my new residence, a small studio apartment, in the working class neighborhood of Neukolln. As I was walking along Sonnenallee, I noticed a number of people window shopping. I thought that was odd, as it was around 1am and the items in the windows were quite ordinary household and food items. At the same time, I couldn't help but become aware of the inordinate number of East German "trabbis"—little cars that used a low-grade fuel and thus gave off an unpleasant smell. One occasionally saw one of these cars in West Berlin but never so many, and so late at night. I hurried to my apartment and turned on the radio to the BBC World Service, my usual news source. The normally staid and emotionless news announcer could not restrain his excitement as he literally blurted out that the unthinkable had happened: The Berlin Wall had opened and thousands of East Germans are streaming into West Berlin. As it was too late for me to go by public transportation to one of the border crossings to witness it firsthand, I had to wait until the morning.

Early the next morning, I headed over to Checkpoint Charlie—the famous spot where Soviet and American tanks faced each other in the height of the Cold War—which was the main border crossing for non-Germans crossing into East Berlin, generally for a day visit. When I reached the spot, I could not believe my eyes. There was a party atmosphere as a continuous flow of East Germans walked through the border crossing, many in tears of joy and disbelief, and West Berliners welcoming them with cheers and a glass of sparkling wine. I stood there for a while, imbibing the excited joy playing out in the streets. I had never thought I would experience anything like this in Berlin. I later heard that it was all a misunderstanding that snowballed from the evening before. The East German minister for foreign travel had announced that East Germans would no longer be prevented from travelling to the West. Apparently some interpreted that to mean that they could go immediately. But that was not what the minister intended. There would, not surprisingly, be some formality and regulation about traveling to Western countries. However, the rumor spread like wildfire and people by the thousands spontaneously rushed to various border crossings. Faced with such a sudden mass of people, the police simply let them pass unhindered into West Berlin, the half of the original whole city that they had been forbidden to visit for nearly 30 years.

As I stood there transfixed by the pandemonium, I shared the ebullience of the East Germans shedding tears of indescribable joy. I couldn't believe that the masses had actually trampled down the impregnable Wall that had stood for 28 years. The scene seemed so unreal, so unlike the daily life in Berlin I had known for so long. I experienced a sense of jubilation as it registered in my mind that I was living in the historical present. And I knew life in Berlin and the rest of Eastern Europe would never be the same as it was before.

The period after the fall of the Wall ushered in the gradual "fall" of my dedication to Georg. The innate instinct—that inner voice I had counted on before—propelled me to seek a new direction in my life. An unexpected event provided the catalyst. One morning in early March 1990, I woke up to discover that one of my eyes was surrounded with little red points. I also could not open that eye fully. I called an American friend of mine living in Berlin, described the symptoms and she urged me to go to the emergency room of the nearest hospital. I hesitated to do so, because I didn't think it could be that serious, but since I did not have a personal physician, I really had no choice. I was glad I listened to her, because evidently I had some type of infection, possibly "shingles," and the doctor on duty recommended that I be admitted into the hospital to begin immediate treatment. I never actually discovered what the infection was, but I was hooked up with an antibiotic drip which I received for about a week. Before going to the hospital, I sat in the kitchen of my apartment and had a cigarette, thinking it may be difficult to smoke in the hospital. I did, however, bring a pack of cigarettes with me, just in case. That cigarette turned out to be my last one. I had no opportunity to smoke at the hospital, especially being hooked up to a drip 24-hours a day. Little did I suspect that I had entered a new period of my life.

When I was discharged and able to go home, I decided not to continue smoking. Having had many hours in the hospital to think about my life and how I would like to direct it, an interest surfaced—one that I had felt intermittently during the past few years: I wanted to study literature at university, with the goal of teaching in the future. I had actually enjoyed teaching English as a foreign language but I recognized that I really wanted to study and teach literature. Thus, the spring of 1990 was a time of rejuvenation for me. Oddly, I didn't think of making a return trip to the Buddhist temple in Frohnau. My re-connection with Buddhism was not to happen for another eight years.

In the summer, I was browsing in the one bookstore in Berlin that had a separate room for books in English. One book caught my attention. It was *The History of the English Language*, by Albert Baugh. Thumbing through it and noting how in narrative form, the author takes the reader on an exhaustive journey through the linguistic, cultural, sociological, and historical development of English, I felt excitement welling up within me. I was fascinated with the subject and immediately decided to purchase the book. For the next week, I read it with as much zealous interest as if I was reading a stimulating literary narrative. What struck me most was the Middle English period (1100-1450), and the discussion of the works of the great medieval poet, Geoffrey Chaucer. I now knew my future plan: I would seek admission into the Freie Universitaet Berlin and study English language and literature, what the Germans call *Anglistik*, focusing on the period of the Middle Ages. But after two semesters, I realized that it would be much more worthwhile to pursue advanced study in the U.S. than in Berlin. And thus I prepared to end my long self-imposed exile in Europe and return to the States.

I set my departure for early summer 1992, thus giving me some time to earn money which I would need for getting settled in the States. About a week before I was scheduled to leave, I noted that there was going to be a Bach concert of all six Brandenburg Concertos in Brandenburg Cathedral. I decided to attend this very special event. The small city of Brandenburg was located well inside the former East Germany and it took some effort to get there. But it proved to be worth the trouble. Sitting in the simple yet majestic cathedral, so close to the chamber orchestra, I allowed my mind to be lifted up and carried on the exquisite melodic tones of the music. I was grateful to the musicians, grateful to the city of Brandenburg, grateful to the newly re-unified Germany, and, most of all, grateful to old Europe that had been my residence for the past eleven years. As I sat there, I thought what better way could there be to bid farewell to Europe than listening to Bach's magnificent concertos in this cathedral.

The official farewell occurred on July 17. Georg accompanied me to the airport. As we were early, we sat at a café in Tegel airport and chatted. We somehow lost track of the time and then had to rush to the gate. There was no time for long good-byes. I was actually relieved about that because I didn't know what to say to Georg. It was unlikely that I would be returning to Berlin anytime soon, if ever.

As the plane took off I experienced incongruent feelings of joy and sadness, and I discovered that tears were streaming down my face. There was a lump in my throat as I realized that a major era in my life had ended.

The Heart of the Journey

CHAPTER 5

Academic Diversion and Re-Discovery of Buddhism

I had not anticipated how difficult it would be for me to readjust to being back in the States. I had made several brief visits to New York during the years I had spent in Europe, but now I was back for an indefinite period of time. How strange it seemed to be using monochrome dollars instead of the colorful currency I had become accustomed to. One pleasant surprise I encountered was that New York seemed to be a much nicer place than it was in the 1970s when I last resided there and even in comparison to conditions in the 1980s. Eleven years in Europe actually made me appreciate my home city. For, despite my long absence, it certainly felt familiar, and after my initial period of adjustment, it was as though I had never left.

I found a reasonably priced studio apartment to rent in a four-story walk-up in the predominantly Greek neighborhood of Astoria, Queens. During the summer, with the window air conditioner unit on, I wasn't too disturbed by street noise, but when the weather turned cooler, I would periodically be jolted by the ever-occurring sound of sirens and car alarms. The latter were often triggered by extremely powerful radios bellowing out from cars waiting for the traffic light to change.

I elected to begin graduate school by first entering the master's program in English at Queens College, CUNY. I thought it best to move through graduate study in stepwise fashion, moving on to doctoral study later. I was motivated to pursue graduate study not only because of my strong interest in studying English literature, particularly of the medieval period, but also in order to live what at the time was my ideal life: an English professor at a small college in a beautiful rural location (preferably in the northeast), with attentive students and a community of friendly faculty. I anticipated balancing my life among teaching, research and summer travel. Once again, I was attempting to shape my ideal world. Needless to say, it did not work out at all as I had fantasized.

After successfully making it through my first semester, I was ready to celebrate my 40th birthday, which occurred in late December. I, like many Jewish New Yorkers, enjoyed New York at Christmas time. The large department stores on Fifth Avenue went all out in creating stunning holiday windows, and there was, of course, the magnificent tree at Rockefeller Center. I spent my birthday alone, traipsing around Manhattan in the freshly fallen snow. Everything that day seemed so perfect and out-of-the-ordinary. Years later, I reflected that it was perhaps the last time I actually experienced the special excited feeling of celebrating the anniversary of my birth. I capped off the day by attending a youth orchestra concert at Carnegie Hall directed by the famed violinist, Isaac Stern. The day was just one pleasurable experience and I sensed that my forties would be a time of personal growth and development—I would be generating a new persona: the academic.

After completing the master's program, I seamlessly entered the doctoral program at the CUNY Graduate School in midtown Manhattan. Besides having to write longer seminar papers, I would also begin teaching English Composition at Queens College. I would be very busy indeed. I decided to join the East Side Y and further develop my lap swimming ability. I had begun swimming in Berlin and continued at Queens College, but not on a daily basis. Now, I would go just about every day. I looked forward to my daily swim and gradually was able to swim a mile without stopping for a break. I counted the laps, making slight adjustments in how I swam after every ten laps. It became so automatic that despite keeping part of my mind focused on counting laps, I was able to just *be* with the activity of swimming. Mind and body were in unison as I moved through the water; there was no discursive thought and I was totally present in the moment. I realized later that swimming had become my spiritual practice. Although I wouldn't become familiar with walking meditation as practiced in Buddhism for a few years yet, I had inadvertently—and unknowingly—discovered meditation in motion.

After completing all of my coursework in the doctoral program, I was set to spend the summer of 1997 preparing for the biggest hurdle: the oral exam. I systematically went through the enormous reading list I had developed in consultation with my future dissertation director, and by the end of the summer, I felt I was as ready as I would ever be. The date of the exam was September 5, the day before the funeral of Princess Diana. I had made an effort to block out the extensive media coverage of that tragic event during the last week before the exam as I knew it would distract me. The exam was held on the fortieth floor of the Grace Building on 42nd Street across from the New York Public Library. The room had a panoramic view of midtown Manhattan, with the Empire State Building appearing startlingly close. Fortunately, I was told to sit with my back turned to the window so that I could remain focused on the panel of examiners who would be facing me. Despite being thrown for a loop by the opening question, I remained extremely concentrated throughout the two-hour ordeal. In fact, the exam seemed to be playing out in a sphere where time did not exist. I was not aware of it as we moved through the recurring rhythm of question followed by answer. I was asked to make a statement at the end of the period, and I found myself returning to the initial question that had stumped me. The seemingly effortless answer that emerged from me met with obvious approval by the committee. I then was asked to leave the room while they discussed my performance in the exam. I was called back in and congratulated for having passed "with distinction." The two-hour exam seemed unreal—almost a fantasy—in a way, which I was unable to articulate to myself nor to the chair of the exam committee who had invited me to have a coffee with him in a café in Bryant Park.

I view my spiritual journey up to this point as being in its preliminary stages. My early, inchoate interest in Buddhism morphed into the devotional path of Ananda Marga. Visiting a variety of spiritual communes from different religious traditions and experiencing spirituality as practiced in communal life planted the seed that would eventually sprout in my decision to continue my journey in a monastic community. In San Francisco, drifting away from Ananda Marga, and channeling my spiritual quest into dancing in New Wave clubs as well as expressing my observations of the world through a poetic lens, steered me away from structured spiritual practice. During my long sojourn in Europe, I dived into the mundane world and particularly during the eight years I spent in Berlin, I both observed and experienced *dukkha*—the key Buddhist term referring to suffering or gnawing dissatisfaction. Yet, I surfaced periodically to catch a breath of the supramundane, whether through writing stories or experiencing my environment otherwise. Attending graduate school allowed me to strengthen my concentration faculty, as I focused intensely on writing seminar papers and eventually my doctoral dissertation.

In the summer of 1998, I was about to cross a threshold ushering in a change in focus which would eventually lead to a monumental development in my spiritual journey.

After spending a number of hours in the dingy room reserved for doctoral candidates in the otherwise majestic New York Public Library, I decided to take a long walk to the multi-leveled Barnes and Noble store across from Lincoln Center. I didn't have a particular purpose for going there other than just browsing and perhaps drinking a cup of coffee in the café. I found myself in the Eastern Philosophy section, directly in front of the shelves with a diverse collection of books on Buddhism. Glancing at the titles, one caught my eye, *Western Buddhism*, by Kulananda, an author

I had never heard of. I thumbed through the pages, read snippets here and there, and recalled my general interest in Buddhism during my early time in Ithaca, more than twenty years before. What appealed to me about this book though was that despite his exotic name, the author was a Westerner and his targeted readers were Westerners who already had an interest in Buddhism or were drawn to finding out more about it. I realized that nearly all the books on Buddhism I had read back in Ithaca, with a few exceptions, were written by Asians. Without any hesitation, I decided to purchase the book.

It soon became clear that this was the right book to read at the right time. It offered me respite from the rigors of doing research and drafting my dissertation. What was most appealing to me about this book was not only the author's clear and coherent presentation of basic Buddhist teachings, but also his efforts to make those teachings relevant for modern life, especially in a Western country like the U.S. He depicted meditation not as a special esoteric practice but rather as a practical means for becoming more alert in one's daily life. Reading this book prompted me to review my life over the last twenty years. I noted that I had neglected periodically to stop external activity and draw my attention inward. I remembered the trip I had taken to the Buddhist temple in Berlin and how I felt just sitting in that meditation hall, allowing the external silence to seep into me. I closed the book and sat in my reading chair with my eyes closed. A thought soon materialized. Why not check out Buddhist meditation centers in New York? I went to my computer and waited patiently for my dial-up connection to become activated. I found a few listings of meditation centers in Manhattan and decided I would check out the

Zen Center of NYC. For my earlier exposure to Buddhism had been mostly related to Zen. I thought it best to go on Sunday morning when there was not only a group sitting but also a "Dharma Talk" by a teacher.

I gave myself more time than needed to arrive at the Zen center on West 23rd Street before the start of the meditation session at 10am. It was located in one of the office loft buildings that were common in that neighborhood just north of Chelsea. I got out of the elevator on the eighth floor and was a bit nervous as I walked down a long corridor to the entrance into the meditation hall. It was a fairly large space, about what one would expect in that type of building. Unadorned with artwork, there were just blank white walls all around and a bare wooden floor. The room felt like a space for cultivating inner stillness, for there was nothing external upon which to divert one's gaze. There were thick square meditation mats spread about, each with a black round meditation cushion on it. I had seen these high black cushions when I had attended a few group meditation sessions in a private home in Ithaca. I stood and waited for a signal of when to sit. Some of the people there wore plain gray robes, a few with black "bibs" in front. I assumed they were more senior practitioners. But most of the people, like me, wore regular clothing.

A sharp sound from a wooden instrument summoned everyone to take their places. We would all be facing the wall and when I quickly glanced at my neighbor, I noticed that he kept his eyes open. I remembered that from Ithaca as well. I didn't know what method to follow, so I just tried to concentrate on watching my breath. Some minutes later I was startled out of a lengthy inner monologue by the sound of a stick hitting something. I didn't dare turn around to see what it was. A short time later I sensed someone standing behind the person on my right. He made a slight nod and then I heard that same sound as the stick came down hard on the man's shoulder. He nodded again and the person holding the stick moved on. I hoped I wasn't going to be hit as well, but I reassured myself that it would be unlikely since hitting someone who had not given permission to do so could lead to a lawsuit. Needless to say, my attempts at concentration were doomed to fail after witnessing that startling, yet apparently normal, behavior at this Zen center.

I was relieved when the sitting session ended and walking meditation began. I had never done it before but had expected it to be done slowly with concentration. I was surprised then to find the person behind me right up my back as I was slowly making my way around the room. I noticed that everyone was walking rather quickly as if they had someplace to get to and they were late. Because there were so many people, the walking meditation went out into the corridor. During one of the times I was out there, I saw a man, perhaps in his late 60s, dressed in a leather jacket, walk carefully past us along the wall. I assumed he was just late for the meditation. After about 20 minutes we resumed our seats in the meditation hall. I felt a little more relaxed for this second session and braced myself for the inevitable whacking sound.

The session ended and we turned around to face the middle of the room. I recognized the older man whom I had seen in the corridor now dressed in a formal black robe and sitting in the seat of honor. I learned later that he was John Daido Loori, a very respected Zen master who had founded the center. He proceeded to give a talk, the details of which I no longer remember, but it had a positive effect on me. In a calm and gentle manner, he spoke thoughts that seemed to arise spontaneously from within him. After he finished, everyone recited a text called the "Heart Sutra" in a fast-paced rhythmic manner. I thought that this sutra was filled with incongruencies and although I didn't really understand what "emptiness" meant, I liked participating in the energy of the group recitation. At the end of my first exposure to the Zen Center of NYC, I felt content and reassured that I had found a place where I could cultivate greater inner awareness, and thus attain some peace in my mind.

I began making a habit of going to the center two evenings during the week as well as Sunday mornings. I gradually recognized some of the regulars, who I learned were monastic-like students in the Order of Mountains and Rivers. They led normal lives in New York City but occasionally went to an affiliated monastery in upstate New York for a period of intensive practice. I was intrigued by this semi-monastic Zen life and thought that maybe I would explore this upstate monastery one day. In the evenings, there was, as on Sundays, two sitting meditation sessions with a quick-paced walking meditation in between. There normally weren't many people there, so the walking meditation took place only in the room. Since it wasn't that large, I felt that I was literally going in circles many times in twenty minutes.

I also began meditating in my apartment. The mornings in particular seemed conducive as it was relatively quiet. I noticed that I felt more relaxed as I went about my daily life that summer, heading to the library every day to continue work on the dissertation, although my mind was often cluttered with thoughts about the project I was diligently attempting to make progress on. I wanted to have a substantial amount completed that summer since I was very occupied with teaching during the semesters. One late weekend afternoon as I was riding the subway into Manhattan to go swimming at the Y, I had a sudden flash of recognition that how I usually saw the world was not how it really existed. This realization did not manifest in words but rather in a feeling somewhere in the center of my body. I felt a moment of exhilaration there in the subway. I was filled with joy—not fear—as I noted my surroundings without labels, concepts or thought. The moment then passed and my efforts to get that awareness to return proved unsuccessful.

One Sunday at the Zen center a few weeks after this occurrence, a female teacher was giving a talk. She referred to a Korean master, Seung Sahn, whom she admired a great deal, and held up one of his books that had the interesting title, *Only Don't Know*. She proceeded to demonstrate all the ways our minds get in the way of knowing reality. While I understood the point she was making, I had difficulty grasping what exactly it was to "not know." I mulled over it for some time afterwards, but never felt that I had reached any conclusive answer.

During the Fall semester, having become ever more occupied with the tasks of teaching and working on my dissertation, I stopped going to the weekday evening sessions and just went on Sundays. But I never felt quite at home there. I didn't find the "students" of the Order nor the lay people who came there to be particularly friendly. I generally talked to no one, but simply meditated, listened to the talk, and left without uttering a word to anyone. One Sunday, I walked over to the large Barnes and Noble bookstore a few blocks away. Unlike the previous occasion, this time I had a purpose. I wanted to find a book on Buddhism that would offer some guidance in meditation. I really did not know what I should be doing other than watching the breath, counting inhalations and exhalations in order to keep me from getting caught up in wandering thoughts. But boredom always set in and my mind became engaged in all sorts of inner chatter and monologues. One book by the American Buddhist, Joseph Goldstein, *Insight Meditation, the Practice of Freedom*, seemed promising. I discovered that he was a native New Yorker and from his name concluded that he was of Jewish background. I skimmed through a few chapters and it seemed well written. I particularly liked that he gave instruction in a type of meditation called "vipassana." I guessed that was the practice that would lead to freedom, as indicated in the book's title. I didn't see any other book that offered more precise information on this meditation method, and so I decided to buy it.

I was not disappointed with the book as I became acquainted with a form of meditation where one developed awareness of what was arising in one's mind. Goldstein also provided a fair amount of explanation of key Buddhist concepts, such as the Four Noble Truths and karma. At this time, my focus was primarily on developing a meditation practice that could lead to a peaceful state of being as I was in the midst of working on my dissertation and teaching three courses at two different colleges. I was certainly not opposed to becoming more mentally aware and learning about key Buddhist concepts as well. A short time later, while reading through a listing of events in the *Village Voice*, I came upon a notice indicating that an insight meditation practice group met every Friday evening in a room above the Quest Bookshop on E. 53rd St. The location was very convenient as the subway I took home after swimming was just half-a-block away. I thought I would check it out on the next Friday.

The bookshop and the room above it belonged to the New York Theosophical Society. But the group that meditated there was not affiliated with this organization. Apparently the room was rented for the weekly meditation sessions. It was a decent size and could easily accommodate twenty-five meditators. I noticed that most who came were women and the facilitator was likewise a woman. I learned later that she was one of two meditation instructors who offered guided meditation for the first few minutes and periodically interrupted the silence to remind meditators to bring the mind back each time it drifted away from the breath. I saw from the business cards on the table near the door, where there was also a donation box, that both leaders were psychotherapists. About half the 15 or 20 people present sat on folding chairs while the others, myself included, sat on cushions on the floor. After sitting for 45 minutes, there was a period of walking meditation, where everyone lined up in rows walking at a slow pace between the two walls. How different the pace was, I thought, than the racing form of this meditation that I encountered in the Zen center. Since the walking track was no more than about 20 feet, walking slowly meant one wasn't constantly stopping and turning around.

After walking for about 20 or 25 minutes, everyone gathered in a semi-circle, mostly sitting on chairs. The facilitator, Sarah, waited for someone to ask a question or talk about a difficult experience from the past week. It didn't take long for a woman to describe some personal struggle she had had that week. Sarah probed her to give further information about it. Others joined in describing similar difficulties they experienced. I had nothing to offer and was uncomfortable with the format and the fact that Sarah was a psychotherapist, even though she did not obviously treat those voicing their problems as though they were her patients. I really only wanted to meditate in a group session and had hoped that there would be a dharma talk rather than a therapy session. I nevertheless continued to go there on most Friday evenings for the next year and stopped going to the Zen center.

I had in the meantime subscribed to the magazine *Inquiring Mind*, which listed in the back pages where there were meditation retreats. I noted that there would be a weekend "Introduction to Meditation" retreat in early September at the Insight Meditation Society in Massachusetts, the retreat center founded by Joseph Goldstein and three other American Buddhists. There was no fixed fee for the residential retreat, but one was encouraged to make a donation. As money was very tight for me, struggling to get by living in New York on the small graduate school stipend I was receiving, I welcomed the minimal expense. I didn't know until I arrived there that the leader of the retreat was an apparently very well-known Sri Lankan monk, Bhante Gunaratana. The timing of this weekend retreat was perfect. It was at the beginning of the fall semester 1999, and I was preparing to apply for full-time university teaching positions that fall for the following academic year. My 400+ page dissertation was completed and in the hands of the readers of my committee. I didn't expect there to be a need for major revision.

I arrived at IMS (as it is generally known), which had formerly been a Catholic novitiate, and marveled at the beautiful stately brick building and the pleasant rural location. I was a little nervous about spending the weekend in a meditation retreat atmosphere with many other people.

But it went very well. After the light evening meal on Friday, we were asked to keep "noble silence"—speaking only when absolutely necessary—until lunch on Sunday. Bhante Gunaratana gave a wonderful opening talk Friday evening, and I liked him immediately. He was quite small in stature, about 70 years old, and spoke English fluently. His eyes often sparkled when he expressed some important aspect of meditation practice. I felt very fortunate to have the opportunity to receive words of practical wisdom from this master of Buddhist meditation.

I was punctual for the first session and attended every one that weekend. I felt my meditation had been given a needed boost not only by having the opportunity to sit several sessions on Saturday and Sunday morning, but also just being in the presence of Bhante Gunaratana. I learned that the donations collected for the retreat would go towards the operations of his monastery in West Virginia. I happily gave my modest donation and decided that one day I would visit that monastery.

My dissertation defense took place on December 14, 1999. I was now officially a Ph.D., although the graduation ceremony and handing out of diplomas would not take place until after the spring semester. I had meanwhile applied for more than thirty full-time teaching positions at colleges and universities all across the country, and out of that pool, I received six invitations for interviews at the annual Modern Language Association conference held in late December and which that year would be in Chicago. Half of those positions were at small liberal arts colleges and I hoped I would be hired by one of them. For that was commensurate with the ideal life I had hoped to find in academia. It did not, however, work out that way. Out of the six positions I interviewed for, only one resulted in a job offer, and that was at the University of South Alabama in Mobile. The deep south seemed to be a foreign country to me. Of course, Mobile was a medium size city near the Gulf coast and I was hopeful that I would be able to find a few Buddhist practitioners there.

That summer, I moved into a small house, which I rented, that was close to the campus. I was glad to discover that one of my colleagues, Michelle, was also interested in practicing Buddhist meditation. Since there were no practice groups in Mobile, we decided that we would form one. We inserted notices into all the Buddhist books in the local Barnes and Noble bookstore and waited for responses. A few trickled in. None of the people who responded had ever meditated before and knew very little about Buddhism, but we reckoned they were interested enough to find our notice while thumbing through a Buddhist book. We met weekly in my living room and it fell to me to be the leader. I had purchased a small Buddha statue and a "singing bowl" to strike at the beginning and end of the meditation. I didn't feel qualified to offer meditation instruction and just indicated to the two or three people who came to our session that they should just close their eyes and focus on the breath, keeping their attention on the inhalations and exhalations. After the session, I would read a passage from one of Joseph Goldstein's books or from the one he co-authored with Jack Kornfield, *A Path with Heart*. I didn't know how much benefit the attendees derived from these readings since they all had Southern Baptist backgrounds and had little familiarity with Buddhism. But it was certainly helpful for me because I carefully combed these books for suitable passages to read aloud and thus gradually became better acquainted with different aspects of practical Buddhist wisdom.

After completing my first teaching year at the university, I decided to drive up north that summer to see family and friends in New York. On the return trip I intended to stop off at the Bhavana Society Forest Monastery and Retreat Center, founded by Bhante Gunaratana (Bhante G, as he is commonly known) and also where he resided. I had registered to attend a four-day retreat that would prepare me to take the eight lifetime moral and ethical precepts at the end of the four days. In late July 2001, I found, with some difficulty, the secluded monastery and retreat center in West Virginia. As I got out of the car and just looked around, I drank in the warm, inviting peaceful atmosphere. I thought this was indeed a sanctuary for cultivating the mind-heart. Every morning, Bhante G gave a talk, focusing on each of the eight moral precepts we would be formally taking at the end of the retreat. In the afternoons, the assistant abbot, Bhante Rahula, an American monk, presided over a period of questions and answers on any topic related to Buddhism. I took an instant liking to Bhante Rahula. He was about four or five years older than me, and seemed very ascetic. I was inspired that an American Buddhist chose to lead the monastic life in the U.S.

The monastery was situated in a large wooded area. The main building housed the kitchen, dining area, a library, and a lounge with a partition in the middle—one side for monks, the other side for lay people. But the main attraction in the building was the beautiful meditation hall, completed only a few years before. The high ceiling was wood paneled and on the altar sat a very large gold Buddha statue, in the Thai style. The airy room, the windows of which looked out into the woods, was highly conducive for meditation. I looked forward to coming there early every morning. I found that I was better able to calm my chattering mind there than at any other public place where I had attempted to meditate.

On the last day of the retreat, we all were supposed to put on white clothes. I had not thought to bring any. Fortunately I had a white t-shirt and my pants, though not white, were khaki colored, which I hoped would be considered close enough to white. The ceremony was fairly simple. We all recited the refuge prayer, "going for refuge" to the Buddha, Dhamma (the Teachings), and the Sangha (the noble disciples of the Buddha). We then repeated the eight lifetime precepts we were committing ourselves to upholding for the rest of our lives:

> To refrain from intentionally killing a human, stealing, engaging in sexual misconduct (which would include adultery), using intoxicants, engaging in false speech, harsh speech, slanderous speech, and idle chatter.

The last four corresponded to "right speech" in the noble eightfold path, and I thought would be the most difficult to keep. I realized that I would have to be very attentive in order not to speak critically of someone not present. For when having a conversation, I often related an experience or encounter where someone did not act or speak in a way that I approved of and which easily then led to my commenting on the shortcomings or character fault of that person. I also was aware that I could easily get drawn into "idle chatter"—talking about inane topics, or general nonsense, just filling the time. I was determined not to be too rigid about these precepts regarding speech acts, but instead just become aware of my thoughts before they are uttered aloud. It would be a good mental training, I reckoned. When it was my turn to go to the front of the meditation hall, I nervously approached Bhante G and the other monks. It dawned on me that this ceremony marked the moment that I officially become a Buddhist practitioner. Bhante G handed me the certificate that affirmed my taking of the eight lifetime precepts and I saw my new name: *Sanghapala* (one who is supported by the community of noble disciples). I liked the name and began to muse on its importance for my continued journey in Buddhism.

As we sat in the dining room on the floor in front of benches that were used as a table, and I gazed at the five monks sitting on a platform with their alms bowls in front of them, I fantasized what it might be like to be a monk here. There was something about the structured daily life of a Buddhist monk who spent his days and nights in this serene and aesthetically pleasing environment that I found very appealing. But then I felt a shudder run through me as I also considered the monotony of spending most of one's time here, with the same monks, doing the same thing every day, year after year. I was torn between yearning for this monastic life and being repelled by it. I let the fantasy dissolve and decided not to give it any further thought for the time being. I then focused on my upcoming departure and the long drive down to Alabama.

I returned to Mobile feeling that my "Buddhist battery" had been fully charged. I was ready to stimulate my colleague, Michelle, to continue our weekly meditation sittings, perhaps placing another round of notices in Buddhist books at the local Barnes and Noble. Nevertheless, despite my hopes for attracting several more people, we actually only gained two. And only one of them came every week, more out of loneliness I felt than because of a genuine interest in Buddhist meditation. One week, however, an older woman came who informed us of a Laotian temple outside of Mobile that she had visited a few times. There was a meeting there with a teacher on Friday evenings. Michelle and I decided to go there the next week. We were given directions by the woman and hoped we would be able to find it. After turning off the highway at Irvington, we headed towards the fishing village of Bayou La Batre (mentioned in the film *Forest Gump*). We had definitely entered semi-rural Alabama, which made me uneasy. We saw a small sign on the left that said "Wat Lao Buddha Vihara" and were relieved. We drove down an unpaved road for a while, passing some trailer homes and small ranch houses, and then came to what was surely the temple. There wasn't much there, just a modest sized wooden building, where the monk in residence lived, and another larger building where people gathered. There was a small group of women, whom I assumed were Laotians, sitting around eating some food. They smiled at us when we entered but didn't speak to us. We stood for a few minutes not knowing what we should do, when a young monk entered and walked up to us. He fortunately spoke English rather well and said he was from Thailand but the people who came here were Laotian. We indicated that we hoped to sit in meditation there and perhaps hear a talk on Buddhist doctrine. He said he would be happy to lead a meditation sitting, although the Laotian women who came there were not too keen on meditation. He then called them over and we all sat on the floor as he took a position on a flat cushion that raised him a little higher than us. He advised us to try quieting our mind by following our breath at whatever place it was most prominent. He didn't say anything else and we sat for about 15 or 20 minutes. He rang a bell and proceeded to speak about the four noble truths for about ten or fifteen minutes. And that was it. We thanked him and he invited us to come again whenever we liked.

Michelle and I agreed that one would never have expected to find a Laotian temple in this area and were glad the small immigrant community had a place to go where they might feel at home. But we realized that it wasn't worthwhile for us to drive out there.

Gradually, our meditation group fell apart. Even the lonely young man stopped coming. And then Michelle decided to leave Mobile as she had been offered a position at a university in Denver, where she much preferred to live. I was left alone and gave up the effort. I made the decision to likewise search for a teaching position in a geographical location where I might find an established Buddhist group—and possibly even a teacher—with whom I could further develop meditation practice.

Thus, in the Fall of 2003, I went on the job market again. I hoped with three years of full-time teaching experience, and some scholarly publications, I would be able to land a position on either the East or West coast. After applying for more than twenty positions, I received only one interview, which would take place at the annual MLA convention, held that year in San Diego. The position was at Oregon State. I thought that would be a fine location, within easy driving distance of Portland, where I was sure there would be a fair number of Buddhist centers. It was an expensive trip and the interview did not go well. One of the members of the search committee was obviously not in favor of my candidacy. Thus, I was not in a joyful state to celebrate my 50th birthday, which occurred on the day following the interview. I resolved, however, not to give up.

By April, I resigned to remaining in Mobile for another year, trying again the following year. But then, early one morning in June, I received a phone call from my friend, Fred, in New York, also an academic, who knew one of the members of the search committee for the position I had applied for at John Jay College, CUNY. In a conversation, this John Jay faculty member casually mentioned that she was surprised that I had never returned their call several months before requesting me to come to New York for an interview. Upon learning from Fred that I had never received the phone call, she asked if he thought I was still interested. The candidate to whom the job was offered and who had accepted had just changed his mind and if they didn't fill the position by the end of the month they would lose funding for it. As Fred was relating all of this to me, my heart started racing in excitement. He then told me I should expect to be hearing from the committee that day. And sure enough, I received a phone call from the chair of the department asking if I was still interested in the position. I tried to restrain my exuberance when I assured him I was. He then asked if I could immediately fly up to New York for an interview. I said I most certainly could.

It all went seamlessly—the interview was pleasant and relaxed, and after asking me to leave the room while they deliberated, I was called back in and offered the position. When I was out in the street, I nearly skipped in joy all the way back to my hotel. I extended my stay in New York to look for a place to live, and having found an apartment in the Riverdale section of the Bronx, from where I could easily drive down to the college (as I intended to keep my car). I was excited about my return to New York and all the options that I would find for continuing my life as a Buddhist.

CHAPTER 6

A Turn to Tibet

PART ONE
Entering the Diamond Vehicle

After settling into my new apartment and having completed my first week of teaching at John Jay College, I thought it was time to establish my new Buddhist home in New York. I had noted in the listings of meditation centers in *Inquiring Mind* that New York Insight, which had formerly met in the room above Quest Books, now had its own place on West 27th St, just off Fifth Avenue. Yet I could not summon up excitement about going there. I felt that the "miraculous" chain of events that led me back to New York portended the unfolding of a new direction in my Buddhist path. I searched online for Buddhist centers in New York, and one in particular caught my attention: The Chakrasambara Meditation Center, a Western oriented Tibetan Buddhist center. My familiarity with Tibetan Buddhism was limited to the extensive collection of *tangkas* (paintings depicting a deity or mandala) at the Metropolitan Museum I had seen shortly before leaving for Alabama. I found these paintings to be very strange yet their exoticism also appealed to me, even with having no understanding of their significance in Buddhism. Riding on the wave of excitement at finding myself back in New York, I was willing to be adventurous and explore this form of Buddhism. On the home page was a photograph of a Tibetan monk with glasses, whom I estimated was about 70 years old. His name was Geshe Kelsang Gyatso, the spiritual leader of an international organization called "The New Kadampa Tradition," and the Chakrasambara Center was the main New York branch. I read the questions and answers in the margin of the home page. In response to the question of whether the New Kadampa Tradition was Tibetan Buddhism, the reply was that it was "world" Buddhism. I wasn't sure what that meant but it did not dissuade me from checking it out. I noted that there were three different series of classes occurring simultaneously, ranging from "general" to "teacher training." I naturally chose the series of general classes for my introduction to Tibetan Buddhism, and the first class of a new series was to be begin on the next Monday.

The center was located on W. 26th Street, off of 8th Avenue, and thus easy to reach by subway. The class began at 7pm and I made sure that I would arrive early enough to get a feel for the place before committing myself to staying for the class. As I expected, it was a loft office building, and I rode the elevator to the 9th floor. The young man sitting at a table at the entrance, welcomed me with a broad, and obviously genuine, smile. A donation of $10 was requested. As I paid it, I thought to myself that I would certainly stay even if I didn't like the teaching. He gave me a photocopy of the text that would be taught in the eight-week series, *Eight Verses for Training the Mind*, by Geshe Langri Tangpa (A.D. 1054-1123). I knew that Tibetan Buddhism developed much later than other Buddhist traditions, but hadn't reckoned that the teachings would be this late. I, nevertheless, kept an open mind. The main room was quite large, about the same size as at the NYC Zen Center, but here there were at least 40 or 50 folding chairs set up in rows. Some people were already seated near the front. But I stood for a while and just looked around. In sharp contrast with the Zen center, there was much to look at. I was amazed at the collection of different types of Buddhas depicted in statues and *tangka* paintings. The room was filled with bright colors which, after getting over my initial discomfort, I actually rather liked. But one thing that I noticed made me feel not at ease. The chairs faced a platform with a thick cushion where I expected the teacher would be sitting. Behind him was a large golden Buddha statue, in what I came to understand as the Tibetan style. But above the Buddha was a large framed photograph of the same Tibetan monk I had seen on the website, Geshe Kelsang Gyatso. I did not feel comfortable with guru devotion, something I struggled with when I was connected to Ananda Marga. However, I was willing to give Tibetan Buddhism a chance.

As the room was filling up, I took a seat near the rear. A tall man of about 40, dressed in a long-sleeve shirt and pants, walked up to the platform and sat down on the cushion. I knew from the website that his name was Kadam Morten, and he was American. After some general talk to warm up the audience, he began the class with the first of the eight verses: "With the intention to attain/ The ultimate supreme good,/ That surpasses even the wish-granting jewel,/ May I constantly cherish all living beings." (https://tharpa.com/uk/wisdom-print-eight-verses-of-training-th-mind.html) I was struck not only by the beauty of the verse, but how it presented the Buddhist path, linking the goal of enlightenment with the "cherishing"—the acknowledgment of the importance of all living beings, which the teacher explained, included ALL living beings. Listening to Kadam Morten's warm, articulate explanation of this opening verse, I sensed something churning within me. A wave of joy spread in my heart and I felt myself opening up to the world. Instead of looking inward, so preoccupied with myself and my concerns, I could feel my mind embracing all the life around me. I recognized that I could not proceed on the Buddhist path without taking into account, at minimum, the millions of human beings just in the New York area. After the class ended at around 9pm and thinking about what I had listened to at this Tibetan Buddhist center during the long subway ride to the Bronx, I decided I would attend all the classes in the series.

Of the eight classes, the one that had the most profound effect on me was the next to last verse that urged one to take on the suffering of all one's "mothers." Viewing all living beings, even just considering those presently in human form, as my mothers in the unimaginable number of previous lives I had lived, transcended rational thought. Although I had at times, especially in Berlin night life, observed the suffering of others, that was in the extreme conditions of drunkenness in bars. Now I was compelled not only to notice but somehow to take on all the suffering I witnessed or imagined that people were experiencing in everyday life. I accepted the challenge of Mahayana Buddhism in its Tibetan form and, I thought, what better place to become initiated into this mind-expanding practice than in New York.

I soon began also to attend retreat days at Chakrasambara on Saturdays. On those occasions, I was introduced into a very different kind of group meditation practice which one followed by means of a *sadhana*, or practice booklet. There was no silent meditation; rather, the "meditation" was a series of beautiful melodic chants that were sung accompanied by recorded music. After initially going for refuge to the Buddha, Dharma, and Sangha, there was a generating of *bodhicitta*, a new term for me in my Buddhist vocabulary, meaning the mind of enlightenment, which one generated for the benefit of all sentient beings. For here in the Tibetan, or Vajrayana (Diamond Vehicle), tradition, one was not so much focused on personal liberation, but rather on the aspiration to become completely enlightened for the benefit of all living beings. While I thought it was a wonderful ambition, I felt the likelihood of my being able to benefit all beings—even in the far-off future—was unrealistic. Yet, I accepted it as a practice that propelled me to extend my gaze outwards. What I found very different from any Buddhist practice I had hitherto experienced was the envisioning of all the buddhas and the *bodhisattvas* (enlightened beings committed to attaining Buddhahood for the purpose of leading all sentient beings to awakening). I had never considered that there was any other buddha than Buddha Gotama, and I felt some resistance to believing that there were also *bodhisattvas* existing in some non-material form that could be summoned by my mind to be present before me. I, nevertheless, was able to open myself up to imagining rays of light being generated from all the enlightened beings, bathing my mind and that of all living beings. It was an incredibly powerful image and I appreciated that there was a pause in the chanting to engage in this act of imagination. And, associated with this was a request for blessings of "rays of light and nectar" from the Buddha's heart reaching directly into my own. Although it took me a few months to develop such visualizing skills, I pursued this practice without questioning if it really had any substantial effect. I did feel uplifted and joyful while doing it, and thus accepted that as sufficient proof of its efficacy.

In April 2005, I moved into Manhattan, having been able to scrape together enough money to purchase a very small studio apartment on the Upper West Side across from Riverside Park. Since I was now living in Manhattan, it was very convenient to hop on the subway to go to Chakrasambara. I often attended the monthly offering to the spiritual guide. A long service, lasting about two hours with a short tea break in the middle, in which elaborate, mostly food, offerings were set up on the altar and then distributed among the attendees after the service. There were two aspects of this practice that I found unsettling, though. Being of a rather practical nature, I wondered to whom exactly the offerings were being made, and I felt there was some fuzziness in separating Buddha Shakyamuni (how Buddha Gotama is referred to in Vajrayana Buddhism) and the spiritual guide. There seemed to be a merging of the two that I resisted. The other aspect was in the second half, when there was a long service addressed to a "Dharma Protector" called Dorje Shugden. I had never heard of him before, and I thought he did not look like a deity nor a buddha-like figure, for he had a somewhat modern appearance and sported what I considered to be a rather stylish hat. I also mused on why the timeless teachings of the Buddha needed an external protector. This practice that was commonly performed at Chakrasambara, and I assumed at all the NKT centers, did not resonate with me despite not yet knowing that it was controversial.

I continued to become more involved with this center and developed casual acquaintances with some of the regular members. However, I didn't feel that I had fully integrated into the NKT community despite having been going there for about nine months. A few events would change that though in the very near future.

In late June of that year, I participated in a formal ceremony led by Kadam Morten, by which I officially took refuge in the Triple Gem (Buddha, Dharma, and Sangha). I had attended a multi-week course on Monday evenings to prepare for this auspicious occasion. Although I had already done something similar nearly four years prior to that at Bhavana Society with Bhante G, I seemed to have let that memory fade out of my consciousness. Around 40 people took refuge and I found the act to be of profound importance for my commitment to Buddhism in the Tibetan tradition, and truly felt that I now belonged to this large international organization of practitioners. I was ready to take the next step which would be a tantric initiation into the deity practice of Avalokiteshvara, the Buddha of Compassion in Tibetan Buddhism. It would take place in England at the Manjushri Centre, the main temple and center of NKT, and Geshe Kelsang would be giving the initiation.

It was very convenient and inexpensive for me to attend the International NKT Summer Festival since I had obtained a research stipend to spend a month in Cambridge, England, working on a project at Kings College. I would simply work very hard the first three weeks, so that I could travel up to Ulverston, at the southern edge of the Lake District, to spend the first week of the two-week festival. I was very excited about this upcoming experience as I was told that probably 2000 people from NKT centers in many different countries would be attending the event.

The Manjushri Centre consisted of an enormous, sprawling Victorian era manor house and a very large rectangular-shaped temple. Although the manor house looked like it could house a few hundred people, that would not be nearly enough accommodation for the estimated 2000+ attendees. So, placed around the spacious grounds were army tents, separate ones for men and women, each containing about thirty cots. There were also some makeshift toilet and shower facilities. I guessed that many people chose to camp out as I saw a great many individual tents as well. The atmosphere was unique, I thought. It was not a silent retreat by any means. Everyone I encountered was warm and friendly, and I even had the chance to practice my German with a few. I was very much looking forward to the tantric initiation that would occur on the final day of the first week.

The temple where daily teachings and chanting services took place was attractive, and hundreds of small chairs were set up in rows. On the day of the initiation, I did not make an effort to arrive several hours before as some did because I didn't think I could sit that long on an uncomfortable seat. Thus, I ended up about two-thirds back from the area where Geshe Kelsang, or Geshe-la as he is referred to by his devotees, would be conducting the initiation. This would be my first glimpse of him in person, for the preparatory teachings on the previous days were given by the English monk who was the resident teacher at Manjushri. After the enormous crowd had settled into their seats and quietly waited, I saw a small, thin figure walk sprightly up to the stage and take his seat. Fortunately, there were large TV screens in each corner so that I could actually have a good look at Geshe-la. He looked rather old and frail when viewed in close-up but he seemed so energetic and youthful when he came in. The service began with teachings and built up to the actual initiation. It took me a while to adjust to his pronunciation as he couldn't say certain English sounds, such as "f" or "v," and his inflection and stress of English words were quite different. The initiation ceremony was very beautiful and I felt uplifted and privileged to be formally introduced into my first tantric practice. I was confident that I would gradually become familiarized with the elaborate visualizations and powerful prayers intended to lead me, in a sense, to merge into the deity of compassion. I planned for it to be my main daily meditation. I did not feel strongly drawn to—nor devoted to—Geshe Kelsang though. I supposed that it was due to my reluctance to give myself completely to another human being, even if he was to be viewed as an emanation of the Buddha. I did not force myself to do so but I did cultivate a strong feeling of gratitude and respect for him.

Since I was riding high on the experience of my first NKT summer festival, I thought I would give serious consideration to attending a very special, highest yoga tantric empowerment, scheduled for that autumn at a venue about an hour outside of Berlin. My NKT friends encouraged me to go because one couldn't know if there would be another opportunity to receive this initiation given the fact that Geshe-la was getting old and was in frail health. When I returned to New York, I looked at the academic calendar for the Fall semester and was elated to see that the Jewish holidays fell exactly at the time of the Berlin festival, and occurred on days I normally would be teaching. I took that to be a sign, and I began to make arrangements for this unexpected return trip to Europe. I realized that I would have enough time to go to Berlin a few days before the festival and see Georg, who would have just celebrated his 50th birthday.

I arrived in Berlin on a chilly, gray day in early October. Georg met me at the airport. I was, at first, taken aback by his appearance. His gray hair was down to his shoulders and he sported a very wide handle-bar mustache. Otherwise, it was the same Georg, just thirteen years older. I was touched that he came to the airport to meet me and we rode the bus into the city to the hotel where I would be spending a few nights before going to the NKT Fall festival. I was very tired after the long over-night flight and after sitting in a café with Georg for a short while, I said that I would need to rest a bit. We made up to meet in the evening at a certain art gallery, where there was an opening of an exhibition.

After resting for a few hours, knowing that it would be a long night and that I was not used to staying up very late anymore, I thought I would go for a walk and reacquaint myself with the city. I had forgotten how gray Berlin could be, and because the air was damp and chilly, I didn't walk very much. I decided to revisit two nearby places that had been important in my earlier life in Berlin, stopping first in front of the building on Weimarer Strasse where I had spent my first year. It didn't generate any emotional reaction surprisingly. In fact, I felt nothing. I tried to recreate in my mind what it had felt to live there, but all I could bring forth was a vague recollection of my room. I then walked the short distance to Pestalozzi Strasse and the site of Bar Schriller. It was now an ordinary *kneipe* and not yet open as it was still early. I peered in through the large glass window that no longer had the thin blue neon light. It was difficult for me to recreate the unique red bar, for the décor and arrangement of the furnishings were completely different. But here, unlike the previous site, I felt a lump in my throat and tears welled up. But I quickly shook off the mood and walked to a nearby restaurant to have dinner. I felt that I was in a dream, for Berlin, or more specifically, the Berlin that I had experienced did not seem to exist. I did not attempt to color it, viewing it through the eyes of the ex-patriate writer searching for a new Weimar Berlin or for "old Europe." What I saw was familiar but it was like a false façade, as on a movie set. There was no substance, for my mind refused to generate the materials needed to give it all a three-dimensional feel. I was not the person I was in 1981, when I had arrived, nor in 1992, when I departed. For I had come to Germany to receive an empowerment into a highest tantric deity practice and not to relive nor even reimagine my former life.

In the evening I went to the gallery to meet Georg and Svetlana, the woman with whom he now lived. Svetlana was a large, heavy-set woman of Russian background who used her size to create an eye-catching and attractive appearance. She made her own clothes using beautiful silk and satin material, and often had something in her substantial hair as well. She had been among those guests at Schriller who came after the live music program had ended and was very personable. I had always suspected that she was attracted to Georg and was just waiting for the right time when he would turn to her. She found it when his girlfriend, the one who had worked with me in the bar, finally left Georg as she knew he was not someone with whom one could build a long-lasting relationship. As Georg had no money, and was in fact living off of a small social welfare stipend, Svetlana made her move and offered to take him in, basically supporting him. He had already been living with her for about ten years and I sensed that he was not happy.

Later that evening we were to attend a special performance of the musical *Cabaret*, performed in German in an actual cabaret setting. It was a belated celebration in honor of Georg's 50th birthday which had occurred a few days before. He had told all his friends and acquaintances that I had specifically come to Berlin for this occasion. I knew it wasn't true but I allowed him to disseminate this fantasy, going along with it. Georg seemed a bit disappointed by my attire. For in the days of accompanying him in the night scene, and when working at Schriller, I usually wore a black sports jacket and tie. Now, however, I was dressed in a black turtleneck sweater and wearing a brown leather jacket.

The musical performance was good but I lost interest about half-way through. I did my best, however, not to let it show. Afterwards, I accompanied Georg and Svetlana to a nearby bar and nearly choked on the cigarette smoke that hung heavily in the air. I could feel my lungs rebelling but I was determined to stick it out as long as I could. I was bored, tired, and gasping for fresh air and at around 2am, I told Georg I needed to return to the hotel as I was very tired. He tried to persuade me to stay longer, but I was firm. I assured him we would spend the following evening, just the two of us, and that I would invite him to a nice dinner in honor of his recent landmark birthday. That clearly pleased him. He then called a taxi for me and with great relief I returned to a quiet and smoke-free environment.

The next evening, we met at the same café where we had first heard the rumor that the Berlin Wall had been opened. It seemed that that had happened in a different city, for now, sixteen years later, the two Berlins had merged into one sprawling city with no trace of the Wall standing. We soon walked next door to a well-known and expensive restaurant, popular with people in the film industry. During our dinner, I gradually probed Georg about his current living situation. He said he was grateful that Svetlana had taken him in nearly ten years before but he was no longer content and wished he could move out. He said she had become increasingly prone to depression and also had some money problems. She often didn't get out of bed until the evening and he found himself falling into a state of inertia and hopelessness. He felt trapped and was developing resentment towards her because he was, in a way, under her control. We continued the conversation at the Paris Bar, a famous place established in the early postwar years. He restrained himself and ordered only wine and we sat for a few hours. I offered a few suggestions about how he could free himself from his "prison." He listened and said he would consider my ideas. We then headed back to my hotel as I would be leaving early the next morning. I told him I had to withdraw cash from an ATM and he waited outside as I did. I then gave him 200 euros (about $250) which he refused to take at first. I insisted and told him that he was not to use it for drinking, but rather to help him get settled back into his former apartment—the rent of which was paid by the state. He only needed to convince the power company to turn the electricity back on, paying his outstanding bill gradually over time. When we arrived at my hotel, we bid goodbye to each other. It was not spoken aloud but clear to both of us that this could be our last meeting. I was nevertheless startled to see him burst into tears. I was deeply moved and tried to console him, assuring him that everything would turn out well, even though I wasn't convinced. With tears still streaming down, he thanked me for all my support in the past and admitted that he was wrong for not having ever properly expressed his appreciation for all I had done for him when I was living there. My heart melted at seeing him so tormented by his perceived past insensitivity. I smiled and said that it was more than enough that he now acknowledged it. We then embraced and I walked into the hotel, turning back for a moment to wave goodbye. He was still standing there and waved back, making an obvious effort to smile. As I walked up the stairs to my room, conflicting emotions of sadness for Georg's plight and relief that I had left Berlin fought a battle within my heart. Ultimately, relief won.

The NKT Fall festival, at which the highest yoga tantric empowerment would occur, was to take place on the site of a former summer camp for East German officials and their families, and prior to that, in the 1930s it was used for the same purpose by Nazi officials. Apparently Geshe Kelsang chose this location in order to transform its negative energy into something wholesome and positive. The empowerment he would give was for the female deity Vajrayogini, considered a manifestation of wisdom. During the weeks before I left for Germany, experienced members of the Chakrasambara center explained to me some of the benefits of this empowerment, thus fueling my enthusiasm to receive it. I was told that, by being initiated into her practice, I would be able to engage in methods that would prevent ordinary death and rebirth by transforming both into paths to enlightenment. And, moreover, consistent with other highest yoga tantric practices, Vajaryogini practice, which was very powerful, allowed one to transform mundane daily experiences into higher spiritual paths.

The former summer camp had, I thought, a very strange atmosphere. There were some empty buildings with broken windows that were in various states of decrepitude. But there were also a few, the ones that would be used for accommodation and dining, that were fairly modern and in good condition. There was an enormous tent, easily seating 1500 people or more, that was set up in a large open area near a beautiful lake. That would serve as a "temple" where daily preparatory teachings and the actual empowerment would occur. Similar to how the summer festival had been organized, senior teachers gave the preparatory teachings and Geshe Kelsang spoke only on the day of the empowerment. Since a fairly large group from the Chakrasambara center were present, there were many people with whom I could interact.

Vajrayogini was a potent and intimidating female deity depicted with a bright red face and body in an action pose, each outstretched leg crushing creatures under her feet, and her form was framed in bright red flames. I was nervous, apprehensive and excited all at the same time as the ceremony proceeded. After we had been initiated into the practice, which simply meant that we were now permitted to engage in it, we each had to make a silent commitment regarding how many times a day we would recite the mantra specific to this deity. As It was not long, I chose 108—the usual number of beads on a mala. After the empowerment, I had to admit that I didn't really feel any different. I didn't note that I had received anything palpable. I expressed these thoughts to a friend, who had already received this empowerment from a spiritual guide, now deceased. He assured me that one needed to "grow" into the practice and that it would take time. I actually experienced my first glimpse of what might develop over the next months when in the morning, a senior nun, Gen-la Dekyong, led everyone through the entire practice we would be doing every day. The opening verses, sung by Gen-la and unaccompanied by recorded music, had a beautiful, otherworldly quality. It lifted me to an imaginative realm never visited before. After that, the long service continued with music, and all of it had extraordinary beauty. With enthusiasm, I worked out in my mind when I would perform this daily ritual once I was back in New York.

Vajrayogini practice became the central focus of my spiritual life. I set up a corner of my one-room apartment as a meditation practice area. I obtained a small *puja* table where I kept the tantric ritual instruments: a bell, a *dorje*, (also known as a *vajra*) and a small hand drum, a *damaru*. I obtained them all at the little shop inside the Chakrasambara center. Although not part of the deity practice per se, I also performed 108 full-length prostrations on a small rug I had placed in front of the table. I began getting up early so that I would have about 2½ hours to go through the prostrations and the Vajrayogini service before going to the university. The physical exertion of performing 108 purification prostrations to the thirty-five confession Buddhas not only woke me up but also provided an opportunity for me to strengthen my concentration. For I attempted to keep track of the particular color of each series of Buddhas and the type of negative karma the prostration was to purify. It generally took me half-an-hour to do all the prostrations. I would then immediately proceed with the Vajrayogini practice.

Although I was struggling with some parts of the practice, particularly the elaborate visualizations and my lack of clarity about how to develop an intimate relationship with this fierce deity, I was confident that it all would become clear eventually. I was excited to learn that there would be a three-week Vajrayogini retreat in January, held at the NKT temple and retreat center in upstate New York about 1½ hours from the city. Gen-la Dekyong, the soft-spoken Irish nun who had led the service at the Fall festival, would lead this special retreat for those newly initiated into the practice. As with the festival in Germany, here, too, the timing was perfect. The three-week retreat would be during my one-month winter break from the university. I would be back home a few days before the beginning of the spring semester. Everything seemed to be falling in place!

The retreat was intense and beneficial, and allowed me to spend three weeks in a peaceful, rural environment, where the freshly fallen snow stayed white and the crisp, cold air was pure and invigorating. We were an intimate group of eight and thus it felt we were being given private daily instructions by Gen-la, who based her teachings on notes she had recorded from instructions she had received directly from Geshe-la himself. She also made herself available for some informal sessions as well. During the day, I often walked around the grounds and one day stopped into a nearly finished building that would eventually serve as a residence for those living at this center. I explored each of the six rooms and chose the one I would like to live in if I was a resident. I stood there for a while, imagining what it would be like to live there. I even started planning a commuting schedule, whereby I would live there and take the train down to the city on the two or three days I taught each week. My fantasizing took off, and I felt an urge to live a semi-monastic life, perhaps even ordaining as a monk in this tradition. I met one during the retreat who despite being a monk continued to teach at a junior high school on Long Island. He didn't wear his monastic robes, however, when he taught. I liked this young monk and could sense how well his chosen lifestyle was working for him.

Once I was back in the city and occupied with teaching at John Jay College and attending classes and retreats at the center, my fantasy of living upstate faded away. I enrolled in the more advanced "foundation" program at Chakrasambara, attending the multi-week course on the Heart Sutra, the core Mahayana text on "emptiness." Kadam Morten moved through the passages very slowly, offering articulate explanations of the difficult text. To give us further practice, there were also occasional retreat days on Saturdays to foster an experiential understanding of emptiness. On one of these day events, I was sitting on a folding chair next to the window as the teacher was pointing to a table, informing us that there is no "table" and that it was merely a construct, a conventional label, applied to an assemblage of parts. She went on to conclude that there was no inherent existence in the "table"—nothing existed from "its own side." And what was true for the table was true for every object we experienced in our world—everything was, in reality, empty. As I looked out the window at the buildings across the way and the street below, I mused on this far-reaching concept.

I closed my eyes and just kept repeating to myself that the buildings, the cars, even the people had no inherent existence, that they were "empty" of a stable center. Everything was just conventional labels. I felt a moment of panic at the thought that there was nothing stable for me to hold on to. My heart began to race. After a few moments, though, I recovered, and re-established my foundation based on familiar conventional reality.

In early summer 2006, I became interested in learning Tibetan. I was intrigued by this ancient Asian language that had nothing in common with English or any other Indo-European language. At about this time, I came upon an announcement that His Holiness the Dalai Lama would be giving three days of teachings at the Beacon Theater in New York City in September. When I mentioned my interest in attending these teachings to a friend, he said that NKT members did not normally attend teachings by the Dalai Lama and, in fact, he was not highly regarded at all in the NKT. I was stunned to hear this and when I asked why this was so, he proceeded to tell me briefly that the Dalai Lama had forbidden the important practice associated with the Dharma protector, Dorje Shugden. Geshe Kelsang refused to accept the prohibition of a practice that his own guru had regularly done and, thus, in defiance of the Dalai Lama's position, it continued to be performed daily in every NKT center around the world. Upon doing some research, I discovered why the Dalai Lama was opposed to this practice. Dorje Shugden, a wrathful minor deity, was historically called on to protect the Gelug school and was fiercely against the other main schools of Tibetan Buddhism. The Dalai Lama, wishing to create harmony among the various schools, especially given the fact that they were living in exile, thus opposed this practice and urged practitioners in the Gelug school not to do it.

After reflecting on this situation for the next week, I realized I had more faith in the Dalai Lama than I did in Geshe Kelsang, even though he was my spiritual guide and the one who had initiated me into highest yoga tantric practice. I thought I could continue to maintain a connection to NKT—but distancing myself somewhat—and, without publicizing it, I would attend the teachings of the Dalai Lama in September. I proceeded to purchase a ticket before the event sold out. However, I was undecided about attending the NKT summer festival that year. After learning about the Dalai Lama's position on Dorje Shugden, I was certain that I would not attend the first week of the festival which would offer a Dorje Shugden empowerment, but possibly attend the second week. Since it was a long and expensive trip to England, I explored whether there might be another retreat or event I could attend the week before or after.

I discovered that there was a one week retreat at the Jamyang Tibetan Buddhist center, in London, during the same week as the first half of the NKT summer festival. Thus, I could conceivable attend the retreat at Jamyang and then go directly to Ulverston to participate in the latter part of the NKT retreat. Jamyang Centre was part of an international organization, FPMT (Foundation for the Preservation of the Mahayana Tradition), under the spiritual guidance of Lama Zopa Rinpoche. Further research indicated that there was an historical connection between Lama Zopa's teacher, Lama Yeshe, and Geshe Kelsang. In fact, the former had brought the latter to Manjushri Centre in the 1970s. Apparently, some split had occurred, and Manjushri Centre eventually became part of Geshe Kelsang's schismatic group, the NKT. I decided to contact Jamyang Centre and register for the retreat if there was still room. The seamless timing of the two venues solidified my decision to explore the possibility of continuing my Buddhist journey under the auspices of this mainstream Tibetan group which, like NKT, was geared towards Westerners.

I was able to register for the Jamyang retreat and was excited about this new avenue that had opened up. And in a few short weeks, I found myself at the door of a Victorian era courthouse and prison in a somewhat run-down neighborhood in south London. But once inside, I felt immediately at home. The courthouse had been ingeniously transformed into a beautiful meditation retreat center. What had been the main room of the courthouse, where trials were most likely conducted, was now the main meditation hall where the sessions of the retreat would take place. The limited number of rooms for retreatants upstairs had been formerly short-term prison cells. They were all booked by the time I had registered, so I was placed in a large room that would serve as the men's dorm. The other retreatants were a diverse group and I quickly connected with a young Englishman, who, as it turned out, had also been associated with NKT. We had much to discuss. I thought how wonderful everything seemed to work out when I followed my instinct, not having fear to redirect my path.

I took an instant liking to the resident teacher at Jamyang, Geshe Tashi. He was probably in his early or mid-forties, very personable, and spoke very good English. He explained that the retreat would provide intensive teachings on the basic *lamrim* (stages of the path), as delineated by the founder of the Gelug school, Je Tsongkhapa. Every morning we would take the eight monastic precepts, which included not eating after mid-day. In fact, we would have only one meal per day. I was apprehensive about whether I would have enough energy to do the daily rounds of prostrations on such a limited amount of food. But, as it turned out, my fears were unfounded. The combined efforts of the retreatants, all following the same schedule and guidelines, infused me with sufficient energy and I wasn't even hungry later in the day.

After confiding to my new friend, Tom, about my dilemma regarding how to distance myself from the NKT, given the highest tantric empowerment I had received from Geshe Kelsang, he suggested I speak to Geshe Tashi. I followed his advice and I obtained a private interview with him. I felt at ease in his smiling presence, and thus spelled out my situation. He responded that recently there had been a number of former NKT members seeking advice and solace at Jamyang. I told him that I had committed myself to attending the second week of the summer festival but didn't want to go. He recommended that I go, but maintain some distance when there and, by all means, I should feel no compunction to take part in the daily Dorje Shugden practice. As for Geshe Kelsang, he praised his books, assuring me that they were accurate presentations of the teachings, but he did not condone the schism that he initiated, nor his failure to discourage those NKT members who were openly expressing disrespect and criticism of His Holiness the Dalai Lama.

I left the meeting with Geshe Tashi feeling much more relaxed and was ready for the trip up north to the summer festival when the Jamyang retreat ended. I felt that the one-week retreat had strengthened my connection to Tibetan Buddhism and was confident that I would find the necessary support from FPMT teachers, not to mention, Lama Zopa, the spiritual guide, to assist me in deepening my practice. I would look for the next opportunity to be re-initiated into Vajrayogini practice from Lama Zopa or another qualified lama, since that would solidify my connection.

As soon as I had arrived at the NKT summer festival I regretted coming. I felt I had entered an alien world. Masses of attendees were walking around wearing a necklace bearing the picture of Dorje Shugden, obviously as a token of the empowerment they had just received. Fortunately, there were at least a few people who, like me, had not attended the first week of the festival. Nevertheless, I sensed that I was an outsider there. While I attended the teachings that occurred in the mornings and afternoons, I felt disengaged, even on the few occasions when Geshe Kelsang spoke. I avoided attending the daily evening Dorje Shugden chanting service, opting to take a walk at that time to the small beach along the shores of a beautiful bay. I generally kept to myself for the entire week and minimized my interactions with Chakrasambara members.

One afternoon, I arrived rather late for lunch as I had spent the morning walking along the beach. After collecting my food, I sat at a table in the nearly empty dining tent when a man slightly younger than me, dressed in black and not wearing a Dorje Shugden necklace, asked if he could join me. I indicated that he was welcome to and we engaged in some general conversation. He was South African and confided that although he had been involved with NKT for several years, he was feeling dissatisfied with its increasing isolation from mainstream Tibetan Buddhism. In fact, this was going to be the last festival he would attend. I responded that I had the same sentiments and that I regretted coming to the festival. I also told him of my recent introduction to FPMT and my hopes to deepen the association. He was familiar with the organization and said that he had heard only praise for Lama Zopa. In fact, he was planning to attend a future FPMT event in Australia. I would have liked to continue speaking with him, but it was clear that we needed to finish our lunch and let the volunteers complete the clean-up. I asked him if we could meet for a coffee that afternoon. He agreed and we set a time and place. However, he didn't show up and, despite seeking him out the next day, I never saw him again. I began to wonder if the conversation had actually occurred or whether it was a fantasy scenario that had played out in my head.

I also began disappearing in the afternoons, walking into town to use the internet at the local library. I was hoping to find a FPMT retreat in the U.S. that I could attend that autumn. I burst out a cry of joy when I discovered that in September Lama Zopa would be offering initiation into the highest yoga tantric deity, Vajrayogini, at the Vajrapani Institute, a retreat center in northern California. After noting that I could attend without missing any classes since it would occur over a four-day weekend, and I taught on Tuesdays and Thursdays, I immediately registered. I even drafted a letter to Lama Zopa, which I sent to his secretary, asking if it were possible to schedule a private interview with him at the retreat, as I sought his advice on how to break off my connection to Geshe Kelsang. I received a reply from the secretary that she would do her best, but given the number of people attending the special event, it was unlikely that I would be able to meet personally with Lama Zopa.

Although disappointed, I understood that I couldn't expect a personal meeting with this internationally known and revered spiritual leader, who undoubtedly had a great many long-time students seeking a moment with him. Yet, I was joyful that I would be able to be re-initiated into Vajrayogini practice and thus have a new spiritual guide.

The week ended and I was relieved to return to London and fly back to New York.

As I was driving on a dirt road through a forest that didn't seem to be arriving at the Vajrapani retreat center, and as daylight was quickly diminishing, I felt panic rising. I glanced at the directions I had printed out which indicated that it was about a four-mile drive on the dirt road. Since I was driving slowly over the rough path, I figured it had not yet been four miles. I berated myself for not taking an earlier flight to San Francisco. But then, I saw lights in the distance. I knew that had to be the place. For, I thought, what else could be out here in this isolated location. And there was the sign: Vajrapani Institute.

After parking the car, I walked into what seemed to be the main building and found a small group of Western Tibetan nuns sitting around a dining table talking. They smiled as I walked in and warmly welcomed me. A lay man walked up to me and asked if I was hungry. I indicated that I was actually, but I could wait until breakfast. He then went into the kitchen and returned with a bowl of lentil soup. I accepted in with gratitude and the nuns indicated I should sit down and eat. I sensed that the atmosphere during the weekend event would prove to be as warm and friendly as my initial moments.

I soon discovered that my hopes of speaking privately with Lama Zopa would not be realized. He wasn't scheduled to arrive until late in the evening of the day before the initiation. I decided not to be overly concerned about how to disengage myself from Geshe Kelsang and merely adopt Lama Zopa as my spiritual guide. I would keep my eyes open for a senior teacher at the event to whom I could turn for guidance. In the meantime, I had an interesting conversation that would prove to have a profound effect on my life. While drying lunch dishes together with an American monk, I learned that he had been a monk for about five years and had spent some time at Nalanda Monastery, an international Tibetan monastery in southwest France. I mentioned that I felt drawn to living the monastic life but didn't think I was ready. He looked directly at me and said that I shouldn't wait too long. He had put it off until he was nearly 60, and regretted that he hadn't ordained sooner, for it is more difficult to adjust to monastic life when one is older. He turned his attention to the plate he was drying and said, half to himself, that one never knows what the next day will bring. He looked again right at me and said that there was no better way to spend the rest of one's life than as a monk. His words reached me because they were clearly uttered from his heart. I believed what he said and began to consider spending my next winter break at Nalanda Monastery.

On late Saturday evening, all the retreatants, which I guessed were about one hundred, were waiting outside for Lama Zopa's arrival. It was already dark but I could sense the presence of the majestic redwoods that were all around us. We finally saw the lights of a vehicle approaching. The suv came to a stop in front of the house. Someone got out of the vehicle and after opening the front door on the passenger's side, Lama Zopa carefully descended and looked at the welcoming crowd with a bright smile. We all stood with our palms together in respect and followed him with our eyes as he entered the building where he would reside overnight. Although I was unable to get a good look at him because of the limited light shining outside from the house, there was a palpable warm energy emanating from him. I felt assured that I had made the right decision in coming there to be re-initiated into Vajrayogini practice.

The preparatory teachings began on Sunday evening. I was told that Lama Zopa preferred to teach at night and the initiation could very well last all night. I wondered how I would manage that and be able to drive an hour-and-a-half to the airport early the next morning for my flight back to New York. I made an effort to brush those thoughts out of my mind and instead focus on what I would be experiencing during the coming night. While waiting for Lama Zopa to begin the teachings, I sat on a cushion on the floor in the crowded *gompa* (meditation hall) and took in the atmosphere and feel of the place. The room was very inviting with beautiful rugs on the floor, some *tangka* paintings on the wall, and besides the, now familiar, Tibetan (or more likely, Nepalese) Buddha statue, there were several large photos—of the Dalai Lama, Lama Zopa, and the late Lama Yeshe (who had been Lama Zopa's teacher). I was quite happy to be involved in mainstream Tibetan Buddhism. I had faith in the Dalai Lama and Lama Zopa, knowing that my spiritual future was under their guidance and, thus, I was in their hands, so to speak.

Lama Zopa took his place on a prominent seat located on a high platform in the middle of the room. Even though I was sitting towards the rear, and he was small in stature, I was able to see him quite well because of the height of the seat. He led us through the *lamrim* teachings, and after taking us through the paths of those of modest and medium motives, he turned to the path for those of high scope, and the striving for complete Buddhahood for the benefit of all sentient beings. I was already familiar with the basics from the NKT, yet felt I was hearing it all for the first time, as Lama Zopa in his gentle manner elucidated the path. At around midnight, we took a half-hour break. He then began the initiation and teachings that explained all the details of this highest yoga tantric practice. It went on for hours, but I didn't feel tired nor did I notice the passing of time. My eyes were fixed on Lama Zopa as though he were a magnet. He exhibited no signs of fatigue as the hours went by. While I, and most others sitting in my vicinity, occasionally moved a sleeping or cramped leg, he never shifted his position, not even moving a foot. He sat still during the entire night that he instructed us.

The initiation and teachings concluded just as the sun was rising. We all stumbled outside to catch a glimpse of the peaceful beauty of sunrise in this spectacular location. After breakfast, while sitting at a picnic table outside, drinking a cup of coffee, I noticed at the end of the table the Swiss monk, Ven. Rene, who had given an excellent talk on the day before Lama Zopa had arrived. I had only a short time before I would have to leave, but I thought I would try to speak with him. I caught his attention and said that I requested his advice on something. There were a few other people at the table and since they didn't get up to give us privacy, I went ahead and blurted out my dilemma regarding Geshe Kelsang. Ven. Rene was well informed about the NKT and the Dorje Shugden controversy. To my question about how to end my connection to Geshe Kelsang, he said without any hesitation that I should remove his photo from my *puja* table and no longer consider him to be my spiritual guide in any way. However, he stated that I should not maintain any negative feelings towards him, but just be neutral. I later came upon the exact same information online from Lama Zopa in response to someone's question that was identical to mine. When reading that, I was convinced the advice I had hoped to receive from Lama Zopa at Vajrapani was somehow transmitted to me though Ven. Rene!

Not long after returning to New York, I followed the American monk's advice and contacted Ven. Tenpa, the director of Nalanda Monastery, expressing my wish to come there for a one-month stay during the early winter. He responded positively to my request and I proceeded to make flight arrangements, planning to head across the Atlantic the day after Christmas.

Just after Thanksgiving, as the Fall semester was coming to an end and I was getting excited about my forthcoming trip to France, I noticed that a film with an intriguing title, *Into Great Silence*, was playing at the Film Forum in Soho. Reading the blurb in the listing of current films in *The New York Times*, I learned that it was more of a documentary than a feature film, for there was essentially no dialogue and the viewer had the unique opportunity to closely observe life in a remote Carthusian monastery located in the French Alps through the four seasons of one year. I decided to see this film; though not a Buddhist monastery, I would nevertheless get my first glimpse of actual monastic life. I was surprised to find the theatre nearly full and just as surprising was that during the entire 2 hours and 40 minutes, I heard no sound of food being unwrapped or popcorn being munched. The viewers in the theatre mirrored the silence that was unfolding on the screen. I was captivated by the scenes and sounds of daily life in that monastery—the ethereal Gregorian chant by the monks in the candlelit pre-dawn church, the monks' white hoods shielding them from distractions; simple meals consumed by monks in their individual cells; listening to a monk, kneeling in prayer before a simple crucifix in his cell. And, for me, the climactic moment—and the rare intrusion of speech—was an interview with a very old blind monk. The questions were omitted and thus one only heard the responses from the monk that had been seamlessly edited together. He had obviously been asked how he felt about death. Despite the empty eye sockets, one sensed that he was directly addressing the interviewer and us, the viewers, and with a beaming, peaceful smile, in his gentle French, he assured the interviewer—and us—that he did not fear death. He had spent more than 60 years in that monastery and on no occasion did he ever feel separate from God. He was certain that the intimacy would continue after his physical death. At that moment, I shed a few tears of joy and felt love for that monk filling my heart. I was deeply impressed by the film and was grateful to the filmmaker's persistence in requesting permission to film the daily life of the monks. For after fifteen years of being repeatedly denied, he was at last granted permission.

Christmas arrived and on the next day I set out for Nalanda Monastery.

PART TWO

Moving towards Monasticism

As the train was approaching the small town of Lavaur, I was getting nervous because I had never received a confirmation from Ven. Tenpa that someone would pick me up from the station. I feared no one would be there and I would not be able to find a taxi to take me to the monastery. My fears were realized when I got off the train at the very small station and saw no signs of anyone—monk or layman—to welcome me. I stood in the chilly air for a while and waited, hoping someone would show up. After about twenty minutes I went inside the station and approached the ticket window. I asked in very poor French if he could direct me to Nalanda Monastery, which he, surprisingly, recognized and said it was not too far away, maybe 5 kilometers. He gave me directions which I partially understood and thought I could always ask someone later on if needed. As I was walking near the river hoping it was the right road, a small car passed me with a "Free Tibet" bumper sticker. It suddenly stopped and a Western Tibetan monk got out. He called out my name, and after identifying myself, he apologized for getting to the train station so late. I was relieved and delighted as I put my suitcase in the trunk and rode the rest of the way to the monastery.

We turned into a long tree-lined path that led to the nineteenth-century manor house which served as the monastery. I noticed that construction was in progress a short distance from the house. Ven. Tenpa said that when completed, it would be the main monastic building. Meanwhile the old farm house served that purpose. I liked the interior of the old building very much. It had a very lived-in warmth and I was given a short tour of the key places: the *gompa*, the kitchen and dining room, and the library, which was located upstairs, along with a great many rooms for the monks and the few lay men who resided there. I was directed to a small room that faced the back lawn and the river which ran along the property. I was enchanted with the place.

I gradually met the monks, about 13 or 14, all European, with Dutch, British, and Spanish being the prevalent nationalities. The morning and evening chanting services were performed in a moderate size *gompa*, located at the end of the corridor, and had a warm and cozy feel. As at Vajrapani, there were *thangka* paintings on the walls as well as the familiar large photos of the Dalai Lama, Lama Yeshe, and Lama Zopa. The chanting was done in English with a sprinkling of Tibetan words. On my first evening there, I joined the monks for the daily Mahakala protection service. I liked the Tibetan monastic tradition of monks sitting in rows facing each other, each seated behind a small *puja* table upon which the service book was placed. This service, calling on a rather frightening looking wrathful deity, was, I was told, commonly performed at Tibetan monasteries. I needed to get accustomed to the noise of banging drums and other loud instruments which accompanied different sections of the service. Nevertheless, I preferred this service to that of Dorje Shugden, because Mahakala protected all the Tibetan schools, not just one.

At the reasonable hour of 7am, I joined the monks for the daily Je Tsongkhapa chanting service. I was familiar with it from NKT and my stays at Jamyang and Vajrapani. Generating *bodhicitta* (the mind of enlightenment) on this occasion, and on every morning, I wondered how living in a monastic community, unencumbered by the daily duties and distractions of lay life, supported this aspiration. I intended to ask one of the monks about this, but it didn't arise in my mind during the informal encounters I had with them. Occasionally while walking along the country road that led away from the monastery, the well-known teaching by the 8th Century Indian sage Shantideva regarding exchanging self with others popped into my head—a teaching which developed into the meditation practice of taking on the suffering of others and offering peace and joy from myself. I reflected that when rushing around in New York, with ample opportunity to view the physical suffering of some individuals—not to mention the inner suffering that one could only imagine—I never thought of this profound practice. But, here, in the French countryside, where I generally encountered no one, and where I spent most of the day in the company of monks who did not appear to be in need of my meager supply of peace and joy, I considered how freeing this selfless, compassionate practice might be, and wondered if I might be more inclined to engage in it if I lived a monastic life.

    I noticed that there was no assigned cook at Nalanda. The monks rotated duties preparing breakfast and lunch. There was no evening meal, but one could fix himself a snack of bread, cheese, and fruit if he was hungry. The monks and lay residents ate their meals in a rustic room with beams and a somewhat worn tiled floor, sitting at wooden picnic tables. While there was not loud conversation at meals, monks did speak with one another and occasionally broke out into laughter. There was, I thought, an overall friendly, relaxed atmosphere, nothing at all like the secluded stillness of the Carthusian monastery in the film.

During my four week stay, I interacted with just about all the monks. I even openly spoke about my former involvement with the NKT, a group which the British monks were familiar with. I gave expression to the confusion and unease I had felt when I learned more about the schismatic group and that I was relieved and very happy that I disengaged myself from them. I easily integrated into the Nalanda community, and by the time of my departure, felt that I was a resident. I determined to return for a longer stay in the summer.

I spent the spring planning my return to Nalanda Monastery. I was going to have a busy summer. I would leave New York immediately after the final exam period and entering the grades for the spring semester, staying at Nalanda for nearly two months before accompanying most of the community to Hamburg to attend teachings there by the Dalai Lama. I had decided that I would then make a trip to Nepal, spending three weeks at Kopan Monastery, founded by Lama Yeshe and Lama Zopa in the late 1960s to introduce Westerners to Tibetan Buddhism. It had since become a traditional Tibetan monastery for Nepalese Tibetan Buddhist novices and monks as well as a retreat center for Westerners. There was no scheduled retreat for the weeks I had planned to visit, so I would do my own retreat, allowing much time for prostrations and Vajrayogini deity practice, as well as making daily excursions to the ancient stupa (domed shaped structure) in nearby Boudhanath. I would then return to Nalanda for my final two weeks, arriving in New York just a few days before the beginning of the Fall semester. My academic teaching position had become of secondary importance in my life. I spent a minimum amount of time preparing for classes and because I had fortunately already completed a number of publications, I did not need to use the summer for research. My first visit to Nalanda Monastery firmly planted the seed for eventual monastic ordination.

My second arrival at Nalanda was quite different from the first one. As I got off the train, I saw the familiar fiat in the parking area and Ven. Tenpa standing next to it. He warmly welcomed me back and I immediately felt that I was a member of the community. As we drove to the monastery, he informed me that the new building was already being occupied, although the *gompa* and the kitchen were not yet finished. He also said that my room would be in the new building. I was excited that I would experience the enlarged facilities at Nalanda.

Since I was paying a reduced daily rate to stay there for the two months prior to going to Hamburg, I would be working four hours per day. I was given the task of making *tsatsas*, votive offerings in the form of small plaques depicting a deity and usually made in molds with clay. A large tent had been set up on the lawn behind the monastery for producing them. Ven. Tsultrim, an Italian monk in his early 60s, who had formerly been an artist, had created the molds for different deities and instructed me in the process of making the *tsatsas*. He was very patient and always had a warm smile, even when he needed to repeat some directions. I was anxious because I knew from my donut making days that it usually took me some time to become adept at a manual process and here, rather than donuts—which if a few got ruined would not be tragic—I would be making plaques of deities. I feared I would ruin some and hopefully not have to pay the karmic price in this life or in the future. Each of the maneuvers in the process had the potential of ruining the *tsatsa*. First, I had to mix the right amount of water in with the hydrostone (a cement-like substance), then pour it into the molds, careful not to pour in too much, and then 30-40 minutes later, carefully extricate the *tsatsa* from the mold without breaking off a piece or cracking it. I was also supposed to be reciting a series of mantras, one for each of the tasks as I was performing it. After working at this for about two weeks, I realized that I had neglected to recite any of the mantras. I then tried to recite at least one of them, generally while mixing in the water, as that required the least amount of concentration.

After several weeks, and after having made several hundred *tsatsas*, with only a handful of casualties, I moved on to painting them. The most difficult part of this task, and for which I had to be well focused, was making sure I did not get paint on the edges, but rather only on the figure. I worked on this in the workshop rather than in the tent and liked being surrounded by some beautiful artworks that were in the process of being created. By the end of the two months, I had made probably around 500 *tsatsas*. They would be brought to Hamburg, where the Dalai Lama would be giving three days of teachings to an estimated 45,000 people, and given away at the Nalanda booth. I was happy to have been able to take part in this project and felt more integrated into the monastic community despite being a layman.

During that summer, Lama Zopa requested that the monks at Nalanda recite the Golden Light Sutra continuously for 24 hours, which would be live-streamed over the internet. It was reported to be of great benefit for those reciting it, directing their lives towards enlightenment. It also was of enormous benefit for those hearing it and for the world-at-large. The sutra was very long, containing twenty-one chapters, and a schedule was formed whereby each monk signed up for a one-hour recitation. Lay volunteers were sought to sign up for a three-hour period, providing the reciting monk with water or tea as needed. I signed up for the unpopular three-hour early morning slot, from 2am to 5am. As I sat through what turned out to be pleasant and uplifting three hours in the middle of the night, periodically fetching tea for the reciter, I felt the gulf separating me from the monastics. For they were afforded the privilege of partaking in this special event, while I was merely an observer, participating in only a marginal way. I didn't yet suspect that one year later I would be sitting in the high platform seat as a reciter.

Late July arrived and all the monks and a few lay residents, including myself, flew to Hamburg. Although I had purchased my ticket for the teachings several months in advance, hoping to secure a seat fairly close to the front of the tennis stadium, I was in the bleachers on the side about two-thirds back from the stage. I had already attended several teachings of the Dalai Lama, but they were in smaller venues. In this enormous stadium, I felt far removed from His Holiness who was so far away. Of course, the large screens enabled me to see him, but I nevertheless had difficulty remaining focused on the teachings that were being simultaneously translated into English and which I listened to on a small transistor radio. In the period between the teachings, I stopped at the Nalanda booth to bond with the monks. I was glad to see that the *tsatsas* were going fast.

Immediately after the teachings ended, I embarked on my journey to Nepal. I had arrived at the airport early and as I was sitting waiting, I noticed that a very well-known English Tibetan nun, Ven. Tenzin Palmo, was waiting for the same flight. Although I had not read the popular biography, *Cave in the Snow*, which describes the twelve years that the venerable nun had spent alone in a cave in the Himalayas, at 13,000 feet elevation, I had heard that during that time she slept and meditated in an upright box. I couldn't comprehend or imagine how someone could perform such a feat and live in such a rugged, isolated environment. And there she was, sitting by herself, reading a book. I decided to approach her, offering her a bottle of water for the journey. She looked up and I saw her amazingly clear blue eyes. I didn't recall ever seeing eyes so clear. She accepted the water and motioned for me to sit down. I informed her that I was headed to Kathmandu to spend three weeks at Kopan Monastery. I learned that she was likewise going to Nepal, but only for a brief visit before returning to her monastery in India. During the course of our conversation, she expressed her disappointment with the Dalai Lama for failing to re-establish full ordination for nuns in the Tibetan tradition. She said that although he had spoken firmly in support of it at the meeting she attended in Hamburg, she nevertheless expected him to bring about more definitive results. As she was relaying this to me, I was conscious of being disappointed that she was so fixed on this thorny issue. But later realized that not being a nun, I couldn't understand the frustration women felt at being denied the full ordination that was available to men.

After the first boarding announcement was made, I stood up, and after thanking her for the conversation, wished her a good journey.

Despite having spent a few hours in the transit area of the Delhi airport, I was not prepared for experiencing the scene at the Kathmandu arrival hall. Perhaps due to the long overnight flight, I felt I was in a daze as I attempted to navigate the steps to register for a 30-day tourist visa. I spotted Ven. Palmo in the hall and just followed whatever actions she was doing. I was relieved that my suitcase had made it, and after going through customs, entered the main part of the airport where there was a lot of bedlam as throngs of people were arriving and being greeted. I was expecting someone to meet me, a Nepalese friend of the two *thangka* painters who currently resided at Nalanda, painting the enormous buddha statue that was in the new *gompa*. They had emailed him my photo so he knew what I looked like, but I had not seen his photo. So, I waited and hoped he would materialize. Suddenly, a smiling young man approached me and introduced himself as Namgyal. I knew that he, too, was a *thangka* painter and, according to his friends at Nalanda, produced work of extremely high quality. He had formerly been a monk and studied the art of *thangka* painting with a master. I liked him right away. He welcomed me to Kathmandu and led me out of the terminal where there were taxis. He said he wanted to accompany me to Kopan Monastery to make sure I arrived there safely. I was grateful for his company as we made our way through the chaos of crowds of people and secured a taxi.

The taxi drove very slowly through a narrow poorly paved road in the direction of Boudhanath, about 5 miles outside of Kathmandu. I looked out the window and was mesmerized by the foreign and exotic sights. I saw people squatting in front of dilapidated huts, cooking on charcoal fires. As it was warm and humid, the car windows were open, and I caught the strong smells of food, spices, excrement, and many smells I could not identify. I felt as though I was viewing a multi-dimensional film of colors and sounds, in which an astonishing array of people, rickshaws, and animals moved. Everything was occurring in slow motion, the action in the street as well as the pace of the ride. Periodically I would hit my head on the roof of the vehicle as we passed over rough spots. At last, we arrived in Boudhanath itself and I had a glimpse of the huge ancient stupa with the staring eyes. Namgyal said there were many Tibetan monasteries here and that it felt like being in Tibet. I couldn't wait to explore!

The taxi drove up the hill from the town and arrived outside the gate to Kopan Monastery. I bid goodbye to Namgyal who lived in Boudhanath, thanking him for accompanying me. During our conversation in the taxi, I mentioned that I engaged in daily Vajrayogini practice. He said there was a little known temple dedicated to this deity about an hour outside of Boudhanath and offered to take me there, if I wished. I indicated my enthusiasm to go there and we made up to make the trip on the following Saturday. I then entered the monastery complex and went to the main office.

The room where I would be spending the three weeks was in a small building reserved for Western guests when there was not a retreat going on. I was the only occupant but there was a group of single dwellings nearby where two

Western monks were dwelling, and they used the bathroom in the building as well. After settling in, I walked around the monastery. I was struck by the beautiful stupa right in the center, which several old Tibetan monks were circumambulating. I peeked into the main *gompa* in which there was a strong smell of incense hanging in the air. I then walked to a wide terrace that gave a spectacular view of the entire Kathmandu valley. I could see the Boudhanath stupa in the near distance, and to the west, the hazy sprawl of Kathmandu. I was so focused on the distant environs that I didn't at first notice the large monastic residence just below the terrace. I saw a number of maroon robes drying in the sun over the railings. After some time of just standing there, taking in the scene, I noted some activity. A group of monks and some very young novices were walking up the steps from the residence. One novice caught my attention. He couldn't have been more than 6 years old and had the most angelic countenance I had ever seen on a boy. And, in contrast with his young age, he walked and carried himself with the dignity of a senior monk. I wondered if he were a *tulku*, the reincarnate of a high lama.

 The next day, and nearly every afternoon during my stay, I walked down the hill and along a narrow path through a network of huts and shops that formed a type of village until I reached Boudhanath. Although I had got a glimpse of the poverty when riding in the taxi, now walking through the village, I saw it in more detail. It seemed that much of the life of the inhabitants was lived outside. I saw young women washing their hair at an outdoor water pump. A few women squatted outside their huts, cooking food on a charcoal fire. I didn't see any electricity lines and guessed that there was no plumbing in the huts. There were little stalls selling fruits and vegetables as well as an assortment of household items, and small groups of men of all ages sat outside smoking cigarettes, talking, and playing cards. I wondered why they weren't working. Besides a few stray, mangy looking dogs, the only other animal I saw was a cow, which a man was leading, without a rope, through the village. As I made my way to Boudhanath, I thought of my daily aspiration to attain enlightenment for the benefit of all living beings. My heart spontaneously generated compassion for these incredibly poor people. I considered what their future was like. There would be little chance for most of them to rise out of the poverty into which they had been born.

When I entered the center of Boudhanath, gazing in wonder at the magnificent stupa, my compassion and commiseration evaporated as I was continuously harassed by women holding a sleeping—but more likely, drugged—baby, who aggressively pulled at me asking for money for the baby. Although I was sure they didn't speak or understand English, I responded tartly that I was sorry but I couldn't help them. I feared if I gave any money to one, I would be set upon by a swarm of beggars. I thought there would be a better way to offer some charitable assistance to the impoverished Nepalese.

I joined the groups of Tibetan-Nepalese who circumambulated the *stupa*, most remaining on the street level. I then walked up to a higher level where there were fewer people, and progressively went higher, marveling at the astounding view of the Himalayas in the distance. I found myself chanting the famous mantra, *Om mani padme hum*, as I made countless rounds of the stupa. I then returned to the street level and noticed solitary Tibetan monks, mostly old and very thin, sitting in the cool shade of alcoves, some with a mala in their hands, others in meditation, and still others looking at whomever was passing by. I didn't know if they were there begging or simply praying. One smiled broadly at me as I passed by. I stopped and handed him some coins. He bowed his head slightly as a gesture of thanks.

On the next Saturday, in the late morning, Namgyal walked up to Kopan to meet me. He didn't think it would be easy for us to meet in Boudhanath. He asked the gate-keeper to call a taxi, which arrived in a surprisingly short time, and after agreeing on the price for what would be a four or five hour trip, Namgyal and I got into the back seat and we drove off. We headed out into the countryside on an awful road. I constantly hit my head on the roof as we made our way slowly over the deep ruts in the unpaved road. I felt nervous going out into such a rural area, with no sign of a town or even a village, but I trusted Namgyal as my competent guide and viewed him as a friend. After more than an hour of travelling on that torturous road, we came to a small temple. We got out of the taxi and were met by a witch-like old woman, toothless and hair wildly disheveled. She put out her hand, obviously asking for money. I gave her a few coins and Namgyal chased her away.

Outside the temple gate, we noticed a cave. I wanted to have a look inside. It was small and I had to duck when I walked in. Namgyal followed. We were standing inside the cave in silence when suddenly tears welled up in my eyes and streamed down my face. They were falling so profusely that I was blinded and despite wiping my eyes, the tears kept on falling. I was not feeling sad or depressed at the time, nor was I thinking about anything that would have prompted an emotional reaction. Namgyal seemed embarrassed for me and simply asked if I was alright. I replied that I was fine and had no idea why I cried like that. The tears finally stopped and able to see again, I walked outside.

We were about to go into the small courtyard of the temple, when I saw off to the side a small booth that looked like it was a sanctuary. Namgyal seemed to want to go directly into the temple courtyard, but I indicated that I wanted to see what was in the booth. I didn't expect to see what I did. Inside was a man, a wild-looking ascetic, black hair with a hint of gray hanging down to his shoulders. I thought he was perhaps around 40 years old, with a thin, but not emaciated face. He was wrapped in a white garment that was not very clean, but also not too dirty. What stood out the most to me though were his eyes. They were intense, his pupils aflame with burning power, but they were not hostile. He exuded a raw energy force that I found frightening and yet also attractive and intriguing. Behind him was an ornate altar with a deity on it. I asked him if I could come inside to see the shrine more closely. He just looked at me. Namgyal translated. I couldn't of course understand his response but his gestures as he was speaking to Namgyal suggested that it wouldn't be possible. Namgyal told me that if I had ever eaten meat in my life, I would be burned up instantly upon entering the hut. I shuddered as I heard that, and wisely listened to him and didn't enter. I then asked, through Namgyal, if I can make an offering donation. He said it was allowed. I gave him a bank note but he wouldn't touch it. Instead he made a gesture with his open hands and somehow directed it to the altar shrine. It just floated and landed at the precise spot where there was a small tray of donations. He then motioned for us to leave. As we walked away I reflected that he was by far the most intense spiritual ascetic I had ever encountered. And although certainly not Buddhist, I was fascinated by him and admired his apparent unshakeable, total commitment to his spiritual path.

We then entered the courtyard where we found a group of young Germans sitting outside the temple drinking water and complaining that they were not permitted to enter the temple. Namgyal ignored them and led me to the entrance. While speaking with an elderly worn-looking woman who I assumed was the caretaker, he pointed to me. I smiled, not knowing what I was expected to do. I guessed that he was telling her that I had been initiated into the highest yoga tantra practice centered on the deity Vajrayogini. Whatever he said, it seemed to work. She led us inside. It was very dark with an extremely strong smell of incense. I thought how wonderful it was that I had a guide to bring me here, for I never would have ventured to this out-of-the-way place on my own. We followed the woman up a stone staircase and came to a closed off area that had prison-like bars around it. Namgyal asked her about it and she told him that it was a very holy place that Vajrayogini favors. After some persuasion by Namgyal, the woman allowed me to enter alone. I was very apprehensive to go inside but realized it was a great and unforeseen opportunity. I felt that maybe my practice would be energized by this experience. As I sat down in a half-lotus position, I felt ashamed about my lukewarm tantric practice. I took out my mala, closed my eyes, and recited the Vajrayogini mantra silently. I distinctly felt a presence there which I could not articulate to myself—I simply let it be. Warm energy, intense but not threatening, gently filled my body. I had the unmistakable sensation of being protected by someone or something. I generated no vision of the deity, I only experienced warmth. And then it subsided and I could feel the warm energy gradually leaving me. I lingered a while, wondering if anything else might occur. But then, I slowly stood up and walked out of the enclosure.

Namgyal was waiting for me and the woman proceeded to lock the gate. I was silent as we walked downstairs and out to the road where the taxi driver was waiting. We got into the taxi and made the slow uncomfortable journey to Boudhanath where I had planned to invite Namgyal to a late lunch. During the ride, we talked about a range of topics, but I didn't reveal to him what I had experienced in the Vagrayogini temple nor did I express how affected I was by the encounter with the ascetic in the booth. But as we were sitting at an outdoor table of a restaurant across from the stupa, I reflected silently on the events of that day. My mind conjured up the ascetic in the booth and it was as though I were there again. I actually felt his presence, his eyes, the power that was radiating in him and from him. I again experienced the feeling of his formidable but not evil energy. My heart started beating quickly. I must have given some outward indication of what I was reliving because I noticed that Namgyal was looking at me. I said I was sorry for drifting off and that I had just revisited the experience at the temple. I didn't mention to him about the ascetic because I feared that as a Tibetan Buddhist he would have dismissed the ascetic and it might deflate the memory I preserved—and periodically called up in my mind in the years to come.

One morning, a few days later, I spoke to the Western nun at Kopan who was the secretary and liaison for foreign guests and requested a brief meeting with the abbot, Lama Lhundrup. We set up an appointment for later that day. I arrived a few minutes early and sat down in the small lounge outside his office. About ten minutes later, Lama Lhundrup emerged from his office. He smiled warmly at me as I stood up. He then beckoned for me to sit down. After expressing my gratitude for having the opportunity to spend a few weeks at the beautiful monastery established by Lama Yeshe and Lama Zopa, I spoke of my growing interest in entering the monastic life. He was very pleased to hear that I wished to be a monk and said by all means I should follow my instinct. I then explained that although I was prepared to give up my academic position and apartment in New York, I feared that my decision would greatly upset my elderly parents. He understood my hesitation, but also clearly indicated that once the aspiration to be a monk had arisen, one should not let it sit too long, for one's resolve to renounce worldly life was bound to weaken and then it would be too late. He said that my parents would eventually come to accept my decision, for they undoubtedly wished me to be happy. I thanked him for his supportive counsel and felt that I had solidified my decision to ordain in the very near future.

After reflecting on my conversation with Lama Lhundrup and spending periods of time in silent meditation, neglecting the deity practice, I listened to my heart. I waited for the instinctual guide within that I had counted on when faced with the decision of leaving the NKT. I trusted it then and it had proved to be right. And now I sensed very clearly that my inclination to pursue monastic ordination which had been growing stronger over the past year was what my heart was directing me to follow. I emailed Namgyal and we made plans to meet in Boudhanath. He would accompany me to a tailor to have a set of monastic robes made.

We went to a tailor shop across from the stupa that had many shelves of different kinds of monastic robe material.

The tailor was very friendly and seemed to like Americans. His English was limited but he was conversive so that I only occasionally had to rely on Namgyal to translate. He proceeded to take my measurements and then showed me a few different types of material. I enlisted Namgyal, who had formerly been a monk, to suggest which material might be best, considering that I would be living in France, and not Nepal. I then paid a deposit and the tailor said they would be ready in one week. As we left the shop, I felt tremendous joy well up inside me. I had taken the initial step toward becoming a monk!

During the next few days, I spent my days at Kopan without venturing down into Boudhanath. I wanted just to imbibe the monastic environment. As it was the summer monsoon season, it was very humid, and there were periods of heavy rain, but the temperature was not unbearable. I sometimes went to a cool, sheltered place, not far from the main *gompa*, where I would meditate. It was a passageway open at each end, and inside was a lovely Buddha statue. There were also some mural paintings on the walls. Since there were a few cushions about, I sat down and tried to concentrate my mind, generating *bodhicitta*. I then allowed my mind to be empty of discursive thought—which was not very successful. I decided just to sit for a while, gazing at the Buddha statue. I was startled to hear some animated voices outside and the distinct sound of two hands clapping just once. I went outside and saw in the broad terrace area outside the *gompa*, several pairs of monks engaging in some sort of interaction, one seated, the other standing. I couldn't understand what they were saying, but periodically the monk who was standing would take a large step and at the same time clap one hand against the other. I later learned that this was how Tibetan monks engaged in debating one another on a particular concept in Buddhist philosophy.

I also spent time in my room, doing prostrations, going through Vajrayogini practice, or just reading. But I was often disturbed by chanting or loud talking resounding from the monastic dining hall just across the way from my room. I was beginning to understand that Tibetan monasteries were not quiet places. Although I loved the beauty and outstanding location of Kopan Monastery, I knew it was not the kind of monastery I would want to live in. I realized that my ideal monastery had more of an affinity with the Carthusian monastery depicted in the film. I imagined living in a Buddhist version of that monastery, but not as austere and not quite as silent. I would carry this vague ideal image with me into monastic life and measure Nalanda Monastery against it.

A week after I had placed the order for my monastic robes, I walked down to Boudhanath and proceeded to the tailor shop. The robes were ready and I paid the balance of the bill. I declined the tailor's offer that I first try them on because I wanted to wait until my ordination. I took the bundle and immediately went to the great stupa, which I circumambulated several times, reciting aloud *om mani padme hum*. I glanced periodically up at the prominent eyes looking out from the top of the stupa and also at the distant Himalayas. I was so glad I had made the trip—a trip that launched my monastic journey. I was optimistic that everything would work out well and attempted not to imagine how that would be.

Near the end of my stay at Kopan, I attended a guru *puja* (offering to the spiritual guide). It was a spectacular service, attended by perhaps two hundred monks. In addition to the awesome chanting, various tantric instruments accompanied the deep voices, filling the large *gompa* with a richly exotic and thunderous sound. Despite the long service being all in Tibetan, I found it to be a potent experience that was the highlight of my time there.

In the late afternoon of my final day at Kopan Monastery, I walked down to Boudhanath for a last round of circumambulations around the stupa. After walking around several times on a lower level and then climbing up to a higher level so that I could view the Himalayas, I noticed a Tibetan monk, probably in his mid-20s, walking next to me. He greeted me in English and we started a conversation. His English was good and his vocabulary was extensive. After walking around the stupa together for about a half hour, he asked me if I would like to have a cup of coffee with him. Although it was nearly dusk, and I would need to be back at Kopan before the gate was closed at 8pm, I thought I would have enough time and accepted his invitation. He led me away from the stupa area and we then walked down a narrow and nearly dark alley. I stayed alert to my surroundings, relying on my New York training, but instinctively trusted this monk. I was, nevertheless, relieved when we approached a few tables and chairs which was a sort of café. We continued our conversation and I learned that he hoped to be able to attend university in India. I found him intelligent, very personable as well, and enjoyed speaking with him on a wide range of topics. I finally said that I needed to get back to Kopan and that I would be leaving the next day. I was taken aback by his offer to accompany me to the airport. He said I should instruct the taxi driver to stop in Boudhanath at the stupa, and he would meet me. I accepted his offer, thinking it would be nice to have company to the airport as I did when coming from the airport three weeks before. He walked me to a taxi stand and bargained a good price for me for the ride up to Kopan. We then parted.

The next day, shortly before noon, I made my way to the front gate of the monastery, my suitcase nearly bursting with the addition of two sets of monastic robes and a golden Nepalese style Buddha statue. I was glad to see the taxi waiting. When I mentioned to the driver that we needed to stop in Boudhanath to pick someone up, he seemed nervous. I was wondering if he was an experienced driver and hoped he knew the way to the airport. When we arrived near the stupa, we saw a large crowd of people, many carrying flags, on the main street nearby. It seemed that there was some kind of demonstration going on. The taxi was unable to travel down the street and so I got out and looked for the young monk. I was about to give up when he appeared out of the crowd and quickly approached the taxi. He got into the back seat, as I was riding up front with the driver, and we headed out of the town.

I felt that something was not quite right. We were the only car on the main road that led to Kathmandu and the airport. I also noticed a lot of debris, broken glass and many stones strewn about on the road. The silence was eerie. The driver seemed very nervous as we travelled down the deserted road. Suddenly a crowd of young men, maybe one hundred, appeared and started racing toward our car. My response would have been to press down on the accelerator and speed away, but the driver panicked and stopped the car. The crowd soon reached the car and surrounded it shouting at us. Some started rocking the car. Strangely, I did not panic. I felt nervous yet assured that nothing would happen to me. I thought the worst that could happen would be that I would have to walk the rest of the way to the airport with my suitcase, the monk most likely helping me. I then speculated whether I would be able to make my flight. Meanwhile, the monk in the back seat began yelling to the crowd, the only word I could understand was something that sounded like "American." I was shocked that this gentle monk hoping to attend university was able to yell so energetically. I felt safe with him in the car. The group that were rocking the car stopped and came to my side of the vehicle and looked at me. I didn't know what to do. I simply smiled and gave a little wave. They conferred among themselves while the monk was still animatedly speaking to them. They then gave a signal that we could proceed. Again, I would have driven quickly away in case they changed their mind, but the driver, clearly traumatized by the event, drove at a slow pace until we were well beyond the crowd. As we drove on to the airport, I thought how odd it was that I met this monk the day before—such a random occurrence—and that he, barely knowing me, would offer to accompany me to the airport. He possibly had known about the demonstration and out of compassion wanted to make sure I got there safely. Despite the dramatic and potentially dangerous event that had just occurred, I felt serenely optimistic that I was on the right path, that moving towards monasticism was the direction my journey needed to take. Upon reaching the terminal, the monk and I got out. We embraced and I handed him the rest of my Nepalese money. He resisted taking it but when I insisted, telling him to use it towards his higher education in India, he relented and accepted it. As I entered the terminal, I reflected on the unexpected dramatic, yet also uplifting, end to my visit in Nepal.

I returned to Nalanda for the last two weeks of my summer break. I was riding high on the Nepal visit and my newly acquired monastic robes. Ven. Tenpa asked me to proofread and edit the information that would be posted on the monastery website about the five-year basic study program, scheduled to begin the following February. After learning that I already had monastic robes although did not know when I would ordain, he encouraged me to consider coming to Nalanda in February and join the study program.

While exploring the FPMT website, I came across the announcement that Lama Zopa would be in Bodhgaya, India in late December to give teachings and conduct a special ceremony at the site of the Maitreya Project. This was for me the clincher. I would take the initial step of going forth (from the householder life into homelessness) from Lama Zopa in Bodhgaya, the holy site of the Buddha's enlightenment. I immediately sent an email to Lama Zopa's correspondence secretary, requesting the initial going forth—more a formality than an actual ordination—from Lama Zopa in Bodhgaya. I mentioned that I had spent several months at Nalanda Monastery, where I planned to reside after the trip to India, and that I had received the Vajrayogini initiation from Lama Zopa the previous year. I leaped for joy upon receiving a prompt reply that my request would be granted. I figured I could actually ordain as a novice monk sometime in the spring at Nalanda. I was thus following Lama Lhundrup's advice. There was no time to lose, for I would be turning 54 while in Bodhgaya.

CHAPTER 7

Buddhist Monastic Life: Two Colors, Two Traditions

Soon after Labor Day, I made preparations to sell my apartment and began to divest myself of the more than 1500 books I had in my studio apartment. I still had one important task to do before I would be free to go forth into monastic life: I needed to resign from my academic position at John Jay College, CUNY. Although I knew I would not be returning, in order to placate my parents who were justifiably very distraught at my decision to give up my profession and my life in New York to take up monastic life, I decided to request a leave of absence from the university rather than resigning at that time. I met with the chair of the English department and explained what I was about to do. Her response was a combination of shock and admiration for my "gutsiness" in making such a dramatic change and that I was willing to give up what so many people would cherish and hold on to. She indicated her wish that all would work out as I wanted but at the same time hoped I would return.

The Fall semester sped by as I felt my ties to lay life in the "world" falling away, leaving me increasingly lighter and unburdened by materiality. On the 22nd of December, 2007, I set out for India.

After spending the night in New Delhi, recuperating from the sixteen-hour flight, I headed for the main train station. The crowds of people and disorder was even greater than what I had found at the airport. As I already had my electronic ticket, a helpful station attendant brought me to the first-class lounge where I could wait in a peaceful environment until the train arrived. Trains were notoriously late in India and my train to Gaya lived up to the reputation, pulling into the station three hours late. It was already nearly midnight when we left the station and my compartment-mates promptly settled into their bunks for the night. I was on the upper level and was worried about falling out during the night as the train ride was not smooth. Fortunately, my fears didn't materialize into reality and I remained safe through the short night.

As dawn allowed me to see the Indian countryside, I was glad the others in the compartment were awake and I could thus sit on the lower level and look out the window. The train stopped although there was no station. We were in a rural area and I saw the sun rising over an open field. What captured my attention though was a solitary woman in the distance standing straight and tall in the middle of the field facing the rising sun. She then moved with a slow, stately gait towards the sun, her arms at her side, and after a while, turned to the right and continued in the same manner. I found this figure to be in exquisite harmony with the peaceful sunrise and surmised it was some sort of religious practice. As the train began to move, I marveled at the striking contrast between the noisy, crowded scene at the train station and this serenely beautiful vista of humanity and nature in unity.

After arriving in Gaya, I had the choice of different types of vehicles to take for the ten-mile ride to Bodhgaya. I selected a sturdy-looking vehicle, though open on the sides. As it was mid-afternoon, I didn't fear the bandits that were reported to prey on vehicles along that rode at night. The taxi took me directly to Root Institute, a retreat center located in the outskirts of Bodhgaya that was part of the FPMT international network, and the site where Lama Zopa would give teachings.

After checking in at the office, I was directed to a large tent that had been put up on the edge of the property which would serve as a men's dorm. As it turned out, I would only spend one night there. On the next day, upon returning in the early afternoon from a brief initial visit to the Mahabodhi temple and the Bodhi Tree (the site of the Buddha's enlightenment)—I didn't want to be away too long, as the going-forth ceremony could happen at any time—I was met by one of the other candidates who excitingly told me that Lama Zopa would perform the rite in just one hour. I was both excited and stressed to learn that it was happening so soon. I rushed to the tent to find my razor and shaving foam as well as to collect the set of robes I had brought, and then raced back to the main compound. I went into one of the bathrooms, turned on the faucet and waited for hot water. I gave up after a few minutes and proceeded to shave my head with cold water. There was a very small mirror over the sink but I couldn't see the back of my head. My nervousness, and the fact that I had never shaved my head before, caused me to cut myself in a number of places. The process seemed to be taking longer than I had anticipated and I rushed to finish. I hastily put on my robes, which I had not yet tried on, and went to a room outside the place where the ceremony would take place. The three others were there: two women, one from Germany, the other from Australia, and one young man, who was American. They looked at me and couldn't resist laughing at my appearance: blood was dripping down the sides of my head and apparently I had left patches of hair in the back; also my robes were not laying right. To my great relief, a senior Australian monk, Ven. Thubten Gyatso, one of the first Western monks to have ordained with Lama Yeshe, came to my rescue. He got hold of a razor and finished the shaving of my head, and using damp tissues, he stopped the bleeding. He then assisted me in putting on the robes correctly. I couldn't thank him enough for his help.

The four of us proceeded into the small shrine room and waited for Lama Zopa to arrive. I had finally calmed down and managed to focus my mind on the life-changing event that was about to occur. Lama Zopa entered and took his seat, and after paying our respects, Ven. Gyatso directed us one by one to approach Lama Zopa for the auspicious hair cutting ceremony that would signal our going forth into the homeless life of a monastic. This was merely an initial step, indicating our intention to request actual novice ordination at the next opportunity that arose. I was the last one, which had given me ample time to observe how the act was performed. When I approached Lama Zopa, I bent my head forward and waited for him to cut the symbolic remaining strand of hair. However, I had been so thorough in shaving the top of my head that he had difficulty finding enough hair to cut. Thankfully, there was a very tiny stand of hair left, and he was able to snip it off. He then smiled at me and I felt warmth rise from my heart right up to my head. He looked directly at me and said that my new name would be Thubten Palden (Thubten being the lineage, and Palden would be my personal name).

After Lama Zopa left the room, the four of us walked outside, admiring each other in our robes. Sabine, the German woman, asked me if I would also be going to Dharamsala in January to train and then receive novice ordination from His Holiness the Dalai Lama. I replied that I hadn't planned to, thinking I would receive it from the abbot at Nalanda Monastery sometime in the spring. She encouraged me not to wait and instead go to Dharamsala. The American was also planning to go and he said that I shouldn't pass up the chance to ordain with the Dalai Lama, for the karmic benefit would be immense. As I was basking in the joy of having taken the initial step, they convinced me. I thought, 'why wait'? But I nevertheless feared I wouldn't be able to receive ordination since I had not applied before the November deadline and I had no one who I could list as a reference on my application. When I voiced my concerns, Sabine dismissed them and advised me to speak with Lama Zopa's attendant, explaining my situation.

I acted immediately on her suggestion and after locating Ven. Roger, the Western monk who was Lama Zopa's long-time personal attendant, I asked if I could speak to him about a personal matter. He invited me to join him in circumambulating the stupa that stood in the center of Root Institute and tell him about my situation. After explaining it to him, he said I should go ahead and submit an application, which I could do electronically at an internet café in Bodhgaya, and he assured me it should work out. I thanked him over and over, but he just waved it off, smiling broadly at me.

Since it was Christmas, we were to have a special dinner. A long table with another one extending outward from the center was set up as well as several additional individual tables. The four newly gone-forth monastics were given seats of honor on the short table extending outward. Lama Zopa sat at the center of the long table and monks and nuns sat on either side of him. As it turned out, I sat directly in front of him, but not facing him. During the meal, I distinctly felt that Lama Zopa was studying me. I could sense his eyes even without looking at him. He seemed to be reading *into* me and I wondered if he was examining my karma or if he had seen something unusual about my future life as a monastic. After several minutes of enduring this, I turned and looked at him and instantly he turned away.

On the following day, I walked to Bodhgaya and went into an internet café to submit my application for novice ordination to the office of the Dalai Lama. I hoped for the best. That evening, there was to be a very special late night event at the site of the Maitreya Project a few miles outside of Bodhgaya. The FPMT was sponsoring the construction of an enormous stature of Maitreya, the Buddha to come in the next age, and Lama Zopa wanted to hold a one-hundred-thousand water-offering service there. It would begin at 9pm and last into the early morning hours. Although I looked forward to the night event and Lama Zopa's teachings, I feared that it would be very chilly out there in the open, for in late December, the temperature dropped into the 40s, Fahrenheit. I regretted not bringing to Bodhgaya my heavy outer robe, which I had thought I would only need for the cold weather in France.

As I was riding to the site in a bicycle rickshaw with the Australian woman who had also gone forth, we both realized that perhaps it wasn't appropriate for two monastics of different genders to be riding together. But since we passed no one on the way, we figured it didn't really matter. Upon arriving there, each of us found a suitable place to sit on the mats that had been placed on the grass. I was already feeling chilled and it was only half-past eight. My mind was wrapped up in thoughts about how I would make it through the next four or five hours, when someone tapped me on the shoulder. It was the Israeli monk I had spoken to briefly earlier that day. He offered me his outer robe to wear, saying that he didn't need it for he was accustomed to the chilly air. I was deeply touched by his offer and after making sure he would be fine without it, I gratefully accepted it. It was of a woolen material and by wrapping myself up in it, I managed to stay warm.

During the next four hours, Lama Zopa gave general teachings regarding the steps of the path, focusing particularly on generating compassion for suffering beings. Similar to the all night teachings in California, he didn't move during those several hours and, even more astonishing, the outer robe he wore was his usual one and would hardly provide him with protection from the chilly wind that blew through the open area. I mused on the possibility that he provided enough warmth from within through engaging in deep meditation as he spoke to us. At around 1am, he ended. I suspected that he could have gone on longer but out of compassion for us who did not have the ability to generate our own heat from within, he decided to cut the teachings short.

As everyone made their way to the exit, there was an open truck that people were piling in on. I hesitated since

I couldn't manage the steep climb and proceeded to begin walking with a number of others. It was late and I did not look forward to the estimated three-mile walk back in the cold night air. We moved out of the way as a suv was passing us. Suddenly it stopped right next to me, and a monk called to me, ushering me into the vehicle. I got in and my glasses steamed up from the heat in the car. I settled into the back seat and soon discovered that sitting right in front of me was Lama Zopa. He didn't speak and in respect to his silence neither did anyone else until we arrived at Root Institute.

Lama Zopa gave additional teachings in the main *gompa* the next evening and on the following day he departed. We all lined up, monks, nuns, new monastics, and lay people, to bid goodbye to him and hopefully receive his blessing as he walked along the line. I anxiously waited for him to approach where I was standing. The Israeli monk was on my right, and Lama Zopa stopped for a moment to talk to him, asking about his immediate plans. As he was slowly walking past me, he paused for a moment and gently patted my cheeks. I accepted that as his blessing. He continued walking along, patting a few people on their heads, and just smiling at others. And then he was gone. I remained in Bodhgaya for a few more days as there was to be a special New Year's Eve retreat, led by Ven. Thubten Gyatso, the senior monk who had helped me before the going forth ceremony. I also joined a few monks and nuns on a day outing to the ruins of Nalanda Monastery. I thought it an appropriate site to visit since I would be taking up residency at the modern version of that institution. As I am not particularly talented at building in my mind an image of a place from its existing ruins, I didn't come away with any sense about what monastic life might have been like there, living and studying among several thousand monks. Yet I savored merely standing among the silent ruins of that illustrious monastic institution.

One day, after lunch, as I was putting my dishes on the cart, Ven. Thubten Gyatso approached me and asked where I was headed next. I told him I would be going to Dharamsala to receive *getsul* ordination from His Holiness the Dalai Lama and then to Nalanda Monastery in France, with which I knew he was well familiar. Then, looking directly at me, he asked if I was ready to die in the monastery. I was taken aback by his question and hesitated before replying that I hoped I was. With a warm smile that I sensed came from his heart, he said that I should at least aspire to die there. At the time, I assumed that he meant that I should be prepared to spend the rest of my life as a monk in that monastery. But several years later, I recalled his words and realized that he most certainly meant whether I was prepared to let the ego or "self" die in the monastery. That aspiration would periodically arise in my consciousness during my subsequent monastic journey.

January 1st was my last full day in Bodhgaya and I spent a good part of it at the Mahabodhi Temple and Bodhi Tree. The first day of the new year proved to be a popular day for visitors to the site of the Buddha's enlightenment. Large numbers of monks and nuns from just about every Buddhist country and tradition circumambulated the holy site. Many Hindus were there as well, noticeable because they walked around in the opposite direction. As I walked slowly with the internationally diverse monastics and lay people around the stupa and tree, I focused on the significance of this most holy of Buddhist pilgrimage sites. Wearing my maroon robes, I reveled at this historic moment in my life journey. I wanted to savor it as long as possible and thus walked around innumerable times. I finally stopped in front of the Bodhi Tree and sat down quite close to the fence. I had brought my sitting cloth and placed it on the hard ground. Although it was very uncomfortable to sit without a cushion, I managed to do so for at least fifteen minutes. I simply allowed my mind to quietly take in where I was. I successfully blocked out the noise and activity all around me and for a few moments, with my eyes closed, I just sensed the Tree, dismissing my acknowledgment of the fact that it was not the same tree the Buddha had sat under on the night of his enlightenment. I reflected on how many monks, nuns, and lay Buddhists had sat under this very tree, and that, for me, gave it enormous power. I then got up and still carrying in my mind the weight and significance of the occasion, walked out of the temple area into the bustling, noisy, and squalid town.

Back in New York, I elected not to wear my monastic robes. After all, I had merely made the initial gesture—the commitment—to ordain, and I didn't feel it was right for me to don the robes before becoming a novice monk. I, nevertheless, felt different than I did before the trip to Bodhgaya. The brief ceremony registered deeply on my psyche and the "world" appeared less interesting and beckoning; I had indeed begun the process of renunciation. I periodically reminded myself, particularly when riding the subway, that I did not renounce having compassion nor concern for those suffering. Although caught up in preparing the apartment for the closing of the sale that would now take place in my absence, discarding a seemingly never-ending quantity of "stuff" in my two closets, when I sat down to meditate, I regularly generated the still weak aspiration to attain enlightenment for the benefit of all sentient beings.

The two weeks passed very quickly and just before my departure, I visited my parents to say goodbye. They did their best to show some excitement for what lay ahead of me, and good-naturedly gave their permission for me to ordain, something that was required in Buddhist tradition no matter how old one was. I made a commitment to try to visit them twice a year while I was living in France. I could see that made them very happy.

I accomplished everything I had set to do and now was free to make a second trip to India.

Two days later I was riding on the overnight bus from New Delhi to Dharamsala. I hadn't received a confirmation from the Office of the Dalai Lama that I was accepted into the pre-ordination training program, but I rested on the assurance from Ven. Roger that all would be fine. As dawn arrived, we began the long winding assent up to McLeod Ganj, the hilltop region of Dharamsala. I was relieved when we reached our destination after a more than eleven-hour uncomfortable journey. I shared a taxi with an Australian who was also going to attend the pre-novice training. We rode further up the hill from the town to Tushita Meditation Centre. He was surprised that I was not wearing my monastic robes. I instantly felt ashamed that for the sake of comfort, I had not put them on for the bus trip. The Centre in its secluded forested location above McLeod

Ganj seemed like an ideal place to train. I looked forward to exploring the immediate area and catching a glimpse of the Himalayas.

After checking in at the office, where I found Sabine, the German woman who had also gone forth in Bodhgaya, I learned that she was the current director of the Centre. She suggested that I put on my robes before I saw Sr. Jotika, the nun who would be leading the training. As soon as I settled into my room, I immediately put them on, and then paid a call on Sr. Jotika. I knocked on her door and after hearing her permission to enter, I walked in and introduced myself. She gave me a friendly smile and said that she was pleased to inform me that I had been accepted into the training program. I sighed audibly. She then asked if I had any questions and when I replied that for the moment I didn't, she indicated that the program would begin the next morning and our daily routine would be explained then. My initial impressions of Sr. Jotika were that she was extremely competent to lead our group of fifteen candidates, consisting of both men and women from a variety of Western countries, through the training course that had been implemented by the office of the Dalai Lama for Western candidates planning to receive *getsul* (novice) ordination.

I hadn't anticipated the extremely cold and snowy weather in Dharamsala in the middle of January despite the fact that it was in the foothills of the Himalayas, located at an altitude of nearly 7000 feet. I ended up sharing an unheated room with Ben, who was the other American who had gone forth in Bodhgaya. We elected not to use the names we had received from Lama Zopa since we would be receiving new names from the Dalai Lama at the novice ordination. We were both concerned about staying warm at night in the room. Fortunately, each bed had two heavy blankets and with a warm sleeping bag and extra warm sleepwear, I was reasonably optimistic that I would not be cold in bed. Soon after the simple evening meal of soup and bread, we retired for the night. The daily training began with a chanting service at 5am.

The *gompa* that was to be used was not the main one. This was not as large and thus easier to heat. However, the two small electric heaters failed to provide sufficient warmth on those early mornings. We all wore sweaters and scarfs under our robes. No one, I noticed, fell asleep during the sessions. Sr. Jotika went over the daily schedule we would follow over the next four weeks until the ordination which was anticipated to occur around the time of the Tibetan New Year in mid-February. She warned us to be punctual for each class session and not to miss any without her permission. She reiterated on several occasions that she was following the guidelines she had received from the office of the Dalai Lama. I had heard from another participant that Sr. Jotika was the only Western monastic who the Dalai Lama permitted to train Westerners. When I inquired about her unusual title, I was told that she had formerly been a nun in the Theravada tradition but after obtaining full ordination in Taiwan, she became a close disciple of the Dalai Lama. I trusted His Holiness's instincts and gave her my full attention and respect.

The living conditions at Tushita were challenging to say the least. A few days after we began the training, we received about two feet of snow. I didn't expect there to be snow plows to clear the road—and there weren't any forthcoming—and so nothing happened. The snow just stayed on the road. Fortunately, the kitchen staff were well prepared and we had plenty of food on hand. We also experienced a periodic loss of electricity, and given that it was our sole source of heat in the *gompa*, this created more cold misery for us seated in that room. In addition, water would sometimes stop flowing into the pipes. One had to be vigilant about keeping water barrels full in the squat toilets as that was the only way to flush. I surprised myself at my adaptability to these conditions. I wore layers of clothes under my robes and on rare occasions I summoned up the courage to take a shower, having learned what time of day to expect a brief amount of moderately warm water.

I believe what kept our group going—and being Westerners we were not generally accustomed to such living conditions—was that we were all so motivated to enter monastic life and appreciative of having the opportunity to ordain with His Holiness. Sr. Jotika, with her warmth and support, encouraged us to rise above the physical challenges. Every evening, after the service in that cold *gompa*, she closed with a beautiful prayer that I had never heard before and assumed it came from her days when she was a Theravada nun:

> To the Buddha I dedicate this body and life
> And in devotion I will walk the Buddha's Path of Awakening
> For me there is no other refuge, the Buddha is my excellent refuge,
> By the utterance of this truth, may I grow in the Master's way,
> By my devotion to the Buddha, and the blessings of this practice—
> By its power, may all obstacles be overcome.
> (from the Chanting Book of Amaravati Monastery, UK)

Every evening we left the *gompa* and headed into the icy chill of the night air, warmed by that beautiful prayer.

During the third week of the training, we had the privilege of paying a visit to Urgyen Trinley Dorje, one of the two claimants to the title of 17th Karmapa of the Karma Kagyu school of Tibetan Buddhism. Sr. Jotika explained that it was a tradition established a few years before that the Western monastic trainees pay a visit to him about a week before the ordination. We were all naturally very excited about having an audience with the Karmapa. One morning, after breakfast, we walked down the hill to the center of town and got into four taxis for the approximately one hour's drive down into the valley below Dharamsala. When our caravan arrived, we were met at the door of the main building of the monastery and ushered into a beautiful *gompa*. We stood anxiously awaiting the Karmapa. In a few minutes, he walked into the room. I was very surprised to see a tall man in his early 20s who conveyed shyness and a quiet, peaceful demeanor. Sr. Jotika, who had met him before on several similar occasions, respectfully bowed her head to him and after introducing our group, asked him if he would be willing to say a few words to us. He looked down for a moment, as if gathering his thoughts and then in a gentle voice began to address us. His English was quite good and I was able to understand him, although I had to strain to hear his voice. He proceeded to offer a brief talk on the benefits and responsibilities of taking monastic ordination. He didn't speak for very long but I maintained vigilant attention to him, more than the words he uttered. I wondered what it might feel like to be the Karmapa, and to be so young. Sr. Jotika had told us that he was in regular contact with the Dalai Lama, who, I expected, offered him counsel. We then walked up to him in an orderly manner offering him a *khata,* white silk scarf—a Tibetan custom—which he took and then placed around each of our necks. This was the first time I did this and thought it was a beautiful gesture, and it also gave me the chance of spending a few seconds in very close proximity to him. After gathering around him for a photo, we took leave and headed to a nearby monastery for Western nuns where we were to have lunch.

We entered the final week of the pre-ordination training, and spent nearly all of our class time going over the 36 novice precepts, which were elaborations and expansions of the basic ten precepts in the early Buddhist tradition. After giving us a brief description of each of the main precepts, Sr. Jotika then read from a detailed commentary written by a Western monastic. We then broke into groups to further discuss the particular precept among ourselves, focusing on how the precept would be followed in daily monastic life and what challenges could arise that might compromise our obedience to it. I found these informal discussions very helpful and it also gave me the chance to interact on a more personal level with the other members of the group. In addition, we were required to memorize the list of precepts, thankfully only in English.

On the day before the ordination, we all walked down into town and went to a small Indian operated barber shop where each of us would have our heads shaved. The barber used a single blade razor which made me nervous. But once he started on my head, I could tell that he had had a lot of experience. Once back at Tushita, Sr. Jotika had us practice doing full-length prostrations wearing our yellow outer robes on top of the usual upper and lower robes. This robe was only worn for very special occasions. Obviously novice ordination would be one of those occasions. I, and most of the others, had great difficulty keeping it on during the prostration. We would need to perform this several times during the ceremony.

In the pre-dawn darkness of February 18th, we walked down the snowy roadway into town and then through the deserted streets to Namgyal Monastery where His Holiness the Dalai Lama resided. It was only about a mile, but the packed snow made the going slower than it would have been otherwise. When we arrived at the security checkpoint, there were at least 40 or 50 Tibetans already lined up. We got in line and slowly progressed to the metal detector, similar to that at airports. While we were still a distance away, a uniformed guard approached us and collected our passports. It took about two hours to proceed through the security checkpoint. It was very chilly but not as brutally cold as it had been in January. Just as we arrived at the metal detector, the sun's first rays came over the surrounding mountains.

With great relief, we were ushered into a large room that served as a dining room. We all sat on the hard mats that had been placed on the stone floor and gratefully received the simple breakfast. I was still chilled from standing so long outside that I ventured to drink the hot Tibetan tea that I was given. It tasted like rancid salty butter and in normal circumstances I would never have drunken it. But on this occasion and in honor of the tradition we were being received into, I generated a positive mind towards it and, while not actually enjoying it, appreciated the warmth it afforded.

We were then led into the main *gompa* where the ordination would occur. Each of us had brought a small transistor radio with us which would provide us with a simultaneous translation into English. We sat towards the rear of the room, behind the Tibetans. The Dalai Lama came into the room, a big smile on his face, and led the initial chanting. The room was not very large and despite being near the rear, I felt very close to His Holiness. How different it was from viewing him at a great distance at a stadium or large theater. The intimacy of his presence was palpable to me. After the chanting, which went on for quite a long time, he gave teachings that were similar to those given by the Karmapa, but in much greater detail. I was delighted and bubbling in excitement when the actual ordination ceremony began. The Dalai Lama took a folded piece of paper out of a vessel, looked at it, and then handed it to one of his attendants, who then gave it to a monastic candidate. I guessed that the paper contained the monastic name that the Dalai Lama had conferred on him or her. I couldn't contain my nervous anticipation of what my name would be. Finally, an attendant approached me and handed me the folded paper. I opened it and read the name: Tenzin Lamten. The first name was the Dalai Lama's lineage name which all of us would receive. The second one was my personal name. I liked it immediately. I had never met or heard of anyone with that name. I did not doubt that His Holiness had selected that name for me and felt privileged at having been given a unique name. Below the name in parentheses was written "holder of the Path." I promised myself that I would give all of my energy to living up to that responsibility.

 The final part of the ceremony was to go up in groups of three to the Dalai Lama for him to bless our robes. When it came to my turn, I walked up with a Russian candidate on my left and Ben on my right. We kneeled in front of His Holiness and each of us placed our hands on top of one another. Since I was in the middle position, my right hand was on top. The Dalai Lama then placed his hand right on top of my mine and held it there. The warmth of his hand felt comforting and protective. I didn't know what to do with my left hand since unlike that of the two other candidates, it was not on the pile. I then placed it on top of the Dalai Lama's hand. I reflected later that I shouldn't have done it and that it was probably disrespectful. But I recalled that His Holiness did not reveal any annoyance with my action and thus I assumed that he was used to Westerners.

Before exiting the *gompa*, each of us again went up to His Holiness and offered him a *khata*. When my turn came, he placed it around my neck and asked me where I was from. I said I was from the U.S., from New York. He smiled and said, "I love New York." I captured in my heart's camera that moment of experiencing his famous beaming smile in such close proximity, and proceeded to walk outside to join the rest of my group.

Sabine suggested that we hold an all-night vigil at Tushita in celebration of our ordination and to summon all the protective energy of the Buddhas and *bodhisattvas*. We unanimously agreed to do so. I didn't join the others for the walk back to Tushita, opting to spend some time alone in the town, reveling and savoring the auspicious event that had just occurred. While I had felt different after the going forth ceremony in Bodhgaya, the present feeling was of a far deeper resonance. I perceived I was now a different person, not only because I had a new name, but also because something had been transformed within me. As I walked along the busy narrow streets of Dharamsala, I was aware that I had officially renounced the "world." I would still be living in it, but my relation to it would not ever be the same as it was prior to that day. As a novice monk, I was now firmly committed to walking the path leading toward enlightenment, and, unlike lay people, I would be able to devote myself to it full-time. Before walking up to Tushita, I picked up some bars of dark chocolate that would give us energy to chant through the night.

The hours of the all-night chanting session flew by. I didn't feel tired in the least. At dawn, we were joined by Sr. Jotika, and we performed the daily *puja* to Shakyamuni Buddha. I then hurried to gather my things since I would be departing directly after lunch. But first, I walked to a stall outside the meditation center to buy an assortment of hard candy to make into an offering for Lama Zopa, who was scheduled to make a visit to Tushita after I was gone. With Ben's assistance, I prepared the offering, and although it wasn't particularly attractive, I hoped Lama Zopa would appreciate my gesture. I wrote a brief note, informing him of my new name and that I was headed to Nalanda Monastery. I also expressed my gratitude for his support in bringing about my ordination.

After bidding farewell to my fellow recently ordained novice monks and nuns, I got into a taxi for the two-hour ride to the nearest train station. I decided to take an overnight train to New Delhi rather than the bus. Since my flight to France wasn't departing until 3am on the following day, I booked a room in a guesthouse in the Tibetan quarter, where I would spend the day and evening before going to the airport.

I arrived at Nalanda Monastery as a newly ordained *getsul* on the first day of the five-year study program. The monks whom I knew gave me a hearty welcome, and I was introduced to three novice monks who had ordained there two days before. The atmosphere at Nalanda was considerably different than in the previous summer. The new study program had brought a number of lay people to the monastery, both men and women. The women were residing in a rented house down the road. After lunch, I entered the large *gompa* in the new building, that was mostly completed, for the afternoon class session. Since I had missed the morning session, Ven. Tenpa brought me to the front and introduced me to Geshe Jamphal, the abbot and also the principal teacher of the program. He smiled and welcomed me and then I took a seat at one of the red wooden *puja* tables. Geshe Jamphal spoke only in Tibetan which was then simultaneously translated by Ven. Tharchin, a German monk with an excellent knowledge of Tibetan and English. Two other translators, wearing headphones, a Frenchwoman and a Spanish monk, translated from English into their respective native languages. Thinking back to the *pujas* held in the intimate old *gompa*, I felt that I was in a new monastery, and I knew that I would need some time to adjust.

With both buildings being fully occupied, there were about 35 residents at Nalanda. Around ten lay women and nuns, the former coming from the nearby house, the latter from Institute Vajrayogini on the other side of Lavaur, came on weekdays to attend the classes. I gradually acclimated to the new busy schedule. There were classes every weekday morning and afternoon, each lasting for a few hours with a break in the middle. During the first months, since there was no morning chanting service, I got up early and although I was residing in the new building, I walked over to the old *gompa* and performed prostrations there. I then returned to my room and went through the deity *sadhana* (practice booklet), all before breakfast. By the middle of May, I was finding myself increasingly disturbed by the lively conversations being held in the dining room downstairs well into the evening. I also reacted rather negatively to the new evening meal that had started up. I guessed that the lay students, who were paying a considerable amount of money for room and board, had expected three meals a day. Thus, the kitchen volunteers started putting out all the leftovers from lunch, and adding to them when necessary. In order not to generate a critical mind, I avoided going over to the new house at the time that dinner was taking place—an event that included a growing number of monks. Having heard from one of the lay students that a room had opened up in the old house, I requested permission to move there.

I was very happy with my small room in a separate area of the old house where the other occupants were all monks, and of a similar mature age as me. Even in the hot summer weather, the room was bearable. I enjoyed the long narrow window that extended to the floor, where I could sit and look out onto the beautiful front lawn with its stately trees. It was now even more convenient to get up at 5am and walk downstairs to the *gompa* just below my room to do daily prostrations. I also seemed better able to concentrate on my daily practice there but was clearly aware that I was not progressing. I stumbled at the "generation" stage in the Vajrayogini *sadhana*, where I was to dissolve my individual ego-self and generate myself in the perceived form of the deity. I still did not know how to do this nor did I seem to be getting more adept at summoning up the complex visualizations associated with the deity's mandala (field of residence). Yet I didn't question the validity of the practice itself even though I knew most certainly it was not directly derived from the Buddha. I had faith in Lama Zopa and other tantric masters while at the same time being conscious of the enormous gulf separating me from them and even from advanced monastic and lay tantric practitioners.

In June, at the request of Lama Zopa, Nalanda conducted a 24-hour chant-a-thon of the Golden Light Sutra that would be live-streamed over the internet. Besides the benefit such a recitation would offer for the monks who were chanting, the monastery where it was held, and all those tuning in to listen, it was hoped that enough donations would come in to cover the remaining costs of finishing the new *gompa* and other parts of the building. Each monk signed up for at least one one-hour session. As there were not enough monks, I signed up for a second session, planning to read that portion from a German translation. As I climbed up to the high seat in the beautiful new *gompa*, I reflected on the summer before when I was sitting on the floor as a layman, listening and waiting to provide the reciting monk with refreshments. I felt tremendous gratitude to His Holiness and Lama Zopa for granting me the opportunity to join the ranks of the ordained community of monks and nuns.

Also that summer, Ven. Jampa, one of the three recently ordained novice monks suggested that we recite the *Sanghata Sutra* in the center of Lavaur. He informed me that Lama Zopa strongly recommended it to be publicly recited because of the enormous transformative benefit it provided for the reciter and the hearer. Jampa was English, in his mid-30s, and we had developed a good brotherly friendship. I liked his friendly down-to-earth manner, something I had often encountered in Englishmen from a working class or lower middle-class background. After riding bicycles into town, about three miles away, we chose a shady spot on the broad island that separated the two directions of the main road. We sat down on a bench and each of us took turns reading a page from the sutra. Not many people passed by, and those that did simply looked at us and moved on. Nevertheless, we read out loud the entire lengthy sutra, and I tried to keep in mind the benefit we were offering to those passing by, hearing only a very brief section of it in a language they probably did not understand.

As we reached mid-summer, I noted my growing dissatisfaction with life at Nalanda. I found myself rebelling at having to study for exams and feeling pressure to perform well since the grades were posted. Having gone through graduate school and the exhaustive exams I had to take in the doctoral program, I felt I had had enough of studying in an institutional setting. And that was how I was beginning to view the monastery. In addition, Geshe Jamphal encouraged the students in the program to engage in Tibetan style debate. I recalled my impression of that competitive form of study when I was visiting Kopan Monastery. It didn't appeal to be then and I hadn't warmed up to it in the present. Jampa wanted to debate with me, but I indicated my lack of interest. He, along with a few other students, were learning Tibetan. I had attempted this in New York a few years before but eventually lost interest, thinking it really wasn't necessary as important texts were all available in reliable English translations. Thus, Jampa and I grew increasingly more distant from each other as our interests diverged.

Around this time, I approached Ven. Gelek, a relatively senior English monk whom I had a great deal of affection and respect for. I expressed my growing unhappiness with the situation and frustration of not going deeper into a more meditative practice. I told him I just did prostrations and mantra recitations, but did not know how to quiet my mind in order to develop concentration. I also revealed that I had been neglecting Vajryogini practice, because after nearly three years, I still had not gotten a handle on it and felt I was wasting my time. I poured all of this out to him and I could see that he was paying close attention to what I was divulging. When I had finished, he said I might want to consider visiting one of the Theravada monasteries in England that had been established by the well-known and well-respected American monk, Ajahn Sumedho. He went on to explain that while visiting family in north London, he had spent a few days at Amaravati Monastery, the largest of the monasteries in England, and found the atmosphere there conducive for developing meditation. Ajahn Sumedho, he said, who had been a long-time student of the famed Thai meditation master, Ajahn Chah, currently resided at Amaravati. He suggested I familiarize myself with one of his books that were in the Nalanda library and listen to some of his recorded teachings. He said that I would then be in a better position to decide if I wanted to explore this avenue more. I thanked him for this information and already felt something stirring within me—a hint that this may, indeed, be what I was looking for. I still carried within me a vague image of a quiet, contemplative monastic community based on the Carthusian monastery in the film. My mind, fueled by this persistent quest, began to conjure up an ideal image of Amaravati Monastery.

In August, most of the monks and lay residents were going to Nantes, a city in northwest France, to attend teachings by the Dalai Lama. I suspected that Sr. Jotika would be there. Since she had formerly been a nun at Amaravati and was certainly well acquainted with Ajahn Sumedho, I thought she would be an ideal source for counsel. I emailed her and asked if we could meet during that time in Nantes. She responded that she would be happy to meet with me and that I should look for her there so that we could set a day and time. I felt relieved to know that I would be able to discuss my current quandary with her and trusted the advice she would offer.

On the first day of the teachings, I sought out Sr. Jotika, which was not easy given the enormous crowd. Adding to the bedlam was a large group of NKT monastics standing outside the stadium banging drums and loudly chanting in English unfavorable slogans regarding the Dalai Lama. They were also handing out leaflets explaining their position. Nevertheless, I was able to find Sr. Jotika, who suggested we meet for lunch at a particular spot that she described on the front lawn. When I arrived there, she was engaged in conversation with several nuns. I didn't want to interrupt them, so I just stood off to the side. However, Sr. Jotika noticed me, and speaking to the nuns in Spanish, which I could catch the gist of, they got up and I was able to speak with her in private. I expressed to her what I had confided to Ven. Gelek. She said she understood my frustration and agreed that Amaravati or Chithurst Monastery, under the leadership of Ajahn Sucitto, would be good choices. She added that both the Tibetan Gelug and the Thai Forest Theravada traditions each had their strengths and weaknesses and that I needed to judge for myself which would be more conducive for my monastic and spiritual life.

Having been advised by two monastics whose opinions I valued, I slowly let the seed grow that would lead to my departure from Nalanda. During the three-day event, I had, as usual, difficulty concentrating on the teachings His Holiness was imparting. My mind was, instead, occupied with the new developments in my life. On the last day, we all took the *Bodhisattva* vows, something that I had done each time I had attended the Dalai Lama's teachings. As I recited the words this time, I summoned all my power of concentration and let them register in my heart-mind. As the Dalai Lama instructed us to let the *Bodhisattva* promise to achieve enlightenment for the benefit of all sentient beings penetrate deep into "the depths of our hearts" and "marrow of our bones," I realized how lax I had been in actually keeping it in mind. I was so caught up in my own needs and problems that I forgot about my aspiration to free all sentient beings from suffering. I fought off the temptation to lay the blame on the current life at Nalanda. I knew it was my own negligence and summoned the determination to be more attentive to these lofty and powerful vows.

During early autumn, I noticed myself becoming more withdrawn and distant from the monastic community and life at Nalanda. I attended classes and *pujas*, but I was increasingly focused and preoccupied with making a decision about whether to depart. One major hurdle I had to overcome was the denigrating view Mahayana Buddhists held towards the "Hinayana" (Lesser Vehicle)—a label that was, as I discovered later, inaccurately applied to the Theravada tradition. Thus, in the eyes of many, if not most, at Nalanda, including Geshe Jamphal, by leaving Nalanda for Amaravati, I would be turning my back on the great vehicle and embracing the inferior little vehicle. Ven. Gelek was one of the few who did not subscribe to this view and, once I had familiarized myself with some of the clear and profound teachings of Ajahn Sumedho, he encouraged me to follow my heart. He gave me the email address of the guest monk at Amaravati, Ven. Vimalo, and suggested that I write to him and ask if I could make a visit. He offered to write to him ahead of me, introducing me and briefly explaining the difficult situation I was in. I was, needless to say, very grateful for his assistance and relied on his support.

In early October, I wrote to Ven. Vimalo and decided also to write to Ajahn Karuniko, assistant to the abbot, at Chithurst Monastery. I thought it wise to spend a few days at each monastery for a comparison. I received prompt replies from both, indicating that I was welcome to visit for the dates in early November that I had suggested. Thus, in one month's time I would be leaving Nalanda Monastery to explore not only a very different Buddhist monastic tradition but also another vehicle of the Buddhist path. I had now to explain my new plans to Ven. Tenpa and eventually take leave of the abbot, Geshe Jamphal.

I wasn't surprised by Ven. Tenpa's disapproval of my plans and he made a tremendous effort to dissuade me from making what he believed to be a very serious error of judgment. He called on a highly knowledgeable Western monk to convince me from a doctrinal perspective to change my course of action. While I listened to his arguments and even suspected that they were true and accurate, I, nevertheless, trusted my instinct and remained committed to my decision. During those last few weeks, I continued to attend classes but missed a few. My mind was not at all focused and I generally drifted off during the teachings.

The day of my departure approached and I asked Ven. Tharchin, the translator for the classes, to arrange an exit interview for me with Geshe Jamphal. I also indicated that I wished to speak with Geshe alone, without a translator present. I did this as a strategic move. I knew that Geshe Jamphal's English was very limited and that he, therefore, would not be able to express the strong disapproval that I was certain he would have. The meeting was not very long. I appreciated but also discounted Geshe's attempts to dissuade me by presenting the Mahayana doctrine of "emptiness" which was believed to be completely lacking in the path of the "Lesser Vehicle." He finally gave up and with a genuinely warm smile simply wished me well. I left the room greatly relieved that the meeting had not been unpleasant.

On the morning of November 4th, which was oddly the day of the presidential election in the U.S., I said goodbye to the monks that had gathered near the car which Ven. Tenpa would be driving to bring me to the airport. As I made my way down the line, I received friendly, brotherly wishes for progress along the Buddhist path. The last monk on the line was Jampa. After we embraced, I took him by the shoulders and urged him not to let himself get stressed in the program. He smiled and assured me he would try. I then got into the car and we drove down the entrance path of the monastery with its line of stately trees—a path the beauty of which I had never tired of during all of my stays.

In hindsight, I recognize that making the difficult and highly unpopular decision to leave Nalanda, and the Tibetan tradition, was the first of several radical changes in my spiritual path—changes that in each case were neither approved of nor supported by the community I was leaving. From 2008 onwards, I became obsessed with being on the RIGHT path with the RIGHT people and doing the RIGHT practice. I believe it was, at least partly, a result of now being in my mid-50s. I was increasingly aware of the swift passage of my life and that my time to attain the elusive goal—a goal that I was still struggling to articulate to myself—was limited. Inevitably, I would devote so much precious time preoccupied with making future plans for changing my present situation when I found myself *not* in the right tradition and not living in the right environment.

I arrived at Amaravati Monastery at dusk on a chilly, gray day. I was very happy that my taxi was met by Ven. Vimalo. As he led me into the men's dorm, I felt very self-conscious of my maroon robes in a world of dark gold. I guessed that the monastic community was informed that a Tibetan novice monk would be visiting for a few days because no one seemed surprised at my attire. That evening I spoke with a few English monks in the common room over a cup of tea. They were eager to learn about what daily life was like in a Tibetan monastery. One of them also informed me that I had a new president—Barack Obama. I smiled to myself thinking at the oddity of hearing this news first from a Buddhist monk in England. The friendly welcome I received at Amaravati I attributed to the rarity of a monk from the Tibetan tradition coming for a visit, especially with the intention to change "vehicles," so to speak.

As it was the evening before the new moon observance day, when the *patimokkha*, the 227 monastic rules for bhikkhus, would be recited, the monks were shaving their heads and availing themselves of the small sauna in the dorm. I was delighted to see Ajahn Sumedho enter the common room and sit down before heading to the sauna. I sat on the floor along with a small group of monks that had gathered. I obviously stood out in the crowd, and Ajahn Sumedho beamed at me and asked what my name was. I told him, adding that I had just arrived from Nalanda Monastery and that I was interested in transferring to a monastery in this tradition. He clearly approved and even gave forth a deep-voiced laugh—which I came to know was quite common for him to do—and jokingly remarked that I had abandoned the great vehicle for the little one. I smiled back and mentioned that I had been trained in Dharamsala by a nun whom he might recall. I then mentioned Sr. Jotika and he again laughed acknowledging that he knew her well. Conversing with him in that brief conversation, I realized that I had never seen anyone who radiated such genuine happiness, with the possible exception of the Dalai Lama.

Although the Amaravati monastic and lay community was similar in number to that at Nalanda, I felt that here the emphasis was on meditation. The spacious completely unadorned meditation hall seemed peaceful and conducive for meditation. I liked the morning and evening chanting and group meditation attended by monks, nuns and lay people. There were no classes going on here, no study program, and it seemed that the monastics spent much of their free time in individual meditation practice in their rooms or doing walking meditation on one of the paths. As my brief visit was coming to a close, I asked Ven. Vimalo if I might be able to come back in December for an extended stay. He told me that unfortunately they were full in anticipation of the three-month winter retreat that would begin in early January. When I told him I was going to visit

Chithurst Monastery, he suggested that I might have better luck there, since he believed there was space available. I had seen photos of Chithurst on the monastery website, and it looked quite beautiful. I was excited now to experience it.

On the day I was planning to travel down to West Sussex which would be a complicated journey by taxi, several trains and another taxi, Ven. Vimalo told me that a vehicle would be going there and I could catch a ride. I took that as a positive omen that Chithurst would work out for me.

It was already dark when we pulled up to the enormous Victorian mansion that served as the main building of Chithurst Monastery. The official name was Cittaviveka (the mind free of attachment). There was a note on the front door that said: "Welcome Tenzin, you are in Room 5." It seemed that I was going to be called simply "Tenzin," my lineage name, rather than by my full name "Tenzin Lamten." I knew here it wouldn't cause a problem since unlike in a Tibetan monastery where calling out "Tenzin" would result in many voices responding, I would certainly be the only one here with that name. I thought how very different my accommodation was compared to that at Amaravati. The room was large and had a fireplace which was no longer used. It was also rather draughty. I particularly liked the shrine room on the ground floor that, beyond the golden Buddha, looked out onto the extensive lawn behind the building. I was told it was used only for the twice monthly recitation of the monastic rules and also for the weekly community breakfast. The one hundred-and-fifty year-old house did not exude museum-like stuffiness, but rather seemed warm and lived-in.

The next day, I joined the monastic community for early morning meditation and chanting, beginning at 4:30am (as opposed to 5am at Amaravati). I instantly liked the more intimate-sized meditation hall. The warm clay walls gave one the sense of being in a cave-like shelter. However, I didn't particularly like the very large white stone Buddha statue that had a decidedly modern touch, but I figured I would come to like it over time. During the morning work period, I assisted the male lay guests in raking leaves that were strewn all about the immense lawn and were constantly falling from the huge trees. I enjoyed the outdoor work in the brisk autumn air and did not feel that it was actually labor. I developed a gentle raking stroke and attempted to keep my mind focused only on the act of raking.

I had intended to stay only four days for this initial visit as I planned to fly to the States, keeping my promise to my parents that I would visit twice a year, and this visit would also coincide with Thanksgiving, which I knew would please them as well as my immediate family. I spoke with Ajahn Karuniko, who was in charge since the abbot, Ajahn Sucitto, was away, about the possibility of returning for a long stay. He suggested I write a letter to Ajahn Sucitto expressing my wish and also the reasons why I wanted to reside there. I followed his advice, and drafted a hand-written letter which I left with Ajahn Karuniko. I had a very positive feeling about residing at Chithurst, which I would have preferred over Amaravati even if I had been given a choice, and was optimistic that I would be permitted to return.

While in the States, I received an email from Ajahn Sucitto. He warmly welcomed me to come to Chithurst Monastery and reside there initially as a Tibetan novice monk. He also indicated what my status would be in relation to the *samaneras* (novice monks) and *anagarikas* (white-clad eight-precept trainees) who resided there. Because of the common practice of Tibetan monastics to use money, I would be treated as a senior *anagarika*, yet out of respect for my ordination, continue to wear my Tibetan robes until the time, if it arose, that I wished to become a *samanera* in the Theravada Thai Forest tradition. I thought his conditions were reasonable and I promptly replied that I would be fine with the situation he presented.

In early December, I returned to Chithurst and found myself in the same room with the fireplace. I didn't actually speak with Ajahn Sucitto until after the main meal on my first full day there. We both sat on the floor in the common room of the main house, but he was slightly higher, sitting on a cushion. He was friendly and I went into greater detail about why I made the unusual decision of leaving a Mahayana monastery to take up residency in a Theravada one. As he was knowledgeable about Tibetan Buddhism, having been to Nepal, he was acquainted with some of the aspects of the monastic way of life that did not resonate well with me.

I acclimated myself slowly not only to the daily schedule but, more importantly, to the tradition. At first I missed the elaborate altar and Buddha statue in the Nalanda *gompa* as well as the rich aroma of incense. At Chithurst, no incense was lit on the simple altar before the Buddha except on Saturday evenings when the nuns and a number of lay people attended the group meditation and chanting. On those occasions, a lay person would be invited to approach the altar and light a single stick of incense. It also took some time for me to adjust to the change in color of the monastics. The deep gold of the monks and the dark brown of the nuns seemed so drab in comparison with the maroon and gold trim of Tibetan monastics of both genders. Over time, I came to like the color as I imagined it was probably closer to the color and style of what the monks might have worn in the time of the Buddha and in the centuries that immediately followed. I quickly adjusted to the sound of Pali, which was chanted in the mornings. Although I had no knowledge of this dialect of ancient Sanskrit, since it was an Indo-European language, the sounds were much more in common with modern European languages than Tibetan.

While the simple breakfast was informal, the main meal definitely had a procedure that was followed only by the monastics. We all gathered, sitting on cushions on the floor in the meditation hall, alms bowls on a stand in front of us (I had been given one since at Nalanda they weren't used). When a signal was given, the monks stood up, took their bowls and walked slowly out in single file according to seniority. They were followed by the nuns, and lastly by the novice monks (I followed directly behind the Theravada novice) and the male and female *anagarikas* followed behind me. We all walked along the cloister that ran in front of the meditation hall, and then crossed the path and entered the house through the back door where we left our sandals. We passed the kitchen where the food was laid out on the counter in the middle and assembled, still in single file, in the foyer of the house. After helping ourselves to the food, we walked back to the meditation hall and when everyone was seated, Ajahn Sucitto led the auspicious mealtime chants, in Pali. We then ate our meal from our bowls in silence, using only a small Chinese spoon. When we were finished, everyone except the senior monks washed his own bowl in a sink at the end of the cloister. The nuns, however, washed theirs in the main house. I noted how a junior monk would first take Ajahn Sucitto's bowl or the bowl of another ajahn (a monk with at least ten *vassas*, or rains retreats, that he had observed in his life as a bhikkhu). I later learned that each ajahn had someone assigned to him, either a junior monk or novice, who was his attendant. And the attendant would wash the ajahn's bowl before he proceeded to wash his own. This practice was not followed at Nalanda; for the monks didn't use alms bowls nor was the practice of a senior monk having an attendant maintained. In a few months, I would get first-hand experience of this Theravada tradition, especially as followed in Thai forest monasteries, when I was assigned as attendant to one of the four ajahns currently in residence at Chithurst.

Since I had already been following the monastic rule—both for monks and novices—of not eating after 12 noon, I didn't find the lack of an evening meal to be challenging. As at Nalanda, I very much looked forward to breakfast after the nineteen-hour fast. The food offered at lunch, also similar to that at Nalanda, varied from day-to-day, depending on who was preparing it, and what food was available to cook. Unlike in France, where the volunteer cooks together with one or two monks went food shopping, at Chithurst, all the food that was served was offered by lay supporters of the monastery. In fact, as far as I could tell, no one went shopping for anything, not even household items and toiletries. Everything was donated to the monastery. I liked this form of renunciation practiced at Chithurst. Since we didn't choose the food we would eat, we had to be content with whatever was offered to us. Although the *anagarikas* helped the lay guests prepare the meals, and I was considered one of them, because of my Tibetan robes which I continued to wear, I was told not to assist in the preparation of food. For monks and novices were not permitted to do so, and I was certainly viewed by lay people as a monastic.

I gradually became accustomed to standing out in the community because of the color of my robes, but my attire underwent a step-by-step color transformation during the nine months leading up to my ordination as a Theravada novice. All the monastics wore "work robes" when engaging in manual tasks in the morning work period. But since I didn't have such attire, I was given a golden-colored lower robe and monastic jacket which I wore when working. It felt strange at first, but I eventually became accustomed to wearing them. As winter continued and there weren't as many leaves to rake, I often took part in wood stacking. The main house and the meditation hall were heated solely by wood, all of it collected from the monastery's 150 acre woodland. About six of us would line up and pass to each other cut logs, the last person stacking them in the wood shed. I had never taken part in such work before, and being older and not as strong as most of the monastics and lay guests, I sometimes stumbled upon receiving a heavy log. I was always happy when this task was completed for the day.

What I appreciated the most about my new monastic life was that every day we were free from noon until 7:30pm. I took long walks in the countryside, learning how to navigate the public footpaths that often crossed through private land. These walks were not as meditative as I would have liked mainly because I was generally uneasy about walking across a farmer's field, past grazing cows or sheep, thinking that I was trespassing. I also walked the trail that went through the monastery's woodland. I gazed up at the simple wooden A-frame *kutis* (meditation huts) where the monastics spent six weeks alternating with six weeks in the main house. I knew that I would eventually be residing in one of them and did not look forward to it. I was aware that the huts had no electricity, running water, or even an outhouse. One dug a latrine and used that. My urban background rebelled against such living conditions.

As the last month of the annual three-month winter retreat approached, Ajahn Karuniko offered to take me on a tour of the huts in the woodland, allowing me to select one that I would prefer. When I actually had a look inside one of them, I felt even less inclined to dwell in it. The interior living space was perhaps only 6 ft x 6 ft because of the steeply sloping A-framed roof. A few had small gas heaters, which appealed to me much more than a wood stove. Ajahn Karuiko suggested I dwell in the *Kusala* (Wholesome) hut as it was close to the main path and had a gas heater. It also had a full length glass door without a curtain. Thus, I would have no privacy, I thought. But I considered that no one would be walking around there at night.

In early March, I moved out of my room in the house, left some books and other belongings in a corner of the attic room reserved for such purposes, and took up residence in the *Kusala* hut. I brought a few candles with me as well as my sleeping bag which I laid out on the thin pad on the floor. As darkness gradually descended, I sat on the meditation cushion that was there and tried to calm my mind. Every sound I heard in the woods made me jump, despite being told that the largest animal one might encounter would be a fox. Needless to say, I did not succeed in reaching any deep state of meditative concentration and elected instead to read a book with my pocket led light. Around midnight, an intense sleet storm started, accompanied by powerful thunder and lightning. I felt very vulnerable in the little hut and hoped it was sturdy enough to protect me from the elements. I thought about the other monastics in similar huts and wondered how they managed to meditate in such conditions—for the purpose of residing in a *kuti* was to foster seclusion and deepen one's meditation. I began to have the thought that perhaps coming to a monastery of the Thai Forest tradition was not the right decision. In subsequent days, however, although not completely adjusting to the primitive living conditions, I felt relaxed enough that I was able to meditate, particularly at dusk.

In the middle of the summer, Ajahn Sucitto announced that novice ordination for me and two *anagarikas* would take place in late August. I was very excited despite hearing that we would have to sew our own lower robe. I had never used a sewing machine and dreaded the mess I would surely make of it. Fortunately, one of the monks was an experienced sewer and he helped us enormously, drawing out the traditional pattern of rice fields that would be sewn on the robe. It nevertheless was a long and frustrating process. Innumerable times, I had to pull out a row of stitches that I had done incorrectly. I, nevertheless, was able to finish the robe before the scheduled date of the ordination. What remained to be done was memorize the precepts (in Pali) and familiarize ourselves with the brief ceremony. Ajahn Karuniko provided each of us with an upper robe and a monastic jacket which we would wear under it. He also gave us instructions about how to put on the voluminous upper robe—and keep it on. This was a challenge especially when sitting on the floor at the meal.

The day arrived and the three of us proceeded to the meditation hall where all the monastics awaited us. At the mid-point, we exited with our new robes in hand and in an upstairs room, with the assistance of several monks, put on our robes. I was happy finally to take off my maroon robes and put on the dark gold ones. I was about to become a Theravada *samanera*. I carried no thoughts in my mind about Nalanda, the Dalai Lama, and Lama Zopa nor any uncertainty about what I was about to do. I had completely embraced this new tradition. We returned to the meditation hall, greeted by the smiling faces of the waiting monastics. We then completed the ceremony by reciting in unison the ten novice precepts. We had practiced reciting together and managed to pull it off neatly and in sync. Ajahn Sucitto then gave each one of us our monastic names. I was now *Chandako*, which meant "one with desire or zeal [for the Dhamma (Buddhist teachings)]." I liked it and soon forgot about my previous name.

Wearing the robes of the Theravada forest tradition prompted me to become better acquainted with the early Buddhist scriptures. Although they were all available in very good translations, I developed an interest in learning Pali, the ancient language in which they have come down to us. Using a textbook, I diligently made my way through it during the course of the next year. I found something I could use as a lap desk when residing in the woods, working through the text book in the long summer evenings. I parsed every word in the practice passages, using an answer key to check my work, and by the time I had completed the book, I felt I had a good foundation in the grammar. In early December, when I was back in the forest, I began to shun spending the long winter evenings in the forest hut. Daylight began to diminish rapidly after 4pm and the darkness seemed endless. I was also feeling aches and pains from the cold damp air. When we began the winter retreat, I asked Ajahn Karuniko if I could remain in one of the rooms above the meditation hall for the three-month duration, including the weeks I was entitled to spend in seclusion. My request was granted and as it turned out, I never returned to the hut in the forest.

The entire Chithurst monastic community spent the last two weeks of the winter retreat at Amaravati Monastery, where Ajahn Sumedho gave daily talks. There were also many periods of group meditation. Living in the men's dorm, with convenient access to toilets and sinks, as well as the common room where one could drink tea or coffee any time of day, I developed the strong desire to move up there from Chithurst. It was a larger community of monks and nuns and there was also a retreat center for lay people. An extra attraction was that Ajahn Sumedho was going to reside there only until after the rains retreat and then retire to Thailand. I thus wanted to benefit from the talks he regular gave in this last period of his residence. In addition, since Amaravati was located quite near London, in contrast to Chithurst, many Thai and Sri Lankan people brought generous cooked food offerings to the monastery. Amaravati thus felt far less secluded than Chithurst and this appealed to me at that time.

When we all returned to Chithurst, I expressed my wish to Ajahn Sucitto, who would have preferred me to stay, especially since I had been assisting him in proof-reading a few of his book manuscripts, but he understood my reasons for seeking to move up there.

In late April, shortly before my move to Amaravati, Ajahn Sucitto led all the male monastics on a sangha walk. This was a semi-annual tradition and I had already gone on two previous walks. Each time I had found it to be a thoroughly enjoyable and invigorating occasion. I particularly liked the opportunity to talk to some of the monks with whom I rarely spoke casually. This time, Ajahn Sucitto chose for us to walk along the upper ridge of the South Downs. It would be about ten miles in total, the usual length of these day hikes. We were fortunate that it was a spectacular spring day in southern England: sunny and breezy, with cool, crisp air. When we had climbed up to the ridge, we followed the path and beheld a stunning view of the coast on one side and the beautiful rolling fields with grazing sheep and cattle on the other. In the distance I saw a stone church and could also make out the stone walls around it. I reflected on how my life journey had turned out so differently than what I had expected back in the 1980s when I had spent considerable time in London. I had never imagined that one day I would be walking along the top of the South Downs as a Buddhist monastic along with a group of monks! I noticed that Ajahn Sucitto was nearby and I caught up to him and walked beside him. Knowing of my background in English literature, he brought up the topic of poets inspired by the English countryside. It was a pleasant, easy-going conversation and I realized that I had never felt so relaxed speaking with him as I did as we walked and acknowledged the poetic beauty of the vista. I even felt a moment of regret for my decision to leave Chithurst. But later in the day, when we were back at the monastery, that unsettling thought faded away.

 A few days before I was to depart, I met with Ajahn Sucitto and expressed my wish for bhikkhu (higher) ordination. I knew that it was Ajahn Sumedho's last year at Amaravati before his retirement and I wanted to ordain with him as my preceptor. Ajahn Sucitto approved of my request, noting that he would be my sponsor even though I would be residing at Amaravati; for my training had essentially taken place at Chithurst under his guidance. The ordination would most likely occur on the full-moon observance day just before entering the three-month Vassa (Rains Retreat).

In mid-May, I left Chithurst, with a large collection of monastics—monks, nuns, and *anagarikas*—waving goodbye as we drove out of the parking area. After settling into my room at Amaravati, I proceeded, together with another candidate, Jotiko, to prepare for the arduous task of sewing all three robes. I dreaded it knowing that it would be weeks of frustration and despair because of my inept skills in using a sewing machine. During the next two months that I worked daily on sewing the robes, I would periodically call on Jotiko's help in straightening out the mess I had made on the particular robe I was sewing at the time.

At Amaravati, pairs of monks occasionally went to the nearest town, Berkhamsted, with their alms bowls to stand on the sidewalk and collect food from the passersby. A monk asked me to join him one day on this traditional monastic activity. As a novice, I would be able to carry back extra food that a bhikkhu would not be permitted to do, since bhikkhus were not allowed to store food overnight, or even past midday. I looked forward to this adventure as we hiked about three miles along forest trails until we reached the High Street of the town. I felt very self-conscious standing on the sidewalk holding my alms bowl as people passed by, some smiling, some ignoring us. After about fifteen minutes we walked to another spot. We received some fruit and a package of bread. I was beginning to think that it would be a very meager meal when we noticed two Thai women emerging from a Thai restaurant carrying containers of food. My hopes were immediately lifted. They approached us and kneeling on the ground placed the packages of cooked food into our bowls. I looked to my companion to see if he was going to recite the traditional auspicious prayer, but he didn't. We then walked to a small park behind a church and enjoyed out lunch. I reflected how different it felt to eat food that was placed into my bowl—which is what the monks in the Buddha's time did, and which was still done in Burma and Thailand—compared to helping myself to food set out on a buffet table.

After two months of blood, sweat, and tears, I completed sewing the three robes. They would certainly not win a blue ribbon, I thought, but they would serve the purpose for which they were meant. And once I was a bhikkhu, all three would have to be within close proximity at every dawn. The ordination date was set for July 26, the day before we would enter the Vassa. A third candidate, an American novice from Ratanagiri Monastery in northern England, was joining us. Under the guidance of several senior monks, we rehearsed the choreography of the ceremony during the last few days leading up to the 26th. It was expected that many people would attend, especially since it might be the last ordination that Ajahn Sumedho would conduct. On the day before the ordination, I felt a sudden pang of recognition that I had failed to inform His Holiness the Dalai Lama as well as Lama Zopa about what I was about to do and to ask for their blessing. I realized that I should have done this prior to becoming a Theravada novice. I immediately went to the building where there was internet access and fortunately found the contact email address for each. I wrote separate letters to the Dalai Lama and Lama Zopa, explaining briefly why I had made the change in tradition, and that I was grateful for having had the opportunity to be a *getsul*. I didn't, however, request their permission, since I already was prepared to be ordained without it, but simply asked for their blessing. About two weeks later, I received a brief response from the Dalai Lama's personal secretary indicating that His Holiness offers his blessings to me as I continue my monastic life in the Theravada tradition. The response from Lama Zopa, which seemed to have been written personally by him, said that I should follow whatever His Holiness recommends and he understood that I was merely following my karma. A memory suddenly flashed through my mind. I recalled the dinner following my initial going forth in Bodhgaya when I noted that Lama Zopa was looking steadily at—or, perhaps, in—me. I now wondered if he had foreseen my unusual move.

The ordination ceremony, with its prescribed rituals, proceeded without any problems or embarrassments. For the actual ordination, the three of us walked on our knees up to the front of the meditation hall where the assembly of at least 30 bhikkhus were waiting. As I was much slower at crawling the long distance on my knees than the other two, who were only in their 20s, I arrived somewhat later at my spot. I thought how interesting that, as in the novice ordination with the Dalai Lama, I again was in the middle position. Thus, I was directly in front of Ajahn Sumedho. The formal announcement was made, the day and exact time of each of our ordinations was recorded, and then Ajahn Sumedho gave the traditional instruction of the four "defeats" that would nullify our status as bhikkhus. We all were then individually congratulated by the monks present. Ajahn Sucitto came up to me and with a joyful smile, patted me on the shoulder and told me that I had done well. We three newly ordained bhikkhus then walked to the refectory where we received gifts from the nuns and some lay people.

The next day, I entered the Vassa as a bhikkhu.

CHAPTER 8

An Unexpected Detour

After the euphoria of becoming a bhikkhu died down during the summer, in early September, I discerned a subtle undercurrent of dissatisfaction with my meditation practice which I perceived was not progressing. I couldn't quiet my mind and did not feel I was reaching any depth of concentration. I wasn't clear about what I was trying to achieve. While at Chithurst, I had read some sections from the *Visuddhimagga* (the Path of Purification), the great 6th century treatise on all aspects of Theravada Buddhist practice that dealt with methods of developing *samadhi* or profound mental quietude, but the meditative states described seemed far out of reach for me. I had listened to many Dhamma talks at Chithurst and at Amaravati about dealing with hindrances and defilements, which I attempted to keep in mind, but still I sensed that something was missing in my spiritual life—I felt no real joy, no sense that I was heading towards attaining freedom from disturbing states of mind. When I managed to take a good long look within me, I noted how I was still gripped by the root defilements of greed, hatred/criticism, and delusion regarding my "self."

I also began to miss the powerful teachings on compassion that had profoundly affected me during my years in Tibetan Buddhist practice, despite the fact that at the time they did not weaken my self-centeredness. Yet, I recalled that by reflecting on them periodically, I was able to at least acknowledge how unfocused I was on the suffering or even simply the needs of others. I did not, however, miss the complicated tantric practices and thus felt no inclination to return to Nalanda. I tried to make do with the Metta (Loving Kindness) Sutta, even though I found that it lacked the transformative power of the Tibetan teachings on training the mind.

In the weeks that followed, I became increasingly conscious of these feelings of dissatisfaction and a general sense of not feeling at home in the Thai Forest tradition. I had been so motivated to become a fully ordained bhikkhu, and very occupied with sewing the robes, that I failed to pay attention to a quiet rebellion gathering strength within me in regard to certain aspects of monastic life in this tradition. Especially during my daily walks in the beautiful countryside, I would stop at a particular picturesque spot and attempt to articulate to myself the origin of this disquieting attitude towards the monastic tradition I had voluntarily entered. Despite my efforts, I couldn't put my finger on it and then a thought surfaced that sent a shudder through my body: Maybe Mahayana practitioners were right—perhaps the Theravada *was* the "lesser" vehicle and would not lead one to complete enlightenment. I shook off that deeply unsettling thought and reminded myself of a number of meditation masters in the Thai Forest tradition, some of whom I had read or heard others refer to, who had without a doubt become *arahants* (fully enlightened beings).

In early autumn, a number of factors came together to generate a dramatic change in the direction of my monastic life. These causes and conditions if occurring singly would most likely not have produced the same effect. This potent mixture of influences that joined forces in my mind at the right place and time were the following: Two topics that Ajahn Sumedho brought up in his regular Dhamma talks: the passage regarding the "unborn, uncreated, unformed, unoriginated" from the *Udana* and "the sound of silence"—the mysterious underlying sound within us that is always present but only noticed when our minds are completely still; While browsing the monastery's large inter-faith library, I picked up a copy of Thomas Merton's famous autobiography, *The Seven Storey Mountain*, and was captivated by his narrative—particularly the passage where he describes how the world seemed transformed after attending his first Catholic mass at Corpus Christi Church in Manhattan's Upper West Side; I happened upon a psalm verse from the Hebrew Bible/Old Testament: "Be still and know that I am God"; I read D. T. Suzuki's *Mysticism, Christian and Buddhist*, focusing on his comparison between the 13th Century German mystic theologian, Meister Eckhart, and the Buddhist doctrine of emptiness; Having picked up a copy of the New Testament from the small library in the monastic dorm, I read the Sermon on the Mount from the Book of Matthew, and several verses resonated so deeply within me that I felt momentary intimacy with Jesus; I found a book in the monastic library with photos of the beautiful gothic cloister and church of a Trappist monastery in Spencer, Massachusetts.

But there were a few more synchronic influences that proved to be the clincher in sending my spiritual journey on an extended detour. Three books, also from the small library in the dorm, prompted me to engage in a daily writing task which clarified, articulated and gave further expression to what was occurring within me. One was *Benedict's Dharma*, in which four prominent Western lay Buddhists reflect on the 6th century Benedictine Rule for monastics; the other two were Thomas Merton's lyrical homage to monastic life, *The Silent Life*, and the Benedictine Rule itself. As a result of reading these works, I began writing my own reflections on the Benedictine Rule, focusing mostly on the magnificent prologue and the twelve steps of humility.

All of these forces together led me to adopt several new daily practices during that autumn: Early in the morning, before the group meditation, I would walk around the very English cloister that stood in front of the Thai-style meditation hall and reflect on the "unborn, uncreated, unformed, unoriginated" alternating with "Be still and know that I am God." And while doing this for a considerable length of time, I held in my mind the picture of black and white clad Trappist monks in their cloister—as well as conjuring images of monks and monasteries in the Middle Ages in general. I described this daily meditative activity and the ideal monastic environment I carried in my mind in the introduction to the reflections on the Benedictine Rule that I was writing:

> I imagine the sacred space of the cloister, the silence of my footsteps, the calm of my mind, the dark, musty smelling ancient stones, a place where so many black-robed monks gave their minds and hearts to the other-than-worldly, the supra-mundane, the spiritual—this draws me in. I see the Buddhist Monastery where I now live through these

eyes. I walk the rectangular cloister in front of the Thai-style temple around and around. I consider my vocation: I am a monk, one who has renounced worldly life. I am striving for liberation from the mundane, from ignorance, seeking to re-unite with my pure Buddha-Nature. (*Dilatato Corde* 1:2 July - December, 2011)

While Buddha-Nature is not a Theravada concept, I seemed to have carried over this idea from my Tibetan Buddhist period, fueled by Ajahn Sumedho's teachings on the "Unconditioned."

In addition, during my daily afternoon walks in what turned out to be the most colorful autumn I had yet seen in England, I often paused at one particular location and setting my unfocused gaze on the autumnal scene before me, I would stand perfectly still for a considerable time. On one occasion something occurred that I had not anticipated and catapulted me into a stunning realization. About two months later, I actually wrote an account of the process, the culmination, and my reflection on it. This is the text, slightly edited:

> During these autumn months, throughout the day I paused to listen to 'the sound of silence' as a means to tap into the Unconditioned, the realm of ultimate reality. It was especially when I engaged in this practice during my daily walks in the countryside that I began to sense something stirring within my mind-heart. And on one day in early November, while standing immobile, directing my unfocused gaze at a distant hillside ablaze in autumnal color

and resting in the stillness, the 'sound of silence' grew increasingly more powerful. My absorption into that silent scene got deeper and I experienced a surge of rapture that prompted a smile so wide that I thought the edges of my mouth would burst. I was in touch with something beyond my control, something supra-mundane and that sent a sudden fear through me. As the fear dissipated there was a slight relaxation of my broad smile and I let out a cry of release with the words, 'it doesn't matter, it doesn't matter.' I immediately interpreted that to mean that I needn't be worried or frightened about the struggle raging inside me regarding my monastic vocation—i.e. Am I in the right tradition and religion? Do I have the courage to recognize that I may not be? I decompressed with the experiential reassurance that my fears don't matter, because all will be well.

I wasn't sure at the time if what I had actually experienced was the non-theistic "Unconditioned" or the presence of God. But I came away from it with the clear sense I was being led in a direction that I had not been intending to go. For when I had first begun exploring parallels between Buddhist and Christian spirituality, I wasn't consciously aware that I was being directed towards an actual religious conversion. The only point of stability I had as I felt the ground shifting beneath me was my unwavering determination to lead my life as a monk.

A few days later, I decided to "test" my experience by stopping into the 13th century St. John the Baptist Church in Great Gaddesden, the village just below Amaravati

Monastery. I had been there several times before and never experienced anything extraordinary. But this time I walked up to the altar and directed my unfocused gaze at the simple gold cross. I immediately experienced a surge of rapture at my heart center which caused me to grin so widely that I felt my cheeks would pop. It was so strong that I nearly lost my balance. Again fear broke in, thoughts rushed through my mind. I wondered if I was going too fast, I was afraid of the unknown ahead of me, dread of the upheaval in my monastic life. I cringed at the prospect of having to explain this to my fellow Buddhist monks, the abbot, my Jewish parents and other family members. I then thought that I should just forget the whole thing and avoid coming to this church. Just go on as if nothing happened. But as I stood there, gazing at the cross, again I felt the warmth at my heart and knew that my connection to the "Cosmic Christ" was unmistaken. I walked back to the monastery knowing that there would be no turning back, it was only a matter of time before I would have to follow this new direction.

I had become convinced that the Buddhist path—in two different traditions—that I had been following diligently for the past six years, the last three in monastic robes, was not going to lead me to ultimate liberation (salvation). Something was not working for me. As a result of this deeply felt realization, my faith in Buddhist practice and the monastic form that was to support the practice seemed to collapse like a flimsily constructed house built on shifting sand; obviously my "house of faith" had not been firmly constructed on a "rock." While I recognized that the Buddha's teachings are enormously helpful for weakening and uprooting defilements of greed, selfishness, and attachment to the ego-self as well as offering methods of quieting and focusing the mind, I perceived that a crucial element was missing—namely, the cultivation of an intimate relationship with the Ultimate, the Transcendent, i.e. God manifested through Jesus Christ.

Merton noted that one remained speechless while experiencing the mystical presence of God. Mystical silence had been what I sought out—and occasionally experienced—in some of the churches and cathedrals I had visited, especially in England. Even while residing at Chithurst, I would often sit alone in the 11th Century stone church next to the monastery. The silence there seemed *different* than that in the meditation hall. At the time, I didn't speculate or examine the reason why I liked to spend moments in that church, but I was certainly conscious of seeking it out.

Merton describes loving God as experiencing God in the most intimate place within one's being. I certainly did not have an anthropomorphic view of the Divine, but rather perceived divine energy as the "unconditioned; unborn; unoriginated." I had the need to pour out limitless love—to completely surrender my individual "self" that I carried around—to an intangible, ineffable yet palpable recipient. I understand now that my vague experiential understanding of the Buddhist concept of non-self at the time was not sufficient nor potent enough to weaken the deeply entrenched sense of ego-self that was always present within me. The combining of love and mystical experience was, I believe, my main attraction to Christian monasticism. I was not, however, at all drawn to the institution of the Church. I was somehow able to separate the Church from the monastic life I sought to lead within in. Nor had I fully embraced the tenets of trinitarian belief held by the Catholic Church. I merely suspended my disbelief and remained open without forcing myself to adopt them. First and foremost was my wish to *transfer* my monastic life to the Christian monastic tradition, ideally, the Cistercian Trappists, the order to which Merton had belonged. Only now do I realize how audacious and unrealistic that wish was.

As for Jesus, I considered him to be a special divine conduit—a unique human who in an inexplainable manner embodied divine energy in a way that no one else did. This is, of course, not completely in line with standard Catholic doctrine which maintains that Jesus is *both* human *and* divine. But at the time, I felt that it was through this accessible human who offered believers a window into the unimaginable—beyond the conceptual world—that I could cultivate a supramundane mode of being that eluded me in Buddhism. I had no desire to do so as a lay "parishioner" but only as a monk living among a brotherhood committed to the same goal. I was thirsting after a monastic ideal which I had become convinced only existed in a Christian monastery.

By December, I had written over fifty pages of reflections on the Benedictine Rule and had been making daily visits to either of the two medieval churches within walking distance of the monastery. I discreetly had explored the websites of most of the Cistercian monasteries in the U.S. as well as a few Benedictine ones. I particularly liked that the former observed all seven canonical "hours," from vigils at 3:30am to *compline* at 8pm. I decided that the next step was to actually visit a few monasteries with the hope that I could continue my monastic journey in one of them. I chose to write to the vocation director at three Cistercian monasteries and one Benedictine monastery. My top choice was St. Joseph's Abbey in Massachusetts, the Cistercian monastery

I had seen pictures of and read about in the book I had found in the library. I had also discovered that a few of the monks there had an interest in Buddhism. I thought that might be a perfect place for me. I drafted a rather lengthy letter, expressing the best I could what had transpired in the past months and my wish to continue to be a monk, but in a Cistercian (or Benedictine) monastery. I admitted that I was an unusual case, not omitting my Jewish background, and that I was fully prepared to take the steps to be baptized into the Catholic Church. As I wrote and edited the letter, I reflected that my life had become unreal. Here I was a recently ordained bhikkhu and after less than six months, I was willing to chuck it all for an idealized Christian monastic environment. Yet, these thoughts did not dissuade me at all. Because I was so certain about the rapturous experiences I had had, even though the intensity of the first one was never repeated, and trusting the inner instinct I had relied on before, I did not doubt that I was doing what I needed to do. Fortunately, two monks at Amaravati with whom I enjoyed good friendship were supportive of my highly unusual endeavor, despite not subscribing to it for themselves. I was grateful to have their sympathetic ears as I divulged to them the process I was moving through.

With the clarity of hindsight, I see that I had not so much undergone a religious conversion but rather had become cognizant of the unfolding of a deeply felt need for an accessible and intimate experiencing of the transcendental Unconditioned. Several adventitious causes and conditions, which I have outlined above, ushered in the process that led to my recognizing this need. And I knew—without a doubt—that I had no choice but to follow the promptings emanating from my heart core.

After sending out the letters about a week before Christmas, I received prompt replies. The first reply was from the vocation director at St. Joseph's Abbey. My heart constricted upon reading his kind but terse reply that my readiness to continue my monastic life there was lauded and that it would be a blessing to meet me; however, he regretted that my age, nearly 57, and the fact that I was not yet baptized, closed off any possibility of my being considered as a vocation candidate there. I received a similar reply from a Cistercian monastery in Colorado. Nevertheless, I had two promising replies, one from Gethsemane Abbey in Kentucky, which had been the home monastery of Thomas Merton, and Mt. Angel Abbey, a Benedictine monastery with a seminary in Oregon. The subject line in the email from the latter in capital letters raised my spirits enormously: "YOU ARE WELCOME AT MT ANGEL ABBEY." The vocation director suggested that I plan to come for a three-week visit to get a good glimpse of monastic life there and for the large community of about 50 to meet me. I was delighted at this prospect. The director from Gethsemane suggested just a week. I was overjoyed to be able to visit both places and began to plan my trip.

I would first be making a brief trip to the U.S. for Christmas week to see my parents and brother in Florida. I would at that time break the news to them about the big change about to occur. I anticipated my parents would be delighted that I would be returning to the States but I feared they would not comprehend my embracing of Catholicism—about the worst thing, in their eyes and probably for the majority of Jews, that someone of Jewish background could do. I thought I would find a way to present my case that would soften the blow. I dreaded even more informing Ajahn Amaro, who had taken over the position of abbot at Amaravati after Ajahn Sumedho's retirement and departure in November. But I decided to hold off on that until I returned from my visit to the States.

Because of my intense anxiousness to actually experience these two monasteries, I decided I would make the visits, which would together be one month in duration, from mid-February to mid-March, thus enabling me to return to Amaravati for the last two weeks of the annual three-month winter retreat. I didn't want definitively to take leave of Amaravati, and had no wish to disrobe, before visiting the Christian monasteries, just in case it didn't work out. I realize now what an audacious idea it was to visit—with the expectation of eventually joining—Christian monasteries while still being a bhikkhu. Fr. Odo from Mt. Angel Abbey had explicitly asked me not to wear my Buddhist monastic robes while there, since it was certain to alienate some of the monks in the community. Still, I resisted officially disrobing before spending time at these monasteries. I would simply take the robes off for the duration of the visits without *mentally* taking them off.

My family visit went well. My parents did not seem upset with my decision, choosing, as I thought they would, to focus on the fact that I would be back in the U.S., even if I would possibly be living in Oregon. I considered that Mt. Angel would probably be a more realistic chance for residency than Gethsemane because I suspected that part of the initial welcome was due to my qualification to teach medieval literature at the college division of the seminary, thus saving the monastery the expense of paying a professor to come in from outside.

I returned to Amaravati in January 2011. Early in the morning of the day after my arrival, I left a note for Ajahn Amaro stating my wish to make a trip to the U.S. during the winter retreat together with a copy of the letter I had sent to Fr. Odo at Mt. Angel. I indicated I would stop back later in the day when he had had the chance to read the letter. As I waited a few hours to return to Ajahn Amaro's dwelling, I became nervous and apprehensive about what he would think about my strange request. I had become so used to the idea of what I wanted to do that I hadn't given much thought to how incomprehensible it might seem to him. I soon found out though. The moment I walked into the room, I knew it wasn't going to go well. I regret now that I had not considered the situation better from his perspective. He had very recently been summoned back to England from Abhayagiri Monastery in California, where he had been co-abbot and very popular with the resident monks as well as with the lay community in the surrounding area, to take up a position that Ajahn Sumedho had held for more than 25 years. And given the immense popularity and respect that Ajahn Sumedho enjoyed, Ajahn Amaro had difficult sandals to fill. But, I was too involved in my own dramatic upheaval to consider his. Not surprising, he did not at all support my decision and was also against the idea of my making an extended trip in the middle of the winter retreat. He suggested, and I now think wisely, that I wait until the spring and see if I still wanted to pursue this unusual direction.

But I resisted putting it off until the spring. I knew from former experiences that once I had made a major decision to do something I had to do it very soon, because of the burning desire to set the plan in motion. My impatience for the day of departure I knew would give me no peace and just wear me out in waiting. The meeting with Ajahn Amaro ended with him not giving his permission but also not preventing me from returning after the trip. He did say that I should wait until the beginning of April to return so that I didn't interrupt the retreat. I understood his point and later made plans to visit a few monasteries in England before returning to Amaravati.

My first impressions of Gethsemane Abbey were a mixture of disappointment and awe. I was disappointed with the immense, unattractive gray monastic residence and church, but I was in awe of standing in the monastery where Merton had lived and written his profound and beautifully inspiring works. I was happy to learn that I would be residing in a wing of the monastic residence no longer used by monks, rather than staying in the modern retreat center. For, I was not there to attend one of the ongoing retreats but rather to explore my monastic vocation. The guest master informed me that the vocation director was away that day, but I would have the chance to meet him the next day. I didn't mind the wait as it would give me a chance better to form my overall impressions and interest in possibly residing at the monastery in the future.

On my first morning, I got up at 3am, which was, surprisingly, not difficult for me to do. I was excited to experience my first day at a Cistercian monastery. I walked downstairs and entered the balcony of the large, historic monastic church—historic in an American sense. I read that it dated from 1866. There were only a few other lay guests in the spacious balcony. I looked down into the main church and watched as monks in white robes with black scapulars slowly walked in and took their places in one of the two choir stalls that faced each other. There appeared to be around 40 or 45, mostly of a mature age. This initial prayer service or "hour," the first of seven "hours" spread throughout the day, was "vigils." I hadn't expected to hear ethereal Gregorian chant in Latin, like at the Carthusian monastery in the film, because I knew the service would be in English, but I hoped to experience something equally otherworldly. However, the service was just a reading of psalms. The acoustics of the church did add depth to the reading voice but it was not a chant. The service lasted about 40 minutes and then there was a break of 90 minutes before *lauds*. I returned to my room and had intended to read from my newly acquired Christian bible, but as it was still very early and dark, I opted to rest in bed, setting my alarm clock just in case I fell asleep. This next service was very different. Psalms were chanted in a simple melodic style accompanied by an organ. I found the organ to be an unnecessary intrusion which reminded me too much of church services I had seen in films, never actually having attended one in person. Towards the end of the service, though, came what would be for me the highpoint of this daily service: the singing of the Lord's Prayer in a beautiful and simple melody. Although I had never recited it, I knew the words. Now, in this monastic setting, the words, "give us this day our daily bread and forgive us our trespasses as we forgive those who trespass against us," resonated deeply. My heart melted at these words as I contemplated how we depend on God not for material bread but for providing the absolute prerequisites needed for living a spiritual daily life; namely, faith and the energy to grow in the path toward mystical union. I also reflected on forgiveness of others, "turning the other check," when someone harms us. I then thought of the Tibetan Buddhist mind-training verse of giving the victory to the one who harmed us. I was delighted that this simple yet powerful prayer was repeated in the early evening *vespers*.

I received word that I would be able to meet the vocation director, Fr. Luke, later that morning. He was friendly and, like me, a native New Yorker, but from the Bronx. I expressed, rather hastily, I now realize, my wish to explore the possibility of joining the community. I added, almost as an afterthought, that there is the problem of not being Catholic. He laughed, good-naturedly, and agreed that it was indeed a problem. He also mentioned that I was presently just over the maximum age of 55 for someone entering the monastery, and it would be a few years before I would be eligible to apply for admittance into the community. I already knew that this involved enrolling in a Catholic initiation course, which lasted around 6 months, and then after baptism, one had to spend two years attending weekly services at a parish church before being eligible to enter monastic life. He didn't do the math for me, but he obviously was aware of how old I would be after fulfilling these conditions. He concluded that it would be a "long shot" but not completely impossible. Although my optimism was deflated a bit by this dose of reality, I wasn't prepared to give up. The question I would ponder during the rest of my one-week stay was whether I really *wanted* to join this community.

For the morning work period, I was assigned to a spry 82-year-old monk. When hearing that he had been at Gethsemane since 1955, I asked with obvious excitement if he had known Thomas Merton (or, Fr. Louis, as he was officially known). He merely said, "Yeah, I knew him."—and offered nothing more. I didn't pursue it any further. One thing that struck me was that the monks wore normal clothes during the work period. There apparently wasn't a "work robe." Thus, it was difficult to distinguish between monks and lay volunteers. I also noted that there was nothing particularly "monastic" or "spiritual" about how work was conducted. Monks chatted with each other about practical matters. There was occasional laughter and just normal working behavior. I helped the old monk in the workshop and also aided in delivering some sheets of glass to another building. I was also introduced to a monk who was working in a large storeroom, stacking boxes almost up to the ceiling. He told me that they were fruitcakes ready to be sold the following Christmas season. I learned that fruitcakes and an assortment of whisky-spiked fudge were the main income-generating production tasks for the monastery. I thought how different this was from a Thai Forest monastery!

By the end of the week, I felt I had gotten a good sense about what life would be like at Gethsemane Abbey. I understood why Merton chose to live in a hermitage, away from the activity of the large monastery, which in those days numbered probably two or three times the number of monks currently in residence. The monastery did not at all approach the ideal image I had held in my mind. Although

I had brought that image down a few notches to meet what I began to suspect would be "real" life at a Christian monastery, I felt Gethsemane was not close enough even to my adjusted image. I was hopeful that the yet unseen and unexperienced Mt. Angel Abbey would turn out to be the right place.

Driving up the hill leading to Mt. Angel Abbey, I gazed at the green surroundings, which I had expected to find given the amount of rain that Oregon received during the year. When we reached the top, I caught my first glimpse of the monastery and seminary buildings arranged in a quad as in a college campus. At the head was the large and majestic monastic church and residence for the monks. It appealed to me even though it was not the arched stone-cloister I held in my mind as representing the ideal Benedictine monastery. The monk who had picked me up from the airport, dressed in lay clothes, brought me to the lay retreat center where I would be spending my first three days. I had read in Merton's idyllic treatise on monastic life that newcomers traditionally had to spend three days outside the monastery gates before being admitted. This was to test their determination and zeal for monastic life. I was glad that this custom was no longer followed literally, and that I had a pleasant room for this initial period. I would also be eating in the seminary dining hall during these three days rather than in the monastic refectory.

Fr. Odo, the vocation director, sought me out and we arranged a meeting for the next day. He, like Fr. Luke, was very friendly and welcoming but I hoped there would be more flexibility regarding taking up residency there given my unusual situation. Unlike at Gethsemane where I wore my golden-colored Buddhist monastic jacket, at Mt. Angel I wore mostly black clothing, trying to fit in with the black-clad Benedictine monastics. My initial meeting with Fr. Odo went well. He did not bring up any obstacles that would hinder me from joining the community. He merely said, very reasonably, I thought, that it was necessary to see how I felt about the community and vice versa after I had the opportunity to spend a few weeks. He reiterated what he had written in the welcoming email that he and at least some of the monks were eager to support me in my unique wish to "transfer" from a Buddhist to a Benedictine monastery.

I was very happy to be able to move into the monastic residence after the trial period. I was treated like a member of the community, participating in all aspects of daily life except for the biweekly community meeting. I thus joined the monks and novices in the choir stalls for the "hours," and ate in the monastic refectory. The first service started at 5:30am rather than at 3:30 at Gethsemane. Here, too, an organ accompanied the chanting of psalms, and I made an effort to get over my dislike of organ accompaniment. I also was able to attend the daily mass. Fr. Odo recommended that when the monks went up to the celebrating priests to receive communion, I should join them but place my arms crossed in front of my chest, indicating to the priest that I was not allowed to receive communion. I gladly followed his suggestion and was therefore given a foretaste, so to speak, of this quintessential Christian rite that I would one day participate in. I gradually became familiar and comfortable with some of the customs followed there. I lined up with the monks and novices for the procession into the church, in pairs, for the *lauds* and *vespers* services. The only potential difficulty for me was remembering that for the former, the monastics lined up beginning with the most senior down to the most junior, and for the latter, the order was reversed. I had known that there would be table reading at meals and enjoyed listening to edifying texts while eating. I was not, however, pleased about the meat-oriented diet. It seemed that St. Benedict's recommendation of a vegetarian diet was no longer observed. There was an unusual custom, I thought, of pairs of monks, as they were leaving the refectory, turning to one another and saying "*prosit*"—the German version of "cheers!" I guessed it stemmed from the German Swiss origin of the monastery.

As at Gethsemane, I had the chance to work with the monastic community during the work period. I was assigned to work with different novices or junior monks, doing both outdoor and indoor tasks. Everyone with whom I interacted was warm and friendly, and seemed genuinely supportive of my interest in possibly joining them. There was one part of the daily life that I didn't really like: community recreation. I had seen it listed on the daily schedule and wondered what kind of recreation it would involve. Since it was a fairly large community of about 45 or 50, there were different groups engaging in "recreation." A few watched the news on PBS (the only television station permitted), some played cards in one room, and in the large common room, monks sat in small groups and chatted. I didn't know which group to join, so I alternated among them, but generally sat in the large room hoping to chat with one of the senior monks. A few engaged me in light conversation, but most did not.

What impressed me the most from a spiritual perspective was the Friday evening "adoration," where between 5 and 6pm, one simply sat in the church in silent meditative prayer. Not everyone participated though. I sat in the choir stall at the beginning of the hour and then left for a while, returning near the end and noticed that the abbot, who was probably around 75, was on his knees, without a cushion, the entire time. At the end of my stay, I had the opportunity to meet with him. He had a calm, kind manner and I sensed that he spent his day in close connection with the Divine. He said he was impressed how well I had fit into the community. I was elated that he had actually noticed. He recommended that I obtain a copy of the Catholic Catechism and familiarize myself with it completely. I followed his suggestion, purchasing a copy at the monastery bookstore.

As my three-week stay came to an end, I was convinced that Mt. Angel Abbey, despite not matching my ideal image of a monastery, would be fine. I liked the idea of being able eventually to teach literature at the seminary college and there were a few monks with whom I anticipated forming a brotherly bond. On the day of my departure, I spoke with Fr. Odo, who said that he had conferred with the abbot and if I got the green light from the community to take up residency there, I could officially give up my Buddhist monastic status by symbolically disrobing there and putting on a simple cassock. It would be a very unique event for the monastery. I welcomed the idea as it was in perfect accordance with my idea to "transfer" from one monastic tradition to another. He assured me he would be in touch once the community had met to discuss my unusual situation and request. I thus departed with the optimistic expectation that it all would work out.

I returned to Amaravati in the beginning of April. It felt strange wearing my monastic robes again. During the four weeks I had spent at the Christian monasteries, thoughts of Amaravati—and Buddhist monastic life—were not in my mind. I immediately felt uncomfortable there, estranged from the community. Although one of my monastic friends had left to spend a year in Thailand, a few monks were friendly and interested to know how my visits to the Christian monasteries had gone. Nevertheless, I was glad that I had planned to stay at Amaravati for just three days before returning to the U.S. I had a farewell meeting with Ajahn Amaro and was pleased that Ajahn Sucitto happened to be at Amaravati as well, and thus I met with both together to take leave officially. I did not, however, disrobe. I expressed my wish to disrobe at Mt. Angel Abbey and thus seamlessly move from one monastic tradition to another. Ajahn Sucitto gave what I thought was very good advice, recommending that I made sure to find time for silent meditative prayer, because the daily services involved many recited prayers with little or no silence. I assured him that I would. I also indicated that if for some reason I did not go to Oregon, I would simply disrobe in New York or wherever I ended up. I was aware that a few of the monks at Amaravati had wanted me to disrobe before leaving Amaravati, probably guessing that I would have to use money while travelling. I was grateful that Ajahn Amaro had not insisted on my disrobing there.

The next day I left, feeling relief and no hint of sadness or regret.

I returned to New York in late April 2011 and awaited news from Fr. Odo. He had written to me while I was still in England, asking that I write a brief explanation about why I particularly wanted to take up residency at Mt. Angel Abbey. He would read it at the community meeting later that month. I drafted a concise essay discussing all the positive aspects I had experienced during my stay and emphasizing how I thought that Mt. Angel would provide the perfect environment for my initiation into the Catholic Church and Benedictine monastic life. Feeling optimistic, I had already obtained a one-way ticket to Portland as I feared the price of the ticket would go up if I waited to the last minute. I was planning to fly out in early May. I meanwhile visited my parents and was relieved that they seemed happy about my future life at Mt. Angel Abbey. The day that I returned from the visit I received an email from Fr. Odo informing me that, unfortunately, I would not be able to come there after all. At the community meeting, there was strong opposition from a significant number of monks. He cited my age and the fact that the monastery had never allowed a catechumen to be instructed at the monastery. Fr. Odo suggested I seek out a R.C.I.A. (Roman Catholic Initiation for Adults) program and then, hopefully, I would find a monastery that would accept me (apparently other than Mt. Angel Abbey).

Although I was stunned by the unexpected rejection by the community, I reflected almost immediately that obviously Mt. Angel was, after all, not the place for me to continue my monastic journey. My instincts had not been accurate here. I had convinced myself that it was the right place merely because my options were so few. During the next days I delved into my mind, trying to come up with a plan of action. For I was now, literally, a homeless monk. I wanted to honor my promise made to Ajahn Amaro that if I didn't go to Mt. Angel Abbey, I would disrobe. I didn't feel it was right for me to remain a monk—even in name only since I was not wearing my robes. As I was staying in a friend's apartment in Manhattan, a Tibetan Buddhist, I decided I would disrobe there. That evening, I put on all my robes, including the outer robe, the *sanghati*, which I rarely used. I made a simple statement that I was giving up the monastic life in the Theravada Buddhist tradition in which I had been ordained. I then asked my friend if he had understood the words I had uttered. After affirming that he did, I simply took off the robes and put lay clothes back on. And that was it. I was a lay man again. My unrealistic attempt to "transfer" directly from a Buddhist to a Christian monastery ultimately failed.

I shortly came up with a plan. I would move to Athens, Georgia, where I figured it would be inexpensive to live, and seek a part-time instructor position at the large university there. I needed to acquire some basic necessities first, such as a car, computer, and phone. I thought it best to go to Florida and spend some time with my brother, who would help me obtain these necessary items.

Having leased a car and purchased a laptop and phone, I was ready to drive up to Georgia. I found an inexpensive apartment quickly and contacted the English department at the university. I bought just the minimum amount of furniture I would need and gradually acclimated myself to living in the "world" after more than three years of monastic life. There was a R.C.I.A. program offered at a Franciscan church on campus that would begin in September. Baptism would occur at the following Easter. I would then need to attend weekly mass for two years in order to meet the requirements set by the Catholic Church for converts wishing to join a monastery. After just two weeks, I realized that I couldn't do it. I was psychologically unable to maintain this type of life for the minimum two-and-a-half years necessary. In a conversation with my friend, Fred, the one who had been pivotal in my obtaining the position at John Jay College, I learned that there were a few Benedictine monasteries associated with the Episcopal Church. Fred assured me that I would find more flexibility there. My research led me to a small Benedictine monastery in Michigan, St. Gregory's Abbey, that seemed promising. They ran a one-month vocation program in July for men interested in monasticism. I immediately wrote to the novice master, Fr. Aelred, asking if I could join the program despite not yet having been baptized. After receiving an affirmative reply, my optimism returned that all would indeed work out. I had a good feeling about Fr. Aelred because his patron saint was the author of a famous and beautiful medieval treatise on monastic spiritual friendship.

Since I still had a few weeks before I would be driving up to Michigan, I thought it wise to meet with an Episcopal priest and discuss the possibility of being baptized. There was an episcopal church just a few blocks from my apartment. I wrote to the priest and, after presenting as concise as I could what would undoubtedly be for him an unusual story, requested an appointment to meet with him. When I hadn't heard back from him in several days, I was unable to restrain myself from writing again, using the excuse that I feared he had never received my original email. That did the trick, and I heard immediately from him. He suggested I come the next day. I drove to the church, even though it was not far, because it was nearly 100 degrees outside and I didn't want to be all sweaty when I met him. I found him to be very friendly and approachable. I repeated the important parts of my story in case he had forgotten them, and expressed my wish to be baptized into the Episcopal Church whenever he thought it the right time to do so. I nearly fell off my chair when he suggested we do it the next day in a private ceremony. And so, on June 11, I was duly baptized according the rite of the Episcopal Church. We went through the procedure, which seemed very close to the Catholic ritual I had read about in the Catechism. He provided me with a towel to place over my clothes and then liberally poured water over my head—actually drenching me—rather than just sprinkling water as it was often done, while stating that I was baptized in the name of the Father, Son, and Holy Spirit. I afterwards sat in the beautiful nineteenth-century church and reflected on what I had just done. I definitely felt that something had transpired, though I could not articulate to myself what it was that I had experienced. I then proceeded to a nearby religious shop and purchased a small crucifix to wear around my neck.

 I do not believe that at the time of my baptism I had fully accepted and internalized the belief that Jesus was actually God incarnate, and my experiential understanding of the triune God was—and continued to be throughout the years I spent as a Christian monastic—vague and tenuous. Nevertheless, I had no doubt that my newly discovered faith in and strong attraction to theistic spirituality stemmed from a need that I perceived from the innermost and trusted depths of my heart.

The next Sunday I attended mass, but I did not feel comfortable in the unfamiliar atmosphere of a parish church. I received communion for the first time, but at that moment did not feel any connection with Jesus Christ, whose body and blood I had just received. I expected I would eventually actually *commune* with Christ during this holy rite. I told myself that I just needed time and to be in the right environment. I hoped St. Gregory's Abbey would prove to be that.

At the end of June, I drove 800 miles up to Three Rivers in southwest Michigan. The monastery was far more intimate than Mt. Angel and, of course, lacked seminary buildings. There was just one expansive brick monastic building that was attached to a very simple but stately church with a bell tower. There were also three additional buildings all arranged around a central green leafy area: two guest houses and an office. I was the first to arrive and once settled into my room in the guest house, I explored the very nice library. There were I estimated about 15,000 books covering a very wide range of fields, secular and spiritual. There was also an old fashioned card catalogue the monastery had received from the local library when they digitalized their catalogue. There were paintings on the walls and tables and chairs for reading. I thought I would be happy to spend some time in this welcoming place.

Seven additional men arrived who would be spending all or part of the month. I soon realized that I was the only one who seriously wanted to lead the monastic life. The program was set up so that we would follow the same schedule as the monks, the only difference being that we had daily classes and our "community recreation" was in the guest house, not in the monastic residence. We sat in the choir stalls with the small monastic community of seven and chanted the psalms for each hour. I was impressed that *matins* (vigils in Catholic monasteries) began at 4am, nearly as early as at Gethsemane. I maintained a positive, non-critical attitude during the month, focusing on what I liked, and pushing out of my mind what I was not that happy with. St. Gregory's was my only possibility for leading a monastic life now. I had given up on the Catholic monasteries, of which there was a much larger selection, because I knew I couldn't hold out for another two or three years. I met with Abbot Andrew, who said that despite my age and the fact that I had been baptized only very recently, I was welcomed to join them for the customary probation period.

On August 1st, I drove south back to Athens to move out of my apartment, giving away the furniture, and taking only my laptop with me. And after returning my leased car and paying a hefty early-return penalty, I made plans to fly to Michigan.

Brother Abraham, the youngest monk in the community, picked me up from the airport and we had a pleasant chat in the car as we drove to Three Rivers. I could sense how happy he was that I was joining the community. When we arrived, Fr. Aelred welcomed me and showed me to my room. The accommodations were quite comfortable with all the necessary furnishings and an attached bathroom. I immediately began the generally six-month period of being a postulant and put on the cassock I had purchased. Having recently spent a month at St. Gregory's, I was accustomed to the daily routine. The difference was that now I was living with the monks and not the laymen who had attended the vocation program. I found the simple unadorned wood paneled church to be conducive for focused prayer services. And despite not being a particularly large church, it felt spacious and peaceful. I was very happy that the monks chanted the psalms unaccompanied by music, and there were different melodies for each psalm. The musical notation though was not in modern form but rather in a medieval style of notation using small circles. It was, however, far easier for me to learn than if it had been written in modern musical notes. Despite the paucity of chanters, I found the antiphonal style of Gregorian chant, which I had also heard in the film, serene and ethereal.

During the ninety minutes between *matins* and *lauds*, I went to my room and engaged in the Benedictine spiritual practice of *lectio divina*—a slow interactive reading of scripture. I selected a scriptural passage, either from the psalms or from the gospels, and read over it several times, allowing my mind to take the words in deeply. I reflected on how the words expressed in the passage related to me personally. I would then just sit in meditative silence and let the meaning of the words circulate in my heart. After a few minutes I would continue to read until I came upon a passage that resonated with me. I found it to be generally the most peaceful time of day.

Meals were eaten in silence in the refectory which was an attractive, pleasant, and airy room, looking out on the woods. The table readings during lunch and supper were not particularly spiritual though—mainly biographies, autobiographies, and historical narratives. While the books chosen were not what I had anticipated, I was not surprised to find in the common room a large number of magazines that the monastery subscribed to, as I had also seen a similar selection at Mt. Angel. I reminded myself periodically that Benedictine monasteries were known for being much more connected to the outside world than the more cloistered Cistercians. I was prepared to accept things as they were and not impose my idealistic fantasy onto St. Gregory's. I was determined to make the most of the chance I had been given, and endeavored to do my best to develop a spiritual life that would lead to increased intimacy with God. I took advantage of the rich offerings of the library, and began to read some of the works written by the ascetic desert fathers.

Life at St. Gregory's presented one obstacle, however, that I had difficulty negotiating. There was a recently clothed novice, Br. Jonathan, who I felt should never have been permitted to become a novice as he did not seem at all suited or even inclined to monastic life. I categorized him rather quickly as a middle-aged "loser" who couldn't survive well in the outside world and thus sought St. Gregory's where he would have the necessary requisites for daily life and the freedom to pursue his mainly non-monastic and non-spiritual interests. I wouldn't have had any difficulty with him as a co-resident if he hadn't latched onto me. He was obviously lonely and didn't interact much with the monks. I tried to be kind and compassionate, but after a month or two, I felt I had to put up a boundary, keeping him at a distance. It didn't work well and I found myself getting anxious about how to avoid him. My talk with Fr. Aelred didn't lead to any improvement. I prayed nightly to the icon of Jesus I had hung over my desk that the situation would somehow be resolved, for my mind was rarely at peace. My prayers were answered. In December, Br. Jonathan was informed that it was unlikely that he would be ordained as a junior monk, as novices generally were after a year. He wasn't told to leave, but he certainly read the writing on the wall, and shortly thereafter announced that he would be leaving. In the seclusion of my room, I sighed, grateful that peace would soon return to me. I felt sorry for Br. Jonathan and sincerely hoped he would find a way to survive in lay life. I knew he would simply return to his mother's house and she would continue to support him.

After Br. Jonathan left, I was assigned to assist in the daily mass a few days a week. My main job was to light and then hold the incense censer, a medieval contraption that took a while for me to get used to. I had to carry it to the altar and hand it to the priest-monk who would cense the altar. I also walked to the reader's stand and handed it to the monk fulfilling the role of deacon, who censed the gospel before reading the passage of the day. I would then stand off to the side and slowly, gently cense the church while the gospel passage of the day was read. I liked actively participating in the mass, without being a priest.

What I appreciated about life at St. Gregory's, along with the simply performed prayer services, was the brief meditation period after *vespers* whereby we would sit in silence in the choir stalls for about twenty-five minutes. I didn't know what kind of meditation method I should be following, so I merely allowed myself to relax my mind and soak in the serenity of the sacred space. But the highlight of the day was the final service, *compline*. I welcomed coming into the still church immediately after the rather mundane conversation I had listened to during the "community recreation" (a normal part of Benedictine life I could well have done without). The service began with a brief reading often taken from John Cassian's *Conferences* for monks living in community. Listening to the detailed instructions, written in the early 5th century, I felt, in a sense, transported back in time to the golden age of desert monasticism. After chanting the customary psalms, we would all kneel and recite one of four beautiful prayers to the Virgin Mary. This was the only time we chanted in Latin. And each prayer, recited depending on the time of year, had its individual otherworldly melody. And with these ancient words ringing in my mind, I would leave the church and enter the nightly "great silence."

The daily chapter meetings also resonated with me. Immediately after mass, we gathered in the chapter room, and performed an activity prescribed in the Benedictine Rule. A section of the Rule was read, followed by a list and description of the martyrs commemorated that day, and lastly there was a discussion of business of that day, such as expected guests or special work projects. It was also the time when anyone in the community could bring up a matter of community concern. During those brief, formal chapter meetings, I felt very much that I was living in an authentic Benedictine monastery.

I was offered the opportunity to be clothed as a novice in March, on the feast day of St. Gregory the Great, the patron saint of the monastery. In preparation for that auspicious occasion, I was allowed to spend a week in retreat at the special lodging reserved for that purpose about ¼ mile from the monastic complex in the woodland. I was given $100 to purchase the food that I would need. The retreat house had a full kitchen as well as a lovely living room overlooking a small lake, and several bedrooms and baths. I chose a few books I would read and also brought with me from the video library a DVD of *Into Great Silence*, which I would watch again.

I spent the first week of March in the retreat house. Other than attending Sunday mass, I was completely on my own and I neither saw nor spoke with anyone. I watched the film about the Carthusian monastery on my laptop and, while I was once again absorbed in viewing the daily life there, I was aware that my monastic experiences of the last few years altered my perspective on what I considered to be an ideal monastery. I realized that I did not seek such complete seclusion. I needed to have some interaction with like-minded brothers. For most of the week I was engrossed in reading a biography of Bede Griffiths, the English Benedictine monk who in the mid-twentieth century went to India to live a monastic-like life, bringing together aspects of Hindu and Christian spirituality. I was fascinated by this free-spirited English monk who had become Swami Dayananda, and lived to old age in an ashram named Shantivanam, meaning "forest of peace" in the Tamil language. I was so moved by his successful attempts to bring the two religious spiritual cultures together in a monastic-like ashram, where the daily prayers were recited in English, Sanskrit, and Tamil, that I began reciting daily the Buddhist refuge prayer in Sanskrit. I loved the sound of the language and it brought back memories of chanting it in the related language, Pali, while at the Buddhist monasteries in England. I felt that I was being drawn to India and recalled my visit to Bodhgaya. However, I did not feel drawn back to Buddhism. I believe what gripped me was a desire to bring together the East and West in a monastic form. Thus, on the eve of my initial entry into the Benedictine Order, I was cognizant of an underlying dissatisfaction with spiritual life at St. Gregory's.

When I returned to the monastic community, I pushed these thoughts aside and focused on the upcoming novice ordination, scheduled for March 12th. The multiple-skilled office attendant altered one of the novice cassocks that had been left behind by a former novice and prepared it for me. A scapular was also chosen. I rehearsed the ceremony with Fr. Aelred and hoped I would remember what I was supposed to do at strategic moments. The most memorable one was when Abbot Andrew and Fr. Aelred clothed me in the cassock and placed the scapular over my head. I was surprised that I really felt different, especially since I had already been wearing a similar cassock—only the scapular was new. But it was the Benedictine scapular with a hood that made all the difference. I had requested that John Cassian, the most important figure in Benedictine monasticism after St. Benedict, be my patron saint. Hence I was now addressed as Br. Cassian.

I reflected that my wish for a seamless "transfer" from Buddhist monk to Christian monk did not turn out as smoothly as I had hoped. But, now, slightly less than a year after disrobing, I was a monastic again!

CHAPTER 9

Journey Eastwards: The Call of the Jesus Prayer

In the afternoon of Palm Sunday, April 1st, I was browsing through the collection of recently arrived books in the monastic common room, when one caught my eye: *The Mystery of the Jesus Prayer*. As I skimmed through it, I understood that it was based on a recent trip that two New York filmmakers had taken with the intention of making a documentary about several diverse Eastern Orthodox monasteries in the Middle East and Europe. Their purpose was to show how the meditative practice of reciting the "Jesus Prayer," most commonly spoken as "Lord Jesus Christ have mercy on me, a sinner," dating from the 5th century, was still being practiced in these monasteries. I was unfamiliar with the prayer and knew little about the Eastern Orthodox Church, but the photos of ancient monasteries and the dark-clad bearded monks that lived there were enough to prompt me to bring the book to my room and read it.

I became absorbed with this book during Holy Week, and after Easter I purchased the DVD of the accompanying documentary so that I could actually meet some of the monks who were interviewed and get a look at the monasteries. What appealed to me about Eastern Orthodoxy thus far was that it had retained the early spirit of the Church. While the Catholic Church had introduced major reforms in the 1960s in an attempt to be more in line with contemporary society, I learned that the Orthodox Church, in all its various ethnic cultural forms, refused to modernize. It was extremely conservative and resistant to making any change at all. I familiarized myself with Orthodox theology as well, reading works by the contemporary theologians, Vladimir Lossky and Kallistos Ware, whose books I was pleased to find in the monastery library. I also discovered some works by Greek and Russian hesychasts—extremely ascetic monks who lived in seclusion in forests or the desert, engaged day and night in contemplative prayer. Although I certainly did not feel motivated to live such a life, I found their writings to be potent and inspiring. I thought here were model monastics whom I could emulate in a manner that suited my physical capabilities. I learned about Mt. Athos, the semi-autonomous monastic republic in Greece where monks in both ancient monasteries and in isolated hermitages spent countless hours inwardly reciting the Jesus Prayer.

The more I discovered about Eastern Orthodox monasticism, the desire to change my direction and head east, so to speak, gained strength. I even began to study Greek, in case I decided to explore the possibility of actually residing at one of the monasteries on Mt. Athos. What was a strong deterrent though, was that I would be isolated from family and might not be permitted to visit them. I couldn't imagine my brother making the trip to Mt. Athos to see me and women weren't allowed on the peninsula. I hoped that there were a few Orthodox monasteries in the U.S. but decided to wait several months before making any inquiries. I was conscious of a trend I had noticed in my monastic life—soon after ordination, I developed a wish to leave and go someplace else. I now see that it was like climbing up a mountain, making the arduous hike motivated by the expectation that the view from the top would be so exhilarating, so mind-expanding. While climbing, I would brush away any thoughts regarding what I didn't like about the landscape, my mind eagerly focusing on the reward for my efforts. When finally reaching the summit, though, I would look around and think, 'well, it's O.K. but not the view I had expected.' Yet, at St. Gregory's, I desisted from jumping into making a dramatic change in my monastic life. This time, I would follow the advice Ajahn Amaro had given when I expressed my wish to visit Christian monasteries, and would wait for a period of time to see if this urge was truly coming from that instinct deep within me that I trusted or if it was merely a passing fascination prompted by a perceived dissatisfaction with my present situation.

In the meantime, I changed my morning routine. Directly after the early morning *matins* service, instead of going to my room and engaging in *lectio divina*, I would sit in a side chapel where the reserved Blessed Sacrament was kept. I put up my hood—as I had seen the monks in the Carthusian monastery in the film do when sitting in the church—and recite the Jesus Prayer silently for about twenty minutes, and then just remain in a silent state of unfocused meditation. The church was nearly dark and completely still. I heard neither voices nor footsteps in the hallway outside. I allowed my mind to get a taste of what it might be like in an Orthodox monastery, based on what I had seen in the documentary.

By July, I had already explored the websites of Orthodox monasteries in the U.S., focusing on those where the principal spoken and liturgical language was English. That left me with only a few choices. After more detailed research, I decided on just one, St. Gregory Palamas Greek Orthodox Monastery in Ohio. If it turned out not to be a viable possibility, I would consider one of the other monasteries, or perhaps study Greek in New York for a few months and then go to Mt. Athos. On August 1st, I sent a carefully written letter to the abbot, Fr. James, expressing as coherently as I could why I wanted to leave my present Benedictine monastery for an Orthodox one. To my great delight, he responded within a day, and accepted my request to come for a ten-day preliminary visit in late September. I waited a month before informing the community at St. Gregory's that I would be leaving so as to minimize what could be an uncomfortable situation during my remaining weeks. I didn't expect the reaction to be as negative as it was at Amaravati, or Nalanda, since I was remaining a Christian monastic, only moving to a much more rigorous and ascetic tradition. I also knew that Fr. Aelred had great respect for Eastern Orthodoxy.

During the first week of September, after my class with Fr. Aelred, I asked if I could speak to him. I then gave him the news. He took it quite well and understood my interest and attraction for the Eastern Church, but warned me that each national church was very much steeped in its particular ethnic culture. I thanked him for the caveat and assured him that having spent many years in Europe, I was quite adaptable. Later that morning, at the daily chapter meeting, I made my announcement to the community.

Abbot Andrew, very graciously, I thought, wished me well and thanked me for the service I had provided to the monastery. No one else said anything but I was aware of the disappointment they felt. Fortunately, a new postulant had recently arrived, so that the community would remain at seven after my departure.

On the day before my departure, I shaved, which would be the last time for many years. Orthodox monks neither shaved nor cut their hair. Although it would be some time before I would be an Orthodox novice, I nevertheless wanted to begin adopting that custom. Early in the morning of the next day, the first day of autumn, Br. Abraham, who had picked me up from the airport a little more than a year before, drove me once again. In the pre-dawn darkness, I glanced at the attractive and cozy monastery for the last time and felt a fleeting moment of sadness. But immediately excitement rose and I looked forward to beginning this next chapter in my monastic journey

---

I had rented a car at the Cleveland airport since I did not want to inconvenience the community. I knew it was at least an hour drive from the airport to the monastery. I arrived in the early afternoon and parked near the entrance to the main house. For some reason, I hesitated going up to the door and ringing the bell. Instead, I walked down the hill and entered the church. I was struck by how different it was from a Catholic or Episcopal church. The walls were covered with small icons of various saints. And in the middle were stands where large icons were placed, an oil lamp suspended in front of each. So many eyes looking at the observer gave me the impression that I had entered a holy community. As I was pondering this, the door opened and a tall thin monk with a long scraggly beard walked in. He said in a gruff manner that they had been searching for me. I apologized and followed him outside and up the hill to the main house. I later discovered that although Fr. Cyprian presented a rather harsh directness, he was actually a very warm and generous person, and someone I eventually began to like. Once inside the house, I met the abbot, Fr. James, who invited me into the front room. Shortly thereafter, a young monk, whose beard wasn't as long as Fr. Cyprian's, brought me a cup of tea.

I estimated Fr. James to be five or six years older than me. He had a very warm and friendly manner and was quite easy to converse with. We talked about my reasons for leaving St. Gregory's, a monastery that he had heard of, and also about my New York Jewish background. I didn't bring up my years of Buddhism, although I had mentioned in my letter that I had first heard God's call while living in a Buddhist monastery. He didn't ask about it and I thought it best not to offer any information that wasn't asked for. After speaking amiably for an hour, he asked the young monk to help me with my huge suitcase as I would be staying at the guest house some distance away. As I walked with the monk, Fr. Nektarios (I found it interesting that Orthodox monks who were not priests were all addressed as "Father"), told me that he had been living there for about six years and would, perhaps in the following year, be clothed in the *schema*—in other words, take life vows and thus become a fully ordained monk. He was quiet, soft-spoken, and rather shy but nevertheless seemed friendly. My first impressions of the community at St. Gregory Palamas Monastery were thus quite positive.

I would get my first taste of Orthodox monastic life early the next morning. *Matins*, as at St. Gregory's, began at 4am. But that was the only thing the two services had in common. I arrived a few minutes early and as soon as I walked inside the nearly completely dark church, I felt that I had entered another world, a sacred one. The dim oil lamps were the only light except for a few candles. The faces of the icons were illuminated by the hanging lamps but the background behind each saint's face was barely visible. As I looked around, all I saw were luminous faces—about six in total. There were also full length icon panels that served as a divider, which together with a full-length curtain in the center, blocked off the apse containing the altar. Jesus was depicted on the right and Mary on the left, and two additional saints on either side. Here, too, the oil lamp revealed only the faces. Unlike at St. Gregory's where the monks sat in choir stalls facing each other, here there were two reader stands on either side of the church, and behind each was a set of wooden seats of a type I had never seen before. They served primarily as something to lean against when standing, which I soon learned one did most of the time. One could put down a thin folding wooden seat and use that for sitting. These types of standing-chairs were also placed around the perimeter of the church. There were no pews or chairs in the middle section of the church—only icon stands.

The *matins* service, which to my amazement, went on for three hours, consisted almost entirely of readings. I wasn't sure, but I suspected they were mostly psalms from the Old Testament. At a few points there was a melodic chant in Byzantine style—more sung than chanted. A small reading light shone on the text that the reader was reading from. Other than that, until daylight began to shine about halfway into the service, the only light in the church was from the hanging oil lamps and a few lit candles.

During my ten-day visit, I interacted with all seven monks in the community. I found each one friendly and welcoming and distinctly had the impression that I would be welcomed to join them. But, of course, it would be some time before I could be officially received into the Greek Orthodox Church. Near the end of my stay, I had another informal meeting with Fr. James and expressed my wish to return and try it out. I was very happy and relieved when he told me that the monks thought I would integrate well into the community. I was ready to return soon since I didn't want to spend so much time in the "world," but Fr. James informed me that he would be away for a few weeks in October and I would need to wait until he returned. We then set a tentative date in early November for my return.

Since I would have about a month to spend before taking up residence at the monastery, I thought I would make a pilgrimage to the Holy Land, remaining mostly in Jerusalem. As I drove back to the airport, I went over in my mind the impressions I had collected from the ten-day visit and felt confident that I had made the right decision in changing traditions. The monks seemed pious and serious about their monastic and spiritual path. In this atmosphere I was convinced that my faith and devotion would develop and I would gradually progress to having greater intimacy with God through Jesus Christ.

I headed first to Florida to see my parents and brother, and while there would make my last minute plans for the journey to Jerusalem.

Walking around the old city of Jerusalem, I was certainly aware that it was a holy place for Jews, but the narrow streets were teeming with Christian pilgrims from a great variety of countries. I saw groups, led by a tour leader, tracing the steps of Jesus along the *via dolorosa*, the path he took to Calvary, where he would be crucified. On my first day, however, I was occupied with the question of whether I should book a package tour to St. Catherine's Monastery far down the Sinai peninsula. Besides wishing to see the ancient monastery and one of the oldest and most famous icons of Jesus, I also wanted to climb Mt. Sinai to observe sunrise from the summit. My hesitation was due to the warnings recently issued by the U.S. State Department advising Americans to avoid visiting the Sinai peninsula because of the continuing violent unrest in Gaza as well as an attack on tourists in a resort town in the south. My interest in making this excursion was aroused while at St. Gregory Palamas Monastery where I saw a poster of St. Catherine's in the foreground of the holy mountain. I knew that Jewish tradition did not recognize this mountain as the one where Moses received the ten commandments—the location is unknown—but Christian tradition from very early on claimed it was in fact Mt. Sinai and hundreds of thousands of Christian pilgrims have visited and climbed it since. I stopped into a travel agency near the busy Jaffa Gate and spoke to a young female agent. She assured me it was safe to go there and people had done so in recent months. I then booked a private two-day tour that would coincide with the October full moon. I thought it would be practical and beautiful to climb Mt. Sinai by moonlight.

After leaving the agent, I strolled through the congested alleys of the old city, full of shops selling both Jewish and Christian religious items, and stopped at a shop that had hiking poles. I thought I would get just one in case the path up the mountain was rocky. As I was walking with my new purchase, a young shop-owner standing in front of his shop, asked me what I was planning to do with the hiking pole. I told him I intended to climb Mt. Sinai. He then asked me to come into his shop and join him for a cup of coffee. I accepted his invitation and when I walked inside, I saw many beautiful Jewish religious items displayed. I assumed he too was Jewish as he had dark features and a Semitic appearance but later found out he was Palestinian. After engaging in friendly conversation with this very personable and educated man, I got up to go and, surprisingly, he did not urge me to buy anything. I really wasn't interested in what he was selling but as I reached the front of the shop, I saw a display of different types of star of David pendants. One captured my attention because it was very unique. Engraved on the spokes of the star were the Hebrew letters of the *sh'ma*—the opening Jewish prayer that I still recalled from my youth. It was artistically done and the silver back of the star had a lustrous shine. My new friend walked up to me and said that he himself had designed it. I stood and looked at it, wondering why I wanted to have it. I was after all in the Holy Land on a Christian pilgrimage. Yet something I perceived from my heart was urging me to buy it. I sensed it was in honor of my Jewish heritage, despite being estranged from Judaism since shortly after my bar mitzvah. After bargaining on the price, I put it on and wore it together with the crucifix I had been wearing since my baptism.

I established an early morning routine. Waking up to the beautiful, otherworldly Muslim call to prayer at 4:30am, I would proceed to the chapel in the Roman Catholic guest house where I was residing and go through sets of psalms followed by meditative repetitions of the Jesus Prayer. I was usually alone in the church at this early hour. I would then go out on the roof-top patio and watch the sun rise over the ancient city, and was particularly mesmerized by the beautifully rich colors of the landmark Dome—so holy to Muslims—as it received the first rays of the sun. The soft gold-toned buildings of the old city had a quality that I knew I could never capture in a photo. I stood still and just let the panoramic scene enter my mind. I reflected on all that had transpired over the centuries in this city—how it was fought over and all the blood that had been spilled. But the serene ancient landscape belied such musings and I remained captivated by the beauty.

In the late afternoon of my first Friday, I elected to go to the Wailing Wall. I wanted to get a taste of the welcoming of the Jewish sabbath at this most holy place. After passing through security checkpoints, I found myself on the spacious plaza in front of the remains of the Temple wall where groups of mostly black-clad Hasidim were already engaged in prayer. Standing back so that I wouldn't get called to join one of the non-Hasidic groups—since a minyan of 10 men was required for the service—I had a wide-angle view of the activity. I watched with some sense of awe how the Hasidim did not pray together, but rather each man davened on his own completely focused on his prayers, paying no attention to the men in his group. As I grew up in a very secular family, I had never observed ultra-orthodox Jews at prayer. I recalled from my youth that in the synagogue, the whole congregation sang or chanted prayers together. I also remembered feeling that the sabbath services I had attended were not particularly spiritually uplifting or moving. Here, however, I observed devout Jews whom I expected were actually communing with God. It nevertheless felt rather foreign to me despite having a Jewish background and I soon departed just as throngs of worshippers were streaming in.

Having avoided going to the Church of the Holy Sepulchre because of the enormous crowds, I decided I would go and make the most of it. I wasn't sure of the significance of different places in the vast complex and simply followed some people going up the stairs that led to a small chapel with an elaborate altar. I noticed how individuals kneeled on the ground at one spot, kissing something that was below in a hole. I did the same not knowing what I was venerating but perceived a strange energy at the spot. I discovered later that it was the reputed spot of the crucifixion. There was another chapel on the ground floor where perhaps one hundred people had lined up waiting to enter. I didn't want to join the line and thought I would come back perhaps late in the evening or very early in the morning. I left the area not feeling that I had experienced a holy site. I blamed it on the tumultuous crowds, however, and not on the place itself.

A few days later I was in the back seat of a van, sitting next to my Egyptian guide for the three-hour drive down the Sinai peninsula to St. Catherine's Monastery at the foot of Mt. Sinai. I was surprised to see a brown desert rather than one with white sand. It was the most barren and lifeless landscape I had yet encountered. Once we arrived, my guide arranged for me to check into my room at the guest house adjacent to the ancient monastery. It seemed that the other occupants were either Russian or Italian. There were no other Americans or native English speakers. My package tour, besides including meals at the restaurant (where there was no menu to choose from), included the services of a personal Bedouin guide who would lead me up the mountain, for no one was permitted to walk up unescorted. We would be departing at 1:30am for the climb, thus assuring we would arrive at the summit before sunrise.

I was very excited despite being under the weather with a bad cold. At the appointed time, I met my guide at a coffee bar where I and other hikers were getting some fuel for the climb. There were a number of groups, each with a guide; I appeared to be the only solo climber. We followed the gradual camel path and as I expected the full moon illuminated the lunar-like landscape so that no flashlight was needed. I didn't find the hike difficult at all because the incline was so gradual. About half-way, we stopped at one of the Bedouin tents where one could get some refreshment. The atmosphere inside was cozy, exotic, and otherworldly. Sitting on a bench covered in a rug, incense hanging heavily in the air, I was captivated by the ethereal music playing softly in the background. I would have liked to sit there longer, but my escort, who was on friendly terms with the owner, ushered me to continue the climb. We arrived just below the summit while it was still completely dark, with not even a hint of the coming dawn. I indicated that I wanted to climb up the rest of the way, a very steep and arduous climb, so that I could meditate well before dawn when I expected many people would be arriving. He suggested I rent a camel blanket for warmth as it would be chilly and very windy on the summit. I followed his advice and after procuring a thick colorful blanket, he led the way up the rocky path. Upon reaching the top, I was delighted that no one else was there. He found a nook in a rock where I would have some shelter from the wind, and after being sure that I would be alright there, he said he would wait for me down below in the café-tent. And thus, I was completely alone in this extraordinarily isolated mountaintop where Moses may—or may not—have received the ten commandments. I didn't focus on the question of whether he did or not, for what struck me the most was that the place was imbued with holiness because of the thousands of pilgrims over the centuries who believed that it was the spot. I took out the worn prayer rope that Fr. Aelred had given to me as a farewell present. He said that it had belonged to a monk who lived on Mt. Athos. I let my mind absorb the mystical stillness that engulfed me as I slowly repeated the Jesus Prayer. I didn't have a watch but I was sure that the sun should have risen because I estimated that I had been sitting there for an hour. A few people came into my vicinity and I stood up and immediately was aware that the sun had already risen. I had been facing west, not east! I didn't really mind though because I had had the opportunity to be completely alone whereas on the east-facing side, there undoubtedly would have been many people distracting me.

I found my Bedouin escort and, at my suggestion, we took the alternative route to descend from the mountain—down the 360 steps of repentance. While it was an extraordinary experience to walk, in a sense, *through* the mountain, I soon regretted my eagerness. The "steps" were not normal steps but rather uneven rocks that had to be navigated slowly and carefully. By the time we had reached the bottom, I could barely walk because my knees were wobbling from the exertion. I recovered somewhat after breakfast, and after viewing the ancient and remarkable icon of Jesus, the Pantocrator, which I thought less engaging in the original than my printed copy, we began the long journey to the border crossing from where I would re-enter Israel.

My time in Jerusalem was coming to an end and there was one day trip I wanted to take. I wished to visit Bethlehem and also, if possible, from there take a little trip to the ancient monastery, Mar Saba, in the Judean desert. I was somewhat nervous to take a city bus to the border crossing into Bethlehem, which was inside the Israeli-controlled Palestinian territory. Fortunately, it worked out without any problem. I easily found the Church of the Nativity and was pleased to see far fewer people there than at the Holy Sepulchre. Once inside, I walked over to a closed off entrance to the grotto which marked the spot where Jesus was born. A Palestinian guard was sitting at the entrance to prevent people from entering. I noticed there was also an entrance on the other side where a sizeable line had formed. He ushered me over and said I could walk inside. I smiled and thanked him as I entered the grotto. Inside I found a hole right in the middle and kneeled down to look more closely. I was startled by the strange energy force I felt coming out of it. I wondered, 'could this really be the spot?' I stood up and walked out the other side past those who were patiently waiting to enter. I had no idea why the guard let me in on the opposite side but was grateful that he did.

Once outside, I looked around for a taxi that might take me out to Mar Saba Monastery. Having found one and negotiating a price, we drove about 25 minutes in the direction of the Dead Sea until we arrived at one of the oldest continually occupied Orthodox monasteries, dating from the 5th century. The driver was going to wait for me outside while I would spend, I thought, at least an hour in the monastery. I had read up on this monastery and knew that it was very austere and isolated, with no electricity. I walked through the gate and just stood for a few moments getting a feel for the place. I then entered the modest-sized church and glanced at the icons. There was a faint smell of incense in the air, and despite being still late afternoon, it was very dim inside. I took out my prayer rope and started saying the Jesus Prayer. A monk of middle age came in and with a friendly demeanor, walked up to me. I introduced myself, explaining that I would be taking up residency at a Greek Orthodox monastery in the U.S. and hoped to be received into the Church soon after. I then asked him where the caves were. For I had read that the monks had originally dwelt in individual caves rather than together in one residence. We walked outside and he pointed across the narrow stream that ran next to the monastery and I saw a few structures built into the cliffs. I couldn't imagine living in one of them. As I stood there beside him, I mentioned that I wished I had more time to explore this amazing ancient monastery. When he then said that I could stay in the monastery overnight if I liked, I couldn't believe what I had just heard. Although all I had with me was an umbrella and a book, I wasn't going to pass up this opportunity. I walked out front and told the taxi driver I was going to stay the night and then re-entered the monastery. The gatekeeper closed the gate behind me as the monastery was locked at night.

Fr. Paisios, who was assistant to the abbot, told me that *vespers* would occur in about an hour and that the morning service would begin at 1:30am. They followed the Byzantine clock, according to which midnight occurs at sunset, and thus the new day begins eight hours after sunset. He said the monks got up one hour before and there would be a wake-up bell that I should be able to hear in my room. After *vespers*, a lay person who served as guest master, took me to my "cell." He gave me a kerosene lamp and some matches and then showed me where the toilet was. It was upstairs in the monastic residence and, as I had expected, was very basic. I hoped I would be able to find it in the middle of the night and negotiate my way back to the room. I was nevertheless very excited and grateful for this unexpected adventure.

Even though it was the first of November, it was very hot in the Judean desert. The temperature was near 100 degrees in the daytime, and despite the fact that my room was cave-like with just a small window, it was very warm and breeze-less inside. I read for a while but the dim light was straining my eyes. I did a number of Jesus Prayers on my prayer rope but my mind was distracted. I tried to imagine what the monks were like who had lived here over the course of the centuries. I had read that the monastery was attacked twice by bands of Muslims in the 7th century and scores of monks were brutally killed. I thought about how their faith had prepared them to face what must have been a horribly violent death. I wondered if I would ever have such strong faith even at the time of a peaceful and natural death. I finally drifted off into sleep just as the bell sounded.

I went into the church shortly before the start of *matins*. I saw one other lay guest, dressed in black who seemed to be at home there. I stood at one of the standing-chairs, similar to the ones at St. Gregory Palamas. At one point during the lengthy service, just as the chandelier was being lit, I felt that I was about to pass out. The incense, the candlelight, the darkness seemed to overwhelm me. I slid down to the floor and just sat there for a while. My heart was beating very fast out of fear. But as I sat on the floor, I also felt that I was in an unfamiliar world that didn't seem threatening but rather unreal and timeless. I gradually pulled myself up and sat down on the hard fold-down seat. A palpable sense of joy was rising within me. It wasn't mystical in the sense of feeling the presence of God, yet I was distinctly aware of some-thing that was not ordinary. I recovered completely and experienced the rest of the service and the first part of the divine liturgy (mass) until the time I had to leave the main part of the church, since I was not yet baptized into the Orthodox Church.

After the service, I joined the monks for a post-communion snack of nuts, dried fruit and coffee. The monks only ate one meal per day. Fr. Ephraim came over to me, asking how I was enjoying my stay. I told him it had been an amazing experience that I would always treasure. He then said that there would be a car driving to Jerusalem shortly and I could catch a ride. I was sorry to have to leave so soon but thought it best to accept the offer. I was scheduled to fly back to the U.S. on the following day.

As we drove off, I reassured myself that I had done the right thing in leaving the Benedictine community in order to join an Orthodox one. My initial stay at St. Gregory Palamas and this brief visit to an ancient monastery in the Judean desert indicated to me that my expectation at finding an ascetic Christian monastic life where one could cultivate intimacy with the Divine, living a daily life that kept one apart from worldly distractions, was to be found within the Eastern Orthodox tradition. I was looking forward with great anticipation to beginning my life at the intimate Greek Orthodox monastery in rural Ohio.

On November 5, 2012, I returned to St. Gregory Palamas Monastery and took up residency. On my first day, I was introduced to the art of making beeswax candles. I began my training with Fr. Nektarios who was the principal candle maker and bee keeper. Although the monastery had beehives, the amount of wax needed for the enormous number of candles that were made required a supply that far exceeded what could be obtained from the hives. Unlike at the Benedictine monastery, here the work period lasted a total of six-and-a-half hours, divided between morning and afternoon. The only day off was on Sunday and feast days. Slowly I picked up the skills needed to perform the major tasks of dipping, cutting, and packing up bundles of candles. To make it even more challenging, in addition to the thin tapers—of which usually 1250 were made daily—there were also thick table candles and very tall altar and bishop's candles that required even more skill. I had a generally good rapport with Fr. Nektarios, despite the fact that he was nearly 30 years younger than me and we had completely different cultural and educational backgrounds. Most challenging for me was maintaining respect for someone who was senior to me in monastic life and to keep in mind that he was very sensitive and insecure. At times, I did not rein in my New York impatience when I found his instructions inarticulate. Very helpful was the Orthodox monastic practice of asking for forgiveness immediately after offending someone. And especially humbling and ego-deflating was asking forgiveness even when I knew that I had not done anything wrong. Despite occasional moments of tension during those initial months, we actually worked quite harmoniously together. After about three months, I was left to make the candles on my own. Fr. Nektarios would simply stop in occasionally to see how it was going.

During those initial weeks in November, I slowly got used to the long morning *matins* service. I began to recognize the different segments and came to understand why it was so long. The initial forty-five minutes wasn't actually *matins* at all—it was the midnight office. I presumed that it was originally performed at midnight but in modern times, it was added on to *matins*. I soon realized that the same extremely long psalm, number 118—which had 176 lines—was read at every midnight office. Since I was not only a lay person but not even Orthodox, I couldn't directly participate in the services. I was merely a semi-attentive observer. Spending so much time in *stasidia* (the unique standing-chairs found in Orthodox monastic churches), I began to find them rather comfortable. I could use the arms and back to support myself when standing and the hard fold-down seat proved to be comfortable when I let myself occasionally take a break from standing. I truly loved entering the nearly dark church just before 4am and feeling the mystical stillness. Oddly, I never felt the urge to doze off.

Fr. James had told me to take my time acclimating myself to the practice of venerating the icons upon entering the church. This involved actually kissing the icon, generally on the hands, never on the face. I cringed to think what my Jewish family and friends would think of this! With time, however, it became a normal procedure and although I don't think I ever quite experienced the icons as "windows into the Divine," I did, especially with the icons of Jesus, summon up real devotion and awe. While I came to accept and eventually enjoy the long morning service when there was a divine liturgy (mass) following *matins*, generally three times a week, I had great difficulty maintaining the same positive feeling on Wednesdays and Fridays, when a very long service to the Theotokos (God Bearer, or Virgin Mary), the *Paraklesis*, was performed. It added forty-five minutes to the morning office. I was then obliged to follow the monks in making prostrations to the main icon of the Theotokos after the service, despite not really feeling comfortable in performing them.

I also had the opportunity during my first week to experience one of the periodic vigils on the eve of a feast. These services, which simply added the morning service onto *vespers*—and contained some elements not in the usual morning service—began at 8pm and generally lasted until midnight. One advantage was that the next day, the service, which included divine liturgy, didn't begin until 9am. So one could sleep later, but, of course, one went to bed later as well. I did not figure out the construction of this long service until after attending several vigils. Thus, during my first experience of it, I thought it would never end. I was tired and impatient especially during the final hour. The highlight of the service, however, which I liked very much, was the swinging of the large chandelier hanging in the middle of the church and lit with 24 candles. While the chandelier was swinging overhead, certain festive psalms were recited. I learned that the motion was to suggest the movement of the universe celebrating the Divine. Although it took me quite some time to acclimate myself to the long daily and festive services, I was always cognizant of how the Orthodox services were meant to support and inspire heartfelt prayer and to lead one ever closer to God. I attempted to keep in my mind the Orthodox Christian concept of *theosis*, whereby one could achieve intimate union with God by the process of gradually becoming more God-like. Theologians pointed out that it was indeed possible for humans to actually participate in the divine nature. While this seemed so remote from my current relationship with the Divine, I was inspired to keep myself open to this possibility.

Although I did not confess to Fr. James every week as the monks did, because I had not yet been officially received into the Church, I met with him weekly to discuss how I was acclimating to daily life. On one occasion, I brought up something that had deeply shaken me. I was still on the e-list of Nalanda Monastery, where I had resided as a Tibetan Buddhist *getsul*, and was shocked and distraught upon reading that one day, Jampa, the English novice monk I had befriended, had walked into the garage and after pouring gasoline over himself, set himself on fire. He had left no note explaining his reasons for doing this horrific act. My first reaction was anger at the community for not seeing any warning signs. I then realized that Jampa did not reveal his inner thoughts and thus he might not have shown any indication or hint that he was about to take his own life. I didn't know what I should do. Knowing that suicide was considered a very heavy offense in Buddhism and Christianity, I wanted to pray for him. But I didn't know if it was appropriate in this case. I raised the question to Fr. James who after giving it some thought, said it was best not to pray for him. However, I only partially followed his advice. I sent strong wishes of positive energy to him without asking God's assistance.

During my first Orthodox Lent, where I did my best to adjust to the rigors of fasting—no food for the first three days and during weekdays only one meal—I also looked forward to being officially received into the Greek Orthodox Church through the rite of chrismation. Although the Russian Church and the Churches on Mt. Athos required someone previously baptized in a non-Orthodox Church to be baptized again properly, the Greek Church in America did not require it. The chrismation would take place on Lazarus Saturday, the day before Palm Sunday, when the celebration of Jesus' raising of Lazarus from the dead is commemorated. I thought that was an auspicious day for my being formally brought into the Orthodox Church. It was a simple ceremony performed only for the monastic community whereby Fr. James anointed me on strategic points of face, heart, and hands with special holy oil. The next day, on the festive day of Palm Sunday, I received holy communion. I didn't really experience anything remarkable. I had perhaps built it up too much, thinking that receiving communion in the manner of the Orthodox Church would immediately lead me into momentary, inconceivable union with God-in-Christ. Nevertheless, on a psychological level I felt that I had begun to travel the path bringing me eventually exquisite supernal joy.

In August, I received the news that I would be clothed as a novice. Thus, I would be taking the first step into monastic life at St. Gregory Palamas Monastery. In the Greek Orthodox tradition, one remained a novice generally for about three years before making the next step up the ladder. I looked forward to wearing black monastic garb. I already had my longish hair tied up in the back and my beard was getting full.

During the summer, since candle making business slowed down, I had been working mornings in the enormous organic vegetable garden. I pulled out weeds and also harvested our planted crops. I wasn't new to weeding, as I had done quite a bit while at Chithurst. But I had never picked beans, diverse types of greens, peppers, and other vegetables. Bending over for extended periods of time prompted rebellion from my lower back, not to mention how cumbersome I found it to be once I started wearing a black cassock over my clothing and a hat on hot summer mornings. But I surprised myself in adapting to this arduous work. As in the candle shop, where I developed a rhythm of saying the Jesus Prayer as I was dipping racks of candles, in the garden, I tried to keep my mind on the Prayer as I was weeding or harvesting. I knew that Orthodox monks were supposed to be saying the Prayer throughout the day and avoid unnecessary talk. Although I tried to emulate this ideal, I was more successful with the latter than the former. The inner chatter and monologues in my mind never seemed to cease and I rarely kept my focus on the Prayer for long.

The novice clothing was a very short protocol that took place in front of the closed off altar just before evening *vespers*. Fr. James simply handed me the not-new cassock I would be wearing over my clothing as well as a black belt and hat. I felt different once I had put them on and excited that I was officially an Orthodox monastic. This change in my status also had practical effects—I would now be permitted to participate in services. Since I was unable to read music and sing the various Byzantine melodies, I would be a principal reader, reading aloud mostly psalms from the Old Testament. By actually reading during the service, not only did time pass much more quickly but I found that I really enjoyed reading aloud the biblical texts, and I shortly became very familiar with all 150 psalms.

During those years as a novice, my conversion to (or as I later came to view it, my "unfolding" into) Christianity became complete. I felt that I was a true believer and I gradually cultivated a deep sense of the presence of Jesus Christ as manifestation of God and accepted the "mystery" of Jesus' birth. I came to think that Christ was, in a way, God—that God was somehow channeled through a human body—something that had never occurred before even in the great prophets of the Hebrew Bible. I tended to think of God-in-Christ as a cosmic force and that Jesus' human form made that impersonal force accessible in some way. I realize now that because I never adequately personalized God as Jesus, I never connected with the Jesus Prayer on any profound level. Despite reciting it hundreds of thousands of times, I never penetrated its mystery. I wasn't really addressing Jesus.

I was also conscious of not fully experiencing communion, despite partaking in it hundreds of times. At the moment that the "body and blood" entered my mouth (in Orthodox tradition both are in a chalice and a small amount is put on a long spoon and inserted directly by the priest into one's mouth)—I felt *something*—but did not truly feel I had just ingested the body and blood of Jesus. The moment before receiving it, I would focus my mind on God's transcendent presence and keep that in mind as the tiny—sometimes just a crumb—was put in my mouth. I sometimes walked away thinking that I got "cheated" because it was so tiny. I could barely feel it in my mouth, only sensing the alcohol of the "blood." Yet afterwards, standing in my place in one of the choir stands, I would observe the pious lay people coming up to the chalice, especially the Romanians, with obvious awe at what they would be receiving. I studied their countenance immediately afterwards as they walked to the tray of *antidoron* (blessed but not consecrated bread). Something was registered in their faces that I know I did not feel or experience myself.

Holy Week was without a doubt the highpoint in our liturgical life. There were vigils every night beginning on the evening after Palm Sunday. The vigil that moved me the most was the one on Thursday. After the almost festive like morning service, with divine liturgy, the vigil that night was the immediate precursor of Good Friday and was known as the "Service of the Twelve Gospel Readings." The readings, culled from all four gospels, took us through the events leading up to the Crucifixion. Each reading, alone, would have been emotive but hearing a sequence of twelve during the course of the four-hour service never failed to move me to the point of tears. The stark realism of the passages prepared us for the potent force that we all, I believe, experienced on Good Friday. It was a day of total fasting—not even water was consumed—until after the special *vespers* when Christ was taken down from the cross. That particular service was for me the one time in the year that I truly felt the humanness of God-in-Christ. The large crucifix was in the middle of the church, candles placed on each corner of the cross. And shortly after the moment in the service where he had given up his last breath, two monks would carefully remove the body from the cross and lay it on a cloth on the altar. The cross remained bare until early Pascha (Easter) morning.

In general, I adopted the position of the Orthodox Church which does not try to *explain* mysteries (as is done in Catholic scholasticism). On Pascha I wholeheartedly celebrated the resurrection of Jesus, accepting it as an unexplainable mystery that defies rational thought. For, I reasoned, if God was manifest in and through Jesus, God must continue to exist after Jesus' death. Thus, while Jesus, the man, died on the Cross, God-in-Jesus, not being born could not die. Fueling this non-rational mystery was the Orthodox tradition of singing countless times beginning at midnight on Pascha and throughout the following week, "Christ has risen from the dead, trampling death by death...."

However, I continued to have difficulty venerating the Theotokos (Virgin Mary). In Orthodox monasticism, she holds a position of veneration just slightly below that given to Jesus. I suspended my disbelief regarding the miraculous birth—that Jesus had no human father—but something held me back from offering her the full devotion that I was quite sure the other monks felt in their hearts. In my case, I knew it was contrived and not spontaneously pouring out of my innermost core. I made progress here though when I acquired a copy of the famous Vladimir icon of mother and child. It was unusual in that Mary was not looking at the baby Jesus, but rather at the viewer. It had an extraordinary life-like quality and the Theotokos had an ascetic look that made her appear rather monastic. Gazing at the icon, especially as I recited the prayer to her, requesting her to pray and intercede for me, which was part of my daily prayer rule, I felt closer to her. In general, however, I was always conscious of the fact that my faith and belief was not on the same level as my brothers who were cradle Christians, even if all but one had converted from Protestantism. In fact, I never identified as a "Christian" because of an underlying discomfort I felt with the institution of the Church.

In February 2016, I was clothed as a *rasophore*, one who wears the *rasa*—a cloak-like robe worn over the cassock. I also began to wear the black veil over my hat, thus taking on the full appearance of a Greek Orthodox monk. In addition, I was given a monastic name. The name I had wanted, and actually received, was Savas, after the saint who had founded a number of monasteries in the Judean desert in the 5th century. The one remaining monastery still in existence was Mar Saba, where I had had the unexpected opportunity of spending the night during my trip to the Holy Land. Thus, I was now addressed as "Father Savas." I felt that I had absorbed many of the teachings of the desert fathers, filling several notebooks with quoted passages, and was even more motivated now as a proper monk to put their wisdom into practice. I viewed that momentous occasion as the highpoint thus far of my monastic life at St. Gregory Palamas.

In October of that year, I made a pilgrimage with Fr. Nektarios to Mt. Athos, the semi-autonomous monastic republic on a rugged, mountainous peninsula in northern Greece. It was the spiritual center of Greek Orthodox monasticism, particularly regarding the ascetic, contemplative hesychastic tradition. Our daily life at St. Gregrory Palamas Monastery was based on the Mt. Athos tradition and we derived our inspiration from this ancient and secluded mecca. Fr. Nektarios and I had received our special monastic "passports" that would permit us to visit the peninsula and we had worked out an itinerary, staying generally two nights each at five different monasteries. We would take day trips to visit several others as well. We were both excited to explore the uniquely different monasteries, most dating from between the tenth and fourteenth centuries. I was a bit concerned about hiking on the rugged terrain in a cassock and carrying a heavy backpack. I was nearly 63 years old and although I was in very good physical shape for my age, I feared breaking an ankle or some other injury. I purchased a sturdy hiking pole which I thought would offer me some support. Fr. Nektarios was very considerate and normally walked behind me in case I lost my balance. However, we were cautious, and since most of the monasteries were near the coast, we generally used the ferry to go from place to place.

The first of the three experiences I had during our ten days on Mt. Athos that had the most profound effect on me was at the Georgian monastery, Iveron, one of the oldest monasteries on the peninsula, dating from the tenth century. It was the destination for a day hike on our first full day on Mt. Athos. Hiking for two hours in order to reach it built up an expectation of a reward for our efforts—and I was not disappointed. Emerging from the dense forest we had walked through we suddenly saw the magnificent monastery below us at the water's edge. Although the main church was adorned with exquisite icons, it was for the purpose of visiting a small separate chapel that we elected to hike there. It held one of the oldest icons of the Theotokos, the *Panagia Portraitissa* dating from the tenth century and according to Orthodox tradition, a "wonderworking" icon, meaning that miracles had occurred for people who had prayed in front of it, requesting help from the Theotokos. While I maintained some skepticism about the miracles, I nevertheless wished to observe it closely. The contrast between the elaborate colors surrounding the mother and child and their faces, which were very dark but deeply textured, was striking. And the Mother's face expressed a profound sadness of a magnitude I was unable to articulate even to myself. Her eyes were not directed towards the baby Jesus in her arms, but rather beyond him, perhaps contemplating the fate that awaited him.

After standing in front of it in deep silence for some time, we moved on. I stopped into the monastery shop and found a display of hand-carved crucifix pendants. The shopkeeper informed me that they were all made by hermits living in extremely remote parts of the peninsula. I decided to purchase one to support the hermit who had carved it and also to wear something that was produced in such an environment—a way of life that I had great admiration for but knew that I could never live. After spending a considerable amount of time choosing which one I would buy, I finally made a selection and promptly put it on, wearing it together with the star of David I still wore.

Later in the week, we hiked with our backpacks to the Skete of St. Anne, the saint who, according to the apocryphal tradition, was the mother of the Theotokos and, therefore, Jewish. We opted not to take the ferry because the skete was located on a steep hill, about 1000 feet in elevation, and we thought the climb would be too arduous with our backpacks. So, we walked there from the previous monastery where we had spent two nights. We would still have to climb up the hill, but it would be more gradual, spread out over what we estimated would be an hour. However, our estimation was not very accurate, and as we trudged along, I thought it would have been better to take the ferry. For our hike led us down and up various slopes along the way, and it took us two exhausting hours to arrive at our hilltop destination. I was so focused on watching my step up the rocky path that I didn't engage in the Jesus Prayer. I needed to keep my mind wholly focused on my steps. When we arrived, I forgot all about the enormous effort of the hike and just drank in the exquisite location. From the terrace of the skete (small monastery), we had a panoramic view of the Aegean Sea far below us. We could also glance down and see many small monastic dwellings hugging the steep slope down to the water. I liked the intimate atmosphere of the skete and didn't mind the somewhat primitive conditions. The toilets and sinks were a considerable distance from the guest house, and reaching them involved walking down outdoor stairs which I expected to be challenging in the middle of the night. The morning service with divine liturgy was held not in the main church but in a small separate rustic chapel that I felt was more conducive for contemplation than the large church. We did have a chance to visit the main church for the purpose of venerating the famous relic—the left foot of St. Anne in a shoe encased in a simple box. Seeing the significant sized relic, I suspended my disbelief and kissed it with veneration.

The third memorable event was our last full day and night on Mt. Athos. We were staying in the very beautiful Grigoriou Monastery located right on the water's edge on the west coast. We would that night have the opportunity of experiencing a true Mt. Athos vigil. I thought what better way to end our visit to the place well-known for very long vigils. In fact, it would be eight hours, twice as long as the vigils at St. Gregory Palamas. We prepared ourselves for it, not by taking a nap, but rather by hiking up to the most iconic monastery on the peninsula, Simonopetra Monastery, that rises tall out of a very steep cliff. Besides seeing the famous monastery, we hoped to meet the American monk who had been dwelling there for the last twenty years. Upon finally reaching the top, after a long, steep climb, we inquired at the guest house if it were possible to meet briefly with Fr. Arsenios. As it was unclear if he could be located at the moment, we decided to explore the monastery and hopefully, by some chance, find him. Two English-speaking monks might catch his attention, we thought. He did eventually find us and we had a nice chat with him. Meeting a fellow American who had adapted so well to life there was very inspiring. He told us that he wanted to establish a small English-speaking skete on the property. Fr. Nektarios and I both expressed our support of this venture. When we bid farewell to Fr. Arsenios, he assured us we would be seeing him later that night, since he and a small group of monks would be participating in the vigil at Grigoriou.

The vigil began at 7pm and Fr. Nektarios and I occupied two adjacent *stasidia* in the area of the church reserved for monks. I tried not to think about the many hours that lay ahead, and just open myself up to the ethereal atmosphere of an Athonite vigil. Although the entire service was in Greek, I was able to keep up with it because the vigils at St. Gregory Palamas followed the same sequence. It seemed that everything was done very slowly and repetitively. I guessed that was why it would last eight hours instead of just four. I had no watch with me and had no sense of passing time. I somehow managed to drift along on the timeless flow of the exquisitely chanted and sung prayers. I had heard that monks on Mt. Athos spent many hours—probably months—learning to sing the prayers with the right inflection and tone. One could easily enjoy the fruit of their efforts. During the night, I developed a relationship with an icon of Jesus that was directly in my eye's view. It had an unusual contemporary style that had caught my attention and drew me towards it. My eyes met those of Christ and, periodically gazing at him, we seemed to connect on a more intimate level than I had ever done when venerating the icons of Jesus at St. Gregory Palamas. When the vigil ended, we had a two hour break before divine liturgy. I noticed that my jubilation at having not only survived the marathon vigil but feeling uplifted from it was not at all shared by Fr. Nektarios. He had struggled to stay awake and admitted that he had fallen asleep at a few points. I hadn't noticed because it was quite dark in the church and I was unusually focused on the service.

The next day, tired but elated by the ten-days spent on the holy mountain, we began the long journey back to St. Gregory Palamas Monastery.

Two years later, subtle changes in my relationship to Orthodox monasticism—and Christianity, in general—began to unfold. Having spent a considerable time studying texts of medieval Catholic mysticism, most notably, Richard Rolle's *Fire of Love* and the *Cloud of Unknowing*, both in the original Middle English (the former in translation from Latin), my interest shifted in an unexpected direction. I decided to learn scriptural Hebrew. The fact that I read aloud in church most of the 150 Old Testament psalms every week, and the very long psalm 118 every day during the midnight office, I wanted to be able to read some of my favorite ones in the original language. Both my interest in non-Orthodox mysticism and my subsequent wish to commune more intimately with the psalms in Hebrew were prompted by a growing dissatisfaction with my Orthodox prayer life centered on recitations of the Jesus Prayer. Something was not clicking. I didn't, however, put the blame on Jesus, but rather my failure to reach God-in-Jesus through the Prayer.

Examining my life up to that point as an Orthodox monk from my present Buddhist viewpoint, I see what was not visible to me at the time. I was unable to let go of the "I" who sought some type of unity, or at least, an intimate relationship with Christ. As long as "I" was saying the Jesus Prayer and Christ was somewhere else, not here, I was destined to fail at union. Orthodox Christianity does not have a concept of non-self but rather professes an individual soul that yearns for mystical union. During those years I tentatively accepted the Christian idea of a "soul." Thus, the problem, I believe, was that I could not separate my "I" from my "soul"—for it was the latter that I needed to move towards union. The "I" was a hindrance for it could never unite with Christ. The innumerable repetitions of the Jesus Prayer never brought me closer—for it was "I" who was saying it, not my soul. This problem, so contrary to Buddhism, was what prevented me from making spiritual progress at St. Gregory Palamas. For I was attempting to merge my "soul" that was bound up with my ego/self into the impalpable, inarticulate Other/God. I had come across no method for eliminating the concept of an individual ego-self. The ascetic desert fathers worked on getting rid of their self-centered ego yet they retained a pure, but still individual, "soul" that was devoted exclusively to God-in-Christ.

In the Fall of 2018, I discreetly downloaded a three-hundred page book of instruction for reading scriptural Hebrew, and studied it every night in my cell for one year. I followed the method I had used for learning Latin and, more recently, Pali. I parsed every word in the scriptural passages in the book and slowly gained a good foundation in the grammar. Achieving knowledge of vocabulary would come slowly I thought once I actually started to attempt reading the psalms in Hebrew. During that year, I looked forward to the two hours nightly that I devoted to this project. I reduced my hours of sleep—already fairly meager because of the daily busy schedule and the time I needed to spend on my prayer rule—but I didn't mind. I felt I was preparing myself for a different type of spiritual practice. At the end of 2018, while still in the early stage of my study, in honor of my 65th birthday, I purchased a beautiful leather-bound Old Testament that was intended for those wishing to read the biblical texts in Hebrew. Each word was glossed, providing not only a translation but also grammatical analysis. It would prove to be an invaluable tool for me once I had completed the study of Hebrew grammar in Fall 2019.

Concurrent with this ongoing study of Hebrew, which I mentioned only casually to one other monk and Fr. James, I was cognizant of feeling restless, and doubts started surfacing in my mind about whether I should make the final step up the monastic ladder and be clothed in the *schema*, the rite that marked the taking of life vows. I should have taken this momentous step early that year, three years after becoming a *rasophore*. But there was an unusual delay, one that I interpreted to mean that I was being given extra time to reconsider whether I wanted to make this step. The protocol was for the candidate to receive a completely new set of monastic attire, including the most important item—the *schema*. This was the Orthodox Church's version of the scapular worn by Catholic monks. The Orthodox "scapular" did not have a hood and it contained a series of Greek letters in bold red and a skull and bones representing one's death to the world. It was a very eye-catching piece of monastic attire and was worn only for services where there was divine liturgy and also at the vigils of feasts. The monks at the Romanian skete on Mt. Athos who were sewing the set of robes had made and sent a *schema* that was of the wrong size. Fr. Joseph had sent it back and for some inexplicable reason, after eight months, the new one had not yet arrived. I hesitated revealing to Fr. James my thoughts about postponing this step, even if the long awaited *schema* showed up, because I feared it would compromise my status at the monastery. I always had a suspicion that he did not feel completely comfortable with me because of my Jewish background. And if I expressed my uncertainty about making the life-long commitment, after having already been there for seven years, I feared I would lose his confidence in the validity of my conversion. Naturally, my fears about his distrust, or his feeling uncomfortable with me, might have been my own creation. Yet I couldn't summon the will to expose my uncertainty to him.

In early January 2020, the awaited article suddenly arrived and I, along with the monastic brotherhood, got caught up in the excitement of the upcoming solemn ceremony that would mark my becoming a *schema* monk. The event would occur during the vigil for St. Anthony the Great—the desert monk recognized as the "father" of Orthodox monasticism—January 17. In my meeting with Fr. James prior to that date, I was stunned when he told me not to wear the star of David at the ceremony. I had had no idea that he knew I was wearing it, for I had always kept it concealed under my t-shirt. I guessed that on an occasion it might have slipped out and he obviously had seen it. I complied with his request but after the ceremony, somewhat defiantly, put it back on.

The solemn midnight service was powerful, beautiful, and filled me with awe. Some of the most beautiful prayers

I had yet encountered were read aloud. After ceremonially cutting off a strand of my hair, representing a tonsure, Fr. James handed me each article of my new monastic attire. The climax was putting on the *schema* itself All the doubts I had perceived in the previous months melted away during those moments.

But as Lent approached, seeds of change began to sprout and would grow during the following months into a major upheaval—a revolution—in my monastic life.

CHAPTER 10

Awakening to My Jewish Roots

In December 2019, when it was still uncertain when my clothing in the *schema* would occur, I came upon a reference to a book by Daniel Boyarin, a respected Jewish scholar at UC Berkeley, with an intriguing title: *The Jewish Gospels: The Story of the Jewish Christ*. I had spent a good part of the Orthodox Advent reading essays about the Jewish origins of Christianity. As we approached the feast that celebrates Jesus' birth, I began to focus on Jesus' Jewishness—acknowledged but not emphasized in the Orthodox Church. This alteration in my view of Jesus extended to the apostles, all of whom were, likewise, Jews. Boyarin's book not only underscored this new apperception but planted the seeds for the awakening to my own Jewish roots. His articulate and convincing argument about the Jewishness of the gospels had a potent effect on me. Significant parts of these quintessential "Christian" texts were, in fact, an inventive re-presentation of Jewish concepts and traditions. Boyarin's boldest contention was that the coming of the Messiah was already imagined in ancient Jewish texts and many Jews, including the apostles, believed he was Jesus. The Christianization of Jesus and his teachings developed later. I was so excited about how this book altered my view and understanding of Yeshua (Jesus in Hebrew or Aramaic), and my recognition that I, too, as a Jew, accepted Jesus as the Messiah, led me to write to Professor Boyarin, offering some background information as well as my gratitude: "I am writing to express my gratitude for your book, *The Jewish Gospels: The Story of the Jewish Christ*. It has been enormously helpful for me in clarifying my relationship with Judaism.... During the past year I have been strongly drawn to learning more about Judaism, particularly of the late Second Temple period. As I delved into this subject, also reading essays from the field of Jewish-Christian Dialogue, it became apparent how ignorant I had been about my religious heritage. Moreover, I realized that I had unquestioningly adopted a Christian supersessionist view of Judaism! While my reading up to this point prompted me to discard my misconceptions about Judaism, it is your book that has radically altered my understanding of Christianity; namely, how Jewish its foundation and definitive beliefs are. Most importantly, I have gradually come to perceive my Jewishness—and Judaism itself—as the heart of my Christian monastic life. *The Jewish Gospels*, and several of your essays, have contributed significantly to my arriving at this profound, very personal recognition." In a subsequent response to his inquiry about how to properly address me, I replied that I was "Father Savas" officially, but thought of myself as "Monk Yehuda," having resurrected my Hebrew name.

Becoming a *schema* monk did not deter me from pursuing further my investigation of early Jewish spirituality. I developed a keen interest in the Qumran community, an ascetic sect of Jews who lived a proto-monastic life in the Judean desert, near the Dead Sea, from 150 BCE until CE

68, when the community dwellings were destroyed by the Romans. I was intrigued by the highly regimented ascetic monastic-like life they led with periods of communal work, study and prayer. There was speculation that John the Baptist might have been at one time a member of the community and that Jesus was most likely familiar with it as well. I regretted that Judaism did not continue an ascetic monastic tradition after the destruction of Qumran.

I couldn't seem to get enough information about Jewish spirituality and mysticism. I delved into Ashkenazic Hasidism of late twelfth-century Germany and the pietists. Their view that the will of God was not fully revealed in the Torah, i.e. in the commandments given to Moses, and thus the *Hasid* had to dig deeper to find God's words hidden in scripture, appealed to me. I was very interested in text-based mysticism as I was generally much more concentrated while reading than while listening to prayers or teachings. Learning also about the belief of Jewish mystics that the individual letters of the Hebrew alphabet each had a specific mystical significance prompted me to give greater effort in reading scriptural texts in Hebrew and learning to write the letters.

Thus, during my first Lent as a *schema* monk, I devoted much time and effort to writing out in Hebrew the entire three paragraphs of the *sh'ma*—one of the most significant Jewish prayers recited several times a day. I naturally did not tell any of my monastic brothers about this activity, for they most assuredly would not have approved of it especially during the Lenten period of repentance. But I was feeling far from repentant as I carried on this task, slowly drawing the Hebrew letters in pencil and then later going over them in ink. I also added grammatical glosses for most words and a literal English translation. I was gradually putting together a little prayer book that I would soon use each morning. After completing the *sh'ma*, I added the Lord's Prayer in Hebrew as well as selections from my favorite psalms. I decided, however, not to start using it until after Pascha/Easter. Meanwhile, in preparation for my new daily ritual, I ordered a *tallis* (a traditional Jewish prayer shawl) which my brother would send so as not to arouse suspicion about my clandestine activity.

Immediately after Pascha week, I got up one morning at 2:45, put on the *tallis* and *yarmulke* that my brother had sent me, and stood in front of the icon of Jesus on the wall over my desk. I just stood for a few moments in silence and tears started rolling down my cheeks. I thought about my parents, now both deceased, and the fact that I had attended both of their funerals as a monk of the Greek Orthodox Church. I reflected about how happy they would have been to know that I had not only re-discovered my Jewish roots but that I was integrating my Jewish identity into my daily monastic life. I slowly recited the *sh'ma*. The opening line, "*sh'ma Yisrael Adonai eloheinu Adonai echad* (Hear O Israel, the Lord our God, the Lord is One)," resonated in my heart. It was the one prayer I recalled from my youth, more than fifty years ago. I paused at the final word, *echad*—the mystical oneness with God, the unfathomable, inconceivable presence that I yearned for. I continued with the other prayers from my handwritten Hebrew prayer book, gazing periodically at Yeshua. I recognized that I was reciting these prayers not only as a spiritual practice but also in honor of my family that had provided me with a loving childhood. I established the daily routine of getting up at 2:45, thus giving myself enough time to perform the prostrations and prayers required by my Orthodox Christian monastic prayer rule as well as twenty minutes of Jewish prayer. I also began reciting the Jesus Prayer in Hebrew, addressed to Yeshua, especially while I was working outside. It was a perfect accompaniment during the hours I spent weeding the gravel walkways around the monastery. For candle-making had slowed down considerably because of the spread of Covid.

In May, as the pandemic took hold and essentially closed the monastery, I undertook a quest to find a way of more thoroughly integrating my Jewish identity into my Orthodox Christian monastic life. This led me to exploring theological writings of Messianic Jews and Jewish Christians. I discovered that there was an annual international conference, the Helsinki Consultation, that had begun in 2010 as a forum for theologians to present and discuss papers focused on how Jews, who identify as Jews, navigate the theological waters of recognizing the Messiah in Jesus/Yeshua. A paper by a prominent American Messianic Jewish theologian, Mark Kinzer, resonated strongly with me. Kinzer, who had been raised as a Conservative Jew (as I was, but in my case, we simply belonged to a Conservative synagogue—my parents never actually attended services) and came to believe in Yeshua at the age of nineteen. He remarked how astonished he felt to actually experience the presence of Yeshua in the synagogue, noting that even the name "Yeshua" would never be heard there. ("Praying the Amidah as an Extension of the Eucharist" [Helsinki Consultation, Oslo, 2013])

I also read a series of papers by the French Jewish-identified Dominican priest, Fr. Antoine Levy. In one essay, he laid out his quandary of how he as a Jew can follow the

Torah within the space of the Catholic Church. He came up with no satisfactory solution. Yet I was so moved by his eloquently argued dilemma that I decided to write to him, first to express my appreciation for his papers that were helping me clarify my own quandary, and second, to ask if he knew of any Orthodox or Catholic Jewish-identified monks. For I was hoping to develop a virtual community of like-minded Jewish-Christian monks. In late May, I wrote: "With warmth, honesty, and eloquence of expression you have articulated the conundrum that I find myself in: How can I, an Orthodox Christian monk-Jew, allow my newly acknowledged inner Jewishness to develop and nourish my daily spiritual life within a monastic community that places no value on the ongoing validity of Judaism? By pondering the salient points you make in your papers, I believe I can clarify for myself the path G-d wants me to follow." Regarding my query about other Jewish monastics, he had just one in mind—a Russian Orthodox monk of Jewish background living in a monastery in Belgium. He gave me his email address and suggested I contact him.

I wasted no time in doing so, and in my letter, I explained my current daily clandestine routine: "Early in the morning, before the community meets for *matins*, in the privacy of my cell, I put on a *tallis* and read the *sh'ma* (Dt 6:4-9, 11:13-21; Num 15:37-41). Before doing this, however, I meditate on 18 'commandments,' which are short phrases from psalm verses that I have collected, such as, 'be humble, lowly,' 'speak truth from your heart,' all of which are directed to love of God or love of neighbor/brother. In the evening, I again put on the *tallis* and after meditating on the same 18 commandments from the psalms, I read the Beatitudes and the Lord's Prayer, first in Hebrew, and then in Aramaic (transliterated using English letters)." I went on to explain how these formalities anchored me in my inner Jewishness, allowing me to be "Torah observant" in the more expansive way expressed by Yeshua especially in the Sermon on the Mount. I ended by revealing that I felt isolated being the only Jew in the community and was hoping to make a connection with one or two Jewish identified monks.

I was disappointed that he didn't respond to my letter but I didn't give up. Fr. Antoine had also given me the email address of a Jewish-born Russian Orthodox married priest living in Jerusalem, who was trying to form a community of primarily Russian Orthodox of Jewish background, synthesizing the two religious traditions. I engaged in a helpful and reassuring communication with Fr. Oleg, despite his limited English knowledge. During the weeks that followed, I became increasingly frustrated with the impossible situation of living as a Jewish-identified Orthodox Christian monk. I felt more and more isolated from the other monks because I could not share with them this pivotal self-realization. My faith in God-in-Jesus, however, was unshaken by this awakening to my Jewishness. With Fr. Oleg's encouragement and support regarding my hesitancy to break my recently taken solemn life vows, in mid-July I made the monumental decision to leave the monastery and emigrate to Israel as a member of the clergy. I would not be able actually to leave though for several months because my brother in Florida, to whom I would go to prepare for emigration to Israel, was in uncertain health and thus it wasn't a good time for me to stay there. I thus needed to be patient and carry on the best I could.

During the vigil of the feast celebrating the birth of the Theotokos (Virgin Mary) on the night of September 7th, an astounding realization would jolt me and irreversibly end my relationship to the Orthodox Church.

At around 10:45pm, I felt restless and left the church to go to the main house to get a drink of water. This had become my habit during vigils—sneaking in one last glass of water before midnight, after which no water was allowed until after diving liturgy the next morning. As I was walking up the hill, I thought the quarter moon and the brilliant panorama of stars in the dark rural landscape was especially beautiful. I sensed that this night was special, not because of the feast, but for an impalpable reason I could not articulate. I looked at the digital clock in the dining room. One more hour to go. I then counted the weeks until I could depart, expecting to be able to leave sometime in November as my brother's health seemed to be improving. As I walked back down to the church, I was going over in my mind whether I was a Messianic Jew or a Jewish Christian or a Christian Jew. I looked down at my *schema* as if expecting it to provide the answer. I realized that I liked the *idea* of wearing it more than this actual piece of monastic attire.

Shortly after 11pm, during the final hour of the vigil, a thought jolted me, shaking me to the core of my being: 'I don't believe that Mary is the mother of God. I don't believe that she gave birth virginally, and without a human male, to God.' I very nearly collapsed onto the seat on my *stasidi*—which at that moment in the service would have been inappropriate. This was immediately followed by the sickening recognition that maybe Jesus is not God Incarnate. The floor under my feet appeared to give way and I nearly fell. I held on to the arms of the *stasidi*. My heart started racing, the lit chandelier got so bright that I thought I would be blinded by it. I took a few deep breaths. Panic was rising. For a few moments I didn't know where I was nor who I was. I looked at the monks in the church and wondered who they were. The church, the icons, all seemed so strange at this moment, as if I was seeing them for the first time and wondering how I had got to this place. I continued to take slow, gentle breaths, in and out, and gradually I calmed down.

I was finally able to sit for a few minutes and thought, 'I am not really a Christian after all.' I clearly realized that I was not like the other monks I had been living with, praying with, working with, eating with for eight years. The calm after the storm set in. I listened to the chanters. The vigil was coming to an end. I panicked when I considered that I would need to receive communion the next morning. For I had never missed receiving communion and if I didn't, especially on such a major feast, I would need to have a valid reason. I didn't want to lie and say that I was ill. I would have to find a way to receive communion without being disrespectful to the holy sacrament even if I didn't believe in it. I would need to carry on as before—at least for appearance sake—venerating the icons, kissing Fr. James's hand for a blessing. I was startled to see Fr. Maximos, the choir master, standing next to me. He reminded me that I had to read the psalms of the first hour, which was done at the end of the vigil. I excused myself, saying I had drifted off.

The vigil ended. After venerating the icons, I left the church and walked up the hill alone. The mild air was very refreshing. I gazed up at the clear sky and just smiled. I perceived that a heavy weight had been lifted from me. My steps were light and effortless. I felt different. Nothing—the house, my room—nothing looked or felt as it did four hours ago. I gladly shut the door to my cell and sat down on the bed. I didn't look at the icons on the wall. I avoided the piercing eyes of Jesus in the Pantocrator icon, an icon that I had treasured and prayed in front of for the last eight years. I didn't look at those eyes that seemed to follow the viewer wherever he stood as in a good portrait painting. As I took off the hat, veil, *schema* and my other robes, I felt I was stripping away my Orthodox monastic life. I would, of course, need to put them all on the next day, but wearing them would henceforth be like a theatrical costume. I would be playing the role of an Orthodox Christian monk who maintained a secret that could never be revealed to the community. When the time came to inform Fr. James, I would need to be discreet and not completely honest.

The next morning, I still felt different, but calmer. I put on my *tallis* as I read the prayers to be recited while putting on the *tallis*. I proceeded to the opening *sh'ma* blessing and the three passages that followed, standing at my desk and looking up at the icon of Jesus with the intense non-symmetrical eyes, my beloved ancient Pantocrator icon from St. Catherine's Monastery in the Sinai Desert. I gazed at the gently smiling friendly eye and the cold, judgmental eye. I just looked at him. I had no words. I thanked him and bowed my head. Although my faith that he actually was God had evaporated, I perceived God's presence through the icon. For I had prayed in front of it for eight years. I asked the face that would not take its eyes off of me: 'What am I to do now?' No answer was forthcoming and I put on all my monastic attire and prepared to go down to the church for divine liturgy.

Once in the church, I did what I had been doing before every festal divine liturgy. After venerating all the icons, I took off my hat and veil and went through the door that led into the sacred altar. I performed three prostrations, walked over to Fr. James, kissed his hand and requested his blessing to receive communion. And then I walked back to the side area and picked up a thick packet of lists of names to be commemorated. During all of this, I had the distinct feeling that I was dreaming. Nothing seemed real.

As we began the actual communion service, I discerned a sickening wave of panic rising. I focused on breathing gently in and out, in and out, and gradually peace arose in my heart. But a few moments later, when I had let down my guard, the panic returned. Fear took hold of me. I thought 'Where am I? What am I doing here?' The lights got blindingly bright, my cheeks were burning and my heart was palpitating. With all the mental strength I could summon, I focused on my breath—long, gentle inhalations and exhalations. After a few minutes, again calm descended. I felt exhausted and sat down on the folding seat. I then walked up to the reader's stand and read the pre-communion prayers, not paying attention to the words. Somehow the words had a calming effect on me. A disquieting nervousness arose in my mind as the time approached for me to receive communion. I wished I hadn't requested the blessing to receive it. But there was no turning back now. I would have to go through it. I assured myself that it was not a sin to receive it in my present faith-less mind. I had no intention to insult the sanctity of the holy sacrament I would be receiving in my mouth. I forcefully turned my attention inward and addressed whatever it was that was causing these panic attacks. Internally, I said 'I am not afraid.' I knew in the deepest region of my heart that God existed in this church and was with me. I slowly walked up to where Fr. James was standing holding the chalice, reciting to myself 'God is One.' He put a spoonful of the body and blood of

Christ into my mouth. In that instant I felt that I was receiving the essence of God—as a Jew.

After the service and the festive meal, I was able finally to spend some time alone. I was aware that something irreversible had occurred the night before. And the church, the monastery, the icons, the monks—nothing was as it was before. I knew it would be extremely difficult to remain in the monastery, acting as though nothing had transpired, and merely go along with life as usual. I had to leave as soon as possible. But there were formidable obstacles. I had no money or debit card, having surrendered all my assets to the monastery prior to being clothed in the *schema*. My monthly social security was now going into the new joint account I had set up with Fr. James. How would I leave and where would I go? I wrote a frantic email to my cousin in New York asking if I could come there until my brother was ready to receive me in Florida. I thought I would take as many precautions when flying so I wouldn't be a health risk. My cousin informed me that there was currently a quarantine imposed and no one could enter New York without first sheltering for two weeks. I thus had no option but to wait it out for the next few months.

Since I now considered myself as a Jew, and not a Jewish Christian or Messianic Jew, I would seek to enter Israel by means of the "Right of Return," whereby any Jew could receive Israeli citizenship. My full awakening to my Jewishness led to a breakdown in my communication with Fr. Oleg. Being a priest in the Orthodox Church, he was much more Christian than Jew. I turned my attention to exploring Chabad, a widely known network of progressive Hasidic communities, expecting there to be many local chapters in Jerusalem. I thought that among one of these communities

I would find help in getting settled.

In November I got the green light from my brother that I could come to Florida and stay with him and his wife while I did all the administrative work necessary for entering Israel under the "Right of Return" program. I devised a plan for obtaining a debit card so that I would be able to rent a car. My brother and I agreed that flying was still a health risk at that time. I now dreaded the inevitable conversation I would have with Fr. James. I thought I would give one week's notice so that I could train the next candle-maker, even though business was still very slow.

The day arrived and having made an appointment to speak with him outside of the weekly confession, I walked into his office. I was sure that he expected I would be talking to him about something of importance and urgency because I had only twice before requested a special meeting—and that was to inform him of the passing of each of my parents and my request to attend the funeral. I had intended to soften the blow by being not completely truthful. I would be expressing my situation as it was prior to the extraordinary revelation on the night of September 7th. As I dropped my bombshell, Fr. James turned white and just looked at me. He said he was shaking inside by what I had just told him. I felt truly sorry that I had caused him such grief and tried to soften the blow by highlighting that my faith in Jesus was unshaken and I would seek out a Messianic Jewish community in Israel. This seemed to defuse somewhat the stunning news I had imparted to him. Fr. James said that I should not read in the church or at table and that he would tell the community that I had a sore throat and had difficulty speaking. I didn't really understand why I wouldn't be permitted to read what was almost entirely psalms from the Old Testament and non-scriptural texts at table, but I certainly didn't want to object. I left thinking that it went better than I had expected.

Later that afternoon, however, he called me into his office and informed me that he had spoken to the bishop who ordered me to leave the monastery immediately. After recovering from the shock of hearing that, I said that it was impossible for me to leave that quickly. For I still had to pick up my new debit card and pay for the rental car twenty-four hours in advance. I told him the earliest I could leave would be on the day following the next. After he offered to simply give me cash to rent a car, I told him that rental car agencies did not accept cash payments. He thus had no choice but allow me to stay two more days. Almost as an afterthought, he said that it was best for me not to come to the church at all but I should continue to wear my cassock and eat at the table with the monks because, while he was obliged to tell the monks about me, he was not going to tell the novices. I was basically not to do anything, not even assist in the after-meal clean-up.

Every evening, after the *compline* service, which was recited in the dining room after the meal, all the monks and novices would venerate the icon of the Theotokos and then kiss Fr. James's hand to receive the nighttime blessing. On that evening, I followed the other monks as usual and thought in respect for the formality I would kiss his hand, but when I attempted to do so, he yanked it away with what I interpreted to be a "knee-jerk" reaction. I didn't look at him but simply bowed my head slightly and walked away.

I was relieved when the day of my departure arrived. Fr. Cyprian, who was the first monk I had encountered at the monastery on the day I arrived for my visit, was assigned to drive me to the Columbus airport where I would pick up my rental car. Just before I left my cell for the last time, I took off the hand-carved crucifix I had purchased on Mt. Athos and placed it on a shelf that had artifacts from the *schema*-clothing ceremony. When I got to the car, I took off my cassock and handed it to Fr. James who was standing by waiting for me. He then said, nearly in tears, that he felt we—meaning he—had failed me. I assured him that he hadn't and that I took full responsibility for my action. And then we drove off.

CHAPTER 11

Lay-Life Interlude

Heading along the interstate, I cried out in elation, 'I'm free!' I had not experienced such a profound release of tension in many years. I then thought about the monastic brotherhood with whom I had shared so many hours during the past eight years and I realized that I held no negative feelings towards my brother monks, nor towards Fr. James. Neither did I harbor resentment towards the bishop who hastened my exit. For I realized that he was merely following protocol. I had broken communion with the Orthodox monastic community and thus was *persona non grata*. Now that I was driving further and further from the monastery, I had gained some mental distance as well. I thought about the *schema* monks I had left behind and respected their full-hearted dedication to the spiritual path they had chosen to walk. Each of them had lived at least fifteen years already as monks and I never detected any wavering in their commitment. I, on the other hand, was still drifting along a non-linear path, the goal of which was still in flux. I hoped in the freedom I would enjoy as a lay person, I would be able to clarify my goal within the framework of Judaism.

By the time I had reached my brother's house in south Florida late the next day, St. Gregory Palamas Monastery seemed a distant memory and I didn't think about it at all as I became completely occupied in planning my emigration to Israel. Just a few days after arriving in Florida, I went to a hair salon and had my very long hair cut. I decided to keep the beard though. During those initial weeks, I focused on the crucial task of proving that I was, in fact, Jewish. What made it very difficult was that I did not belong to a synagogue and thus did not have a connection with a rabbi who would attest in a sworn statement that I was Jewish. But before I could do that, I thought I had better establish a daily prayer life in the Jewish Orthodox tradition. I immediately ordered a *tallis* of the proper size, for the one I had been using was rather small and I couldn't wear it the way Orthodox men did. I also ordered *tefillin*—that strange leather strap that I had occasionally seen ultra-Orthodox Jews and Hasidim in New York wear. Most prominent was the small box containing special verses from the Torah which was worn on the forehead. Both items would be arriving from Israel and I would need to wait a few weeks. Meanwhile, I began a morning prayer ritual, setting up a folding table in the room I was occupying. I followed an Orthodox prayer book that had English translation directly under the transliterated Hebrew so I could gradually become accustomed to the sound of the prayers in the original Hebrew. I also adopted the practice of wearing a *yarmulke* all the time. My brother and sister-in-law were very impressed with my new Jewish look, which they obviously preferred to my Greek Orthodox appearance.

I continued to do extensive research, finding out about different Chabad communities in Jerusalem. But after reviewing how much monthly income I would have from social security and seeing how much even just a rented furnished room would cost, I decided to put my focus on Tzvat (Safed), the small city in the extreme north of Israel where mystical Judaism developed in the 16th century and which still had a new-age, mystical atmosphere, so I read. It seemed an ideal place for me to live not only because it would be much less expensive than Jerusalem, but also I would, I thought, more easily connect with a diverse, international population of mystically-minded people. I was very excited about this prospect.

Once my *tallis* and *tefillin* had arrived, I struggled to learn how to wear them. I watched YouTube videos and tried to imitate the person in the video. The first time I managed to put both on correctly, I felt empowered by this ancient Jewish custom. I stood in front of the little makeshift prayer table, draped in my full-length *tallis*, the *tefillin* strapped around my arm and forehead, and began the morning prayers. I performed this ritual early every morning, never skipping a day. Besides the passages of the *sh'ma*, a highlight was the *Amidah*, the great eighteen-verse prayer that was expressed standing. I would often pause at the second stanza:

> You, O Lord, are mighty forever, you revive the dead, you have the power to save. You sustain the living with loving kindness, you revive the dead with great mercy, you support the falling, heal the sick, set free the bound and keep faith with those who sleep in the dust. Who is like you, O doer of mighty acts? (https://www.amiyisrael.org/)

I was struck at the awesome, magnificent power of God, in particular, raising the dead and maintaining benevolent contact with those "who slept in the dust." This quintessential Jewish prayer seemed so un-Jewish. For I had never come upon a direct reference to life after death in Judaism. But I welcomed this anomaly, especially after the years I had spent within Christianity. I didn't try to reason it away, but rather would stand in silent awe before this unfathomable divine presence.

However, I felt little or no connection to most of the words I was reading during my self-led morning prayer service, even though they were in English. As I took off the *tallis* and *tefillin*, packing them away carefully, I nevertheless felt optimistic that I would warm up to the prayers over time, especially when praying with a congregation. After another two weeks, I thought it was time for me to actually attend a morning service at a Chabad synagogue. It felt very strange walking in as I realized that it had been at least twenty years since I had set foot in any synagogue. I stayed in the back and watched what the other men were doing, how they put on their *tallis* and *tefillin*. It was also very uncomfortable wearing a mask during the service, which periodically fogged up my glasses so I had difficulty reading. But, I was lost in the service and reading wasn't very helpful anyway. I had never attended an Orthodox service and it was not at all like the services I remembered at the Conservative synagogue of my youth. The worshippers here did not chant in unison, each one prayed on his own in a low mumble. I couldn't even recognize the key moment in the service when the *sh'ma* was recited. I felt frustrated and wondered if I would ever manage to participate in the service. Before leaving at the end of the service, I caught the attention of the rabbi and asked if I could make an appointment to speak with him. We set a time for the next day.

I brought all the documentation I could come up with: An invitation to my bar mitzvah, photograph album from the occasion, and my birth certificate. The rabbi was very friendly and supported my plan to move to Israel but he needed further documentation, especially concerning the Jewishness of my mother. The best I could offer was a photograph which I hoped to obtain of my maternal grandmother's grave. For, unlike my mother, she was buried in a Jewish cemetery—actually a famous one in Queens. It would, however, take about a month before I received it. And during that time of waiting, as the idea that I was really going to move to Israel sunk into my mind, I began to waver. After extensively researching and estimating how much income I would need to live in Tzvat, I realized that I would barely have enough to live even an austere simple life. In addition, and what really hit me, was that I would be completely alone there. I knew no one in Israel and I would need to have some workable knowledge of modern Hebrew, since I couldn't expect everyone to speak English, and I would need to be able to communicate and understand the spoken language in order to get settled and carry out basic tasks of daily life. One day, sitting at my desk, having spent the last several hours trying to learn some modern Hebrew vocabulary, I realized that at my current age of 67, I did not have the same adventurous spirit I would have had even ten years before. I felt my whole plan to emigrate to Israel collapse.

Sensing my hesitation to go to Israel, my sister-in-law spoke to my brother, who offered to purchase a small apartment for me in a senior condominium in Florida.

When planning my departure from St. Gregory Palamas Monastery, I never imagined that I would end up living in a retirement community! However, I was grateful for the offer and I accepted it. I thought I would find a way to lead a spiritually-fulfilling life in Florida.

By the time I moved into my apartment in late February, three months after my arrival in Florida, I had given up on traditional Jewish Orthodoxy. It became clear that because I had no foundation in this tradition, I could not find a way to connect. It seemed almost like a foreign religion. I searched for alternatives. I discovered that there was a local group in Florida connected to the Jewish renewal movement. Because of the ongoing pandemic, all activities and classes were via Zoom. I attended a Zoom Passover seder, and while I didn't find it a particularly spiritual experience, it was nice to connect with people. I also viewed some classes where a very articulate rabbi offered innovative kabbalistic interpretations of biblical texts. Yet, I longed for something more experiential, participating in a form of prayerful worship that would lead me closer to God.

I then came upon the Aquarian Minyan. A renewal congregation based in Berkeley, founded by the charismatic rabbi known as Reb Zalman, who after leaving Chabad, became affiliated with the hippie drug culture of the late 1960s. He was now deceased but his legacy lived on in this eclectic group that, thanks to Zoom, would gather from around the U.S. for Friday evening services. I tuned in every Friday for several weeks and found their free-spirited approach refreshing. There was some musical accompaniment, and the prayers were mostly in English, with some original ones added. I also liked that sections of the service were led by different people. But something still was not clicking and, by early June, I was aware of feeling that I had not yet found the right spiritual practice.

On one of my daily walks around the perimeter of the large community, I pondered what wasn't working for me in Judaism. The prayers, even the more personalized ones of the Aquarian Minyan, did not resonate in my inner being. I did not feel in my heart the words I would chant along. Moreover, I couldn't embrace Torah observance, especially what was expected of an "observant" Jew. As I delved deeper, I tried to articulate to myself how I viewed God and if in fact I believed in Him as a Jew. While I continued to walk in inner stillness, having stopped the interior monologue, I waited for some inkling to arise from the innermost depths of my heart. I walked and waited. Nothing arose. And I took that to mean that the goal of my spiritual life was not to be realized in a theistic tradition.

Pondering further, I came to understand that the awakening to my Jewish roots was a necessary but only temporary sojourn on my journey. Becoming cognizant of my Jewish roots restored the inner foundation upon which my spiritual journey rested, a foundation that had been badly shaken by the startling discovery that my faith in the key principles of Christianity was not solid. Although my efforts to embrace Judaism as a spiritual path ultimately failed, by recognizing how my formative years were shaped in a Jewish familial and cultural environment, I knew it was unwise—and not possible—to dismiss and discard my heritage.

I don't recall what prompted my search, but I stumbled upon an essay by the internationally-known, Jewish-born

Buddhist monk, Bhikkhu Bodhi on why rebirth is necessary for Buddhism. Reading his intelligent, highly articulate argument, I not only accepted it, but as a result, I opted to purchase two books by him—one a concise explanation of the Noble Eight-fold Path and the other a collection of essays that had been published over a period of twenty years while he was director of the Buddhist Publication Society in Sri Lanka. In the weeks that followed, it was as if someone had opened a door for me and I found myself on a slide that effortless landed me on Buddhist ground. I imbibed the basic Buddhist concepts as if I had finally discovered the perfect drink to quench my thirst.

My bedroom, which contained not only my bed but also a desk, some books, and meditation cushion, became my monastic-like cell. I once again took up a daily meditation practice. Except when eating, I spent most of my time in that room, never using the living room in the apartment. Towards the end of the summer, I received word from one of the universities in the area I had applied to in search of a part-time instructor position. I was offered the possibility of teaching two academic writing courses that Fall semester. I wasn't particularly motivated to teach again, but financially it was necessary. But about halfway through the semester, I sensed that I did not want to take up that life again. Moreover, living as a lay person in an adult community, commuting a few days a week in awful traffic, I felt like a fish out of water. Having spent most of the previous thirteen years in monasteries, I knew that I had to find my way back to one—a Buddhist monastery. For even living in a monastery as a lay resident would be preferable to living in the "world."

I considered my limited options and thought I would contact the Bhavana Society Monastery in West Virgina, the residence of Bhante Gunaratana, and the place where I had taken life-time precepts more than twenty years before. They encouraged long-term residents to live there at no cost in exchange for helping with the necessary daily tasks at the monastery. And residents had plenty of time for meditation and study while living in a beautiful and peaceful environment. After being interviewed by the office manager and the acting abbot, my application for residency was accepted. I would head up there in December for an initial period of eight months. I very much looked forward to living in an environment where I could further develop my renewed Buddhist meditation practice and, I hoped, live in a mutually supportive atmosphere with the other lay residents. I also expected that living with monks again would be as natural for me as walking.

I took up residency at Bhavana Society on a cold winter day in late December, 2021. Although I needed to adjust to the wintery weather after spending the last year in Florida, I was very happy to be there. Entering the perfect stillness of the meditation hall early on my first morning, I knew I had done the right thing in coming to Bhavana. I effortlessly acclimated to the daily schedule at the monastery and established a disciplined way to use my free time. I soon joined a Pali class with another resident that was offered by one of the Sri Lankan monks in residence. I had forgotten much of the Pali grammar I had learned twelve years earlier at Chithurst, but was pleased to see how quickly I was able to pick it up again. I also studied a variety of modern Western interpretations and commentaries of key Buddhist concepts and, in some ways, I was discovering Buddhism for the first time. My mind was open to becoming more fluent in the practical wisdom of the early teachings. I didn't recall very much of what I had read by the teachers, both Thai and Western, of the Forest Tradition while a monk in England. Now, I broadened my scope and read works by a variety of Theravada monastic teachers as well as the suttas upon which the teachings were based.

In the middle of March, as I was taking one of my daily afternoon walks along the country road that passed in front of the monastery, I considered whether I wanted to seek re-ordination. After nearly three months at Bhavana, I felt more in tune with the monks than with the lay residents; for I alone among them felt that being a monk was the best way to make use of one's life. Renunciation of worldly life was not a hardship for me. There was nothing "out there" that attracted me. I wanted to live in a residential community where outside distractions were limited and where I was afforded the living conditions most conducive for training the mind, weakening the defilements that hindered me from attaining any experiential depth of understanding of the Buddha's teachings. I didn't feel that I had used the opportunities I had been given in my former Buddhist monastic life and developed the wish to try it again. However, later in the day, as I thought about my prospects for ordaining, I realized they were very slim. My advanced age of 68 disqualified me from ordaining at any Western monastery with which I was familiar. I thought I might possibly have a chance in Asia, particularly Sri Lanka or Burma, but I didn't feel a burning desire to go half-way around the world. I was also concerned about the living conditions there. Thus, I let the thought simmer for a while.

In early April, Bhavana officially re-opened to the public and offered a weekend retreat focused on *metta* or loving kindness. I got into a conversation with a serious young man who was planning to go to an international training monastery in Malaysia to ordain as a monk. I thus learned about the Sasanarakkha Buddhist Sanctuary, Monk Training Centre. After carefully reviewing the wealth of information on their website, especially about the monk training program, I became very interested in exploring the possibility of joining the program. I decided, however, to sit with the idea for a few weeks before taking any action. I thought about the advantages and disadvantages of going to Malaysia, with the expectation of remaining there for at least five years after ordination. Research indicated that the standard of living there as well as the general infrastructure was much better than in other countries in Southeast Asia. But I feared it would be difficult for someone my age to adjust to the tropical climate. I thought back to my days at Chithurst Monastery in England, and how I did not find living in a *kuti* (small hut) in the forest conducive for my spiritual practice. And that was in a climate with which I was familiar. I wavered back and forth for two weeks before I made a decision to at least contact the Austrian abbot, Bhante Ariyadhammika, and see how he would respond to my query.

In the letter, I gave a very brief overview of my monastic history, including the years at the Greek Orthodox monastery, and was honest about my age. In his reply, Bhante Ariyadhammika warmly welcomed me to come and try it out. He rightly pointed out that I myself would need to see if I could handle the all-year-round heat and humidity. I made the decision to go there and see how it worked out.

As the months passed, I generated increasing excitement and anticipation about making this enormous move to Malaysia. As I had committed myself to staying at Bhavana for eight months, I thought it right to wait until August to go. But my impatience got the better of me, and I elected to go at the end of July. In the meantime I purchased far too many things to take with me—all that I thought I might need to survive in the tropical environment. And so fitting everything into my two suitcases was an ordeal. But, at last, my departure date arrived. I was touched by the farewell card I was given, with kind messages from Bhante G and the other monks as well as from all the lay residents. I was optimistic that with all those good wishes, everything would work out for me and I went with the expectation of remaining, perhaps indefinitely, in Malaysia.

CHAPTER 12

A Buddhist Monk (Again)

As Lenny, the monastery steward, was driving up the steep slope in a four-wheel-drive jeep, periodically backing up in order to make the extreme hairpin turns, I became anxious about the daily alms round on what I expected to be a steep walking path. I knew that in the early morning the monks and lay residents walked down into town to the Taiping Insight Meditation Center to collect food for their one daily meal. And then they had to walk back up. I had learned from the website that the walk generally took at least 30 minutes in each direction. I wasn't able to detect the elevation from google earth, but it was clear that the monastery was located on a steep forested slope. Our arrival at the monastery ended my musings and fears.

The guest monk, Bhante Khema, from the Czech Republic, warmly welcomed me to SBS and proceeded to give me a tour of the central monastic area. He then, with the offered assistance of an American monk, wheeled my two suitcases to my *kuti* which was not more than a five minute walk away. I then saw the flight of stairs—at least 30—that led up to my new home. It was nicer than I expected, with a fan, and there was a sink outside. The nearest toilet was down the stairs, followed by additional stairs. I quickly saw that the monastery was not only on top of a forested slope, but was actually built directly *into* that slope. The only flat place was the monastic central area with the library, Dhamma hall, classroom and offices. The octagonal meditation hall situated in the middle of a pond was on a slightly lower level. The two monks left me to settle in and I stood outside my *kuti* and just took in the beautiful tropical landscape. I had a fine view of the hills in the distance and could see across the cascading stream to another forested slope. The monkeys in the trees startled me but I came to enjoy watching their antics in the trees, especially how they leaped from branch to branch, never missing. I marveled that I was actually in Malaysia!

I had a very pleasant initial meeting with Bhante Ariya (I learned that the monks used a shortened version of their names). I knew from the photos that the monks walked down for alms every day barefoot. I indicated that I would not be able to manage that. But Bhante Ariya assured me I would gradually adjust to it and that I should just try to walk part of the way barefoot at first. I said I would give it a try.

That next morning, I lined up behind the monks and the white-clad ten-precept "postulants" for my first walk down the hill. I soon saw that the initial part would be going down stone steps, at least 200, if not more. It was quite beautiful and peaceful, hearing the roaring stream running through the gorge below our path. We then crossed through a small Burmese *vihara*, where I learned one of the SBS monks, a Burmese, dwelled. And then the path was paved, but very steep, as it led one in the final descent through an enormous Chinese cemetery. I was amazed that all the monks and the postulants were walking barefoot on this hard rough ground. I knew I would never be able to do it. Just wearing sandals, I found the going strenuous. When we came to the old part of the cemetery, I recalled Bhante Ariya saying that I should try walking barefoot from that point. I saw a grassy area and assumed it would be like that the rest of the way. And so I left my sandals and began walking barefoot. Not long afterwards, I regretted what I had done. The path became very rough and I was distraught to see that we still had quite a distance to walk. I naturally fell behind. When I had thought the worst was over, we came out of the cemetery and walked across a paved area not only covered in hard-edged stones but it was strewn with garbage and even some broken glass. I walked so slowly and carefully that the others were very far in front. The last postulant stopped and turning back towards me, waved me to catch up, as if it was under my control and I had been dawdling to enjoy the landscape! I nevertheless took my time and was elated when I came to the final stretch. I wondered how I would make it back to the place where I had left my sandals. I felt at that instant that I would never be able to stay at SBS and that I should just give up and return to the U.S.

Needless to say, I did not take off my sandals on subsequent walks down and back. I found the walk itself arduous, especially the long steep hike up as the already hot sun was burning my face and wearying me as I trudged up the treeless stretch up to the forest, carrying a heavy shoulder bag containing my food for the day. I knew that the walk down and back was supposed to be a form of meditation—one was expected to maintain silence—but I was preoccupied with the physical exertion and my mind was far from silent and peaceful.

As the weeks passed, which were difficult to note because neither the weather nor the length of daylight altered very much, I gradually acclimated to life at SBS. The community, especially the postulants and the few other laymen in residence, were very friendly. I wasn't surprised to find that I was far older than everyone else, even Bhante Ariya. However, I did my best to keep up with them, but didn't push myself too hard. And I was grateful that no one expected me to.

Although my concentration had been slowly improving during my time at Bhavana Society, in the rugged tropical environment I had great difficulty quieting my mind. I didn't find the heat as unbearable as I had feared, and was delighted that the early mornings were refreshingly cool (in the low 70s). But the humidity was relentless. It was difficult for anything to dry, and clothing, towel, everything in the *kuti*, even with the fan, had a mildewy smell. I found myself tired during the day, probably because I didn't sleep well, having to get up several times during the night because I drank so much water during the day and evening to make sure I wasn't dehydrated. During group meditation at 5am, I was not able to focus well and I often couldn't stop yawning during the 40 minutes of chanting that followed the meditation period. But I generally found the daily *sutta* (scripture) classes very beneficial and especially liked that Bhante Ariya read the *sutta* passages aloud. Monastics would then offer comments or ask questions about the particular passage. Although I had difficulty hearing some of the monks, and thus didn't always catch the comment being expressed, I was able at least to hear the *sutta* passages because Bhante Ariya wore a microphone.

Despite the struggles I had with the climate and topography, I was glad I had come, and when I requested to become a postulant after just one month there, Bhante Ariya agreed. For he was aware that being 68—and the fact that I had been previously a Buddhist monk—I didn't want to wait too long before putting on the monastic robes. On September 10, 2022, in a short ceremony that was performed in Bhante Ariya's office, I became a ten-precept postulant and with freshly shaven head donned white robes, which were comparable in style but not in detail to those of a bhikkhu. I would also use an alms bowl, which I would carry down every day, similar to that of the monks except mine was of heavy ceramic material rather than lighter metal.

I was very happy to be in robes again, even though they were white, a color I had never worn since I had not been an eight-precept *anagarika* when at Chithurst Monastery, but rather a Tibetan novice monk. On the evening of my first day, Bhante Sumana, a lovely Sri Lankan monk, second in seniority, pointed out that my leg was bleeding. I looked down and blood was pouring down my leg and staining my white robe. I rushed into the toilet and tried to wash the blood off before it dried. And thus, I was introduced to leech bites, of which I would, like everyone else, have many during my time at SBS. They always tended to be a surprise, because one was not aware of being bitten. It is the blood that indicated that a leech, generally already dislodged, had had a drink.

During those initial weeks of being a postulant, I gradually became accustomed to leeches, always carrying band-aids in the monastic pouch I wore, but I continued to struggle putting on the upper robe so that it would stay on during the long hike down and back up with the alms bowl strapped around me. However, eventually, I was relaxed enough, and confident that the robe would not fall down, that I even tried to do walking meditation, or at least focus my awareness on the movement of my feet, as I walked down. I began getting a head start, as some of the others did as well, so that I could take my time walking. We all met at a certain spot in the old cemetery and from there walked in single file, in order of seniority, for the rest of the way.

In November, my work task was changed, from sweeping paths under the hot midday sun, to being appointed the monastery librarian, which also included maintaining the cleanliness of the library. As it was the one building, besides the meditation hall, that had air-conditioning, at least during part of the day, I was delighted with the change. I generally spent several hours a day there anyway, mostly assisting the Pali instructor by preparing the answer key for the beginner's course. This involved providing a word-by-word grammatical analysis and close translation of passages mainly from the *suttas*.

By January, I and two other postulants, began sewing our robes and learning the chants for the bhikkhu ordination that would occur in the second week of February. Despite having sewed all three robes for my initial bhikkhu ordination at Amaravati Monastery in England twelve years before, I had great difficulty sewing just the lower robe. That was mainly because at SBS we had to do it the traditional way of cutting individual pieces of material—at least thirty of different sizes—and then sewing them on according to the prescribed pattern. Increasingly frustrated not only with my lack of skill using a very high-powered sewing machine, but also because I could not wrap my mind around the sequence of steps to put together a complete robe from so many different pieces. To my great relief, Bhante Siya, a young German monk, came to my rescue, guiding me through each step. And I was then able to complete the robe in just a week. Having compassion for my plight, Bhante Ariya allowed me to just sew the lower robe. Normally a candidate for bhikkhu ordination was expected to sew the upper robe as well.

The two other monastic candidates and I diligently practiced the correct pronunciation of the Pali chants for several weeks. Then after performing them for Bhante Ariya, we were informed that we were ready for the ordination ceremony. On February 11, 2023, the torrential tropical downpour ceasing moments before the ceremony was to begin, the three of us became full members of the community of Buddhist monks, the lineage of which extended back 2500 years. I was grateful to Bhante Ariya and the monks at SBS who had voted in favor of my ordination in spite of my advanced age. I was now Bhikkhu Nyanadhammika. I reckoned that my name, meaning "one with the quality of knowledge," would provide me with a potent daily inspiration to follow in the footsteps of many revered monks of the present and previous century with the name "Nyana" (knowledge). It felt natural to be wearing the deep gold robes of a monk in the Theravada Forest tradition. I hoped that having taken this step and having acclimated to monastic life in Malaysia, I would have a peaceful mind and thus better inclined to deepen my experiential knowledge of the Buddha's teachings.

Any progress I was beginning to make in strengthening my concentration when practicing Mindfulness of Breathing meditation, was disrupted by two events that occurred in March. On a special occasion when we received our food from the SBS Lay Retreat Center, located about 400 feet in elevation above the Monk Training Centre, as I was walking down the many stairs with my alms bowl around my neck,

I slipped on a wet stair and tumbled down the remaining six stairs. Miraculously I didn't break any bones but my ribs were badly bruised in addition to cuts and scrapes on my legs and hands. The shock of the fall had a deep effect on me. During the weeks it took to heal, and experiencing great pain just getting onto my mattress on the floor of my *kuti*, I began to view SBS with different eyes. I sensed danger in the rugged topography that I had to negotiate daily. I was fearful to walk down stairs and had to summon all my mental strength to stop my knees from shaking as I slowly walked down them.

Just when I was getting back to normal, but still nervous about the stairs, especially after rain, I came down with a strange case of diarrhea. It didn't seem like a normal upset stomach for it lingered on and off for several days and I had no appetite to eat. Feeling increasingly weak, I requested that our steward, Lenny, make an appointment with a physician. As it was Friday, I would have to wait until Monday. But then, Saturday evening as I was getting up from a chair in the library, I collapsed and briefly passed out. Naturally, the monks who aided me, and Bhante Ariya, who was immediately informed, were alarmed and said I would be taken to the hospital the next morning, since it was already late evening. The next day, I was driven to the emergency room, since it was a Sunday. After a preliminary examination and blood test, the physician on call diagnosed that I had *leptospirosis*—a serious bacterial infection, contracted from rat urine, that was fairly rare in humans. I was henceforth admitted into the hospital for immediate treatment.

Perhaps because I was so weak, I took the prognosis and immediate admission into the hospital very calmly. I allowed everything to take its course. Wearing monastic robes in a hospital bed was certainly a challenge I had never expected to have. And having different tubes inserted into me with a drip that would be ongoing during my four-day stay would have been easier to deal with in lay clothes. I soon took off the upper robe and covered my upper body with a blanket. I had just one book with me, the *Dhammapada*. The brief passages of profound poetry were just the right kind of reading material. I only read a few passages at a time. I mostly just lay in bed and thought about the turn of events. In such a short time, and so soon after the ordination, I experienced two formidable blows that seriously weakened by physical well-being. And during those many, long hours in the hospital, the first seeds of a thought to leave Malaysia and return to the U.S. were planted.

After being discharged and spending a week convalescing at the meditation center in Taiping where we received our daily alms, I returned to SBS. Upon Bhante Ariya's recommendation, I immediately moved into one of the few *kutis* that did not have stairs leading up to them. I continued to feel weak for some time and was permitted to ride with Lenny in the car down and back up every day. I pushed myself to try to start walking at first up, and then down, using a sturdy staff for support. But my medical problems were not over yet. One of my routine follow-up exams revealed that I was very anemic. And so, I had an endoscopy which revealed I had developed several stomach ulcers. In addition, I was continuously plagued by swelling in my ankles and insteps which made walking down stairs difficult. All of these factors together led to my decision to make a "rejuvenation" trip to the U.S. I felt that on home soil in a climate that I was accustomed to, my health would thrive again.

I had intended to just stay until after the Rains Retreat and then return to Malaysia. I investigated possible options for my U.S. monastic residence and chose the Sitagu Buddha Vihara, a Burmese monastery in Austin, Texas. I wrote to Bhikkhu Cintita, an American monk who resided there, and explained my situation. Since he had relocated to a branch monastery in Minnesota, I thought I would go there instead, as I looked forward to having contact with another American monk.

And thus in mid-June, I departed SBS and Malaysia. As I began the 24-hour journey, I reflected on the unexpected circumstances that had arisen leading to my departure. After my fall down the stairs, I had already begun to consider that I would not be able to remain in Malaysia for the traditional five years of training with one's teacher/preceptor for newly ordained bhikkhus. But, I was determined to do my best to persevere as long as possible. I never imagined that my time there would end so soon. The past three months had made a shambles of my efforts to concentrate in meditation. But, I did, however, manage to maintain a strong focus on the work I continued to do for the intermediate Pali course at SBS. I also read and took copious notes on books dealing with meditation practice as well as key Buddhist concepts, such as non-self and rebirth. I felt optimistic and excited about my return to the U.S. and knew, instinctively, that my monastic journey would progress smoothly.

After spending two weeks at Bhavana Society Monastery, attending a monastic study retreat, I headed north to Minnesota. The small vihara in rural Minnesota was as different from SBS as was possible. Here there were no *kutis*, for the small community of monks lived in one of two residential buildings. The beautiful Burmese pagoda had nothing in common with the small octagonal meditation hall at SBS. And there were no hills, no outdoor stairs to walk up and down, and no leeches. The summer weather, despite a few hot days, was pleasant and I began a daily procedure of taking long walks twice a day. In a very short time, I felt as energetic and healthy as I had before I went to Malaysia. I knew that it was clearly the right move to return to the U.S.

After just a few weeks in Minnesota, I felt a strong urge to finally write an autobiographical narrative of my spiritual journey. While in Malaysia, I told an abridged version of it on at least five occasions to both monks and laymen who, having heard that I had walked an unusual path that landed me eventually at SBS, were very interested to learn about it. Their reactions all indicated that I should write about it. Now, with the time and peace of mind to engage in such an arduous writing project, I was highly motivated and eager to do it. I thought it might clarify to myself some aspects of my journey that I still did not fully comprehend.

One remarkable thing occurred as a result of writing the narrative of my journey. When I reached the four-year period that I spent diligently practicing in the Tibetan Buddhist tradition, I called to mind the teachings and practices I had done. And in the process of recalling and attempting to articulate them, and thus, in a sense, relive them, I sensed a strong positive force arise from within. Although the tantric practices I engaged in at that time still did not appeal to me, I developed the urge to reread *The Way of the Bodhisattva* by the 8th century Indian monastic sage, Shantideva. And doing so, it resonated with me far more strongly than it did more than 15 years before. I felt tremendously inspired by the spiritually heroic *bodhisattva*, which in Mahayana Buddhism refers to one who has generated the spontaneous wish to attain enlightenment for the benefit of all sentient beings and is committed to following this path for innumerable lifetimes. Having gained in recent years a much greater familiarity with the Pali *suttas*, the foundational texts of Buddhism, I recognized how Shantideva was providing an amazing commentary and expansion of seminal early Buddhist concepts.

This led me to further explore the key meditations of equalizing and exchanging self and other. By turning to several modern interpretations of these practices, and contemplating them, I have come better to understand the monstrous glob of self-centeredness that is so deeply entrenched in my heart; and I am cognizant of the fact that it will take an enormous ongoing effort to dislodge it and remove it. I noted that just sending thoughts of loving kindness or compassion to all beings in all directions was not very effective for me. It was going to take a stronger meditation weapon. I have come to realize that my strong self-cherishing stems from my journey itself. The unpopular changes in monastic and religious traditions that I made met with formidable objection and I received no support to follow my inclination. Thus, I had to build a sturdy fortress around me to protect the inner guide I trusted more than anyone else. That was the theory I have come up with. In any case, I have become aware of the need to give far more attention to reducing and eventually eliminating completely my self-centeredness and lack of consideration for the position—and suffering—of others.

The brilliant verses of Shantideva's seminal text as well as the related topic of generating aspiration *bodhicitta*, the mind of enlightenment (for the benefit of all sentient beings), have empowered me to dig deep and begin at least to make some slight indentation in the muck of self-cherishing. Several times a day, for the first part of my meditation period, I contemplate on the equal status of myself and all other beings, how we are all trapped in suffering caused by our deep-seeded ignorance and delusion. I am attempting to deepen my understanding of the suffering of others—physical, mental, spiritual—so that it is not just on the superficial level. I am trying to actually *know* it and *feel* it.

I have also returned to practicing the powerful Tibetan meditation, *tonglen*, which I had first been introduced to in my days with NKT. In this visualization practice, I take on all the suffering, pain, and negative karma of others (all sentient beings) and in return give them all my happiness and welfare. In just a short time, I have noticed a lightness in my heart and often experience moments of mild rapture as I engage in these compassion meditations. I also try to repeat throughout the day my aspiration to work for the benefit of all sentient beings by seeking enlightenment.

I have realized that I need the Mahayana teachings on compassion to give me the momentum and force to take on this extremely formidable internal battle. Together with the Early Buddhist teachings on non-self—that nothing, including "me," has inherent, independent existence—I hope in the coming years continuously to peel away the unascertainable layers of self-centeredness and self-cherishing that have accumulated over innumerable lifetimes. Although I am a Theravada monk, I feel I am not betraying the tradition into which I have been re-ordained by taking on some of the later Mahayana teachings and meditation practices. While they are not *directly* from the Buddha, in that he did not speak them, I have clearly recognized that these teachings are based on and are derived from those in the Pali canon. And if and when I feel ready and am sure about my aspiration, I will voluntarily observe the vows of the *Bodhisattva*.

I have sharpened the focus of my goal and see now that it is not to reach a transcendent state of bliss, similar to what can be experienced on hallucinogenic drugs, but rather to attain an un-imaginable, un-dramatic, un-spectacular peaceful abiding in the here and now world with the unshakeable wisdom that *knows* definitively how things exist in reality. And the complete extinguishing of the "I" concept. With this wisdom it will be impossible to intentionally harm another living being with body, speech, or mind. For compassion and wisdom are inextricably linked in one who has attained this goal. I know I am far from attaining this mode of being but, at last, I have a clearer view of what it is I am seeking and the best way to realize it.

In the course of writing this narrative of my spiritual journey, attempting to describe the unstable chameleon-like sense of "I" who has tread this eclectic path, I have come to see the key Buddhist concept of impermanence in action, so to speak. One identity after another unfolded during the course of nearly fifty years: Ananda Marga yogi > San Francisco poet/New Wave dancer > Expatriate writer > jazz club manager > English professor and literary scholar > Tibetan Buddhist lay practitioner > Tibetan Buddhist novice monk > Thai Forest Buddhist monk > Benedictine novice > Greek Orthodox monastic > Orthodox Jew > Buddhist lay man > Buddhist monk. Even the Buddhist monk I am today is far different from the one I was in England thirteen years ago, despite both falling within the category of Theravada

Buddhism. I search for a stable "I" within this chain of identities—and even within one particular identity—but cannot articulate it. Yet I discern an underlying impulse, a karmic stream that I *can* put an interior finger on. I observe a relentless quest for clarity, for understanding how best to make use of this precious human life. And this indefatigable motivation has indeed been a constant force through each identity instantiation.

Here in Minnesota, the trees are beginning their annual kaleidoscopic display of brilliant color. The dying process never appears more beautiful than in the autumn landscape. And every day as I walk in the countryside, I see and absorb nature's profound teaching on impermanence. I know my journey is far from over, but the focus of my goal, though ever in movement, has become sharper and clearer. I believe that my spiritual vision, while not 20-20, is closer to that level of clarity than it was fifty…forty…thirty…twenty…ten…one year ago. I hope from the depths of my heart that I will not waver and one day make the commitment to carry on and not rest until I have attained enlightenment for the benefit of all beings!

AFTERWORD

Viewing the overall trajectory of the spiritual path I have tread, I see the detours and diversions I have taken as inherently part of the journey. Each proved necessary at that point in time. And even when the awareness that I was on a spiritual quest faded from my daily consciousness, as it did during my eleven years in Europe, it nevertheless popped up occasionally as a reminder that I had not completely fallen off the path. Experiencing pleasures, sorrows, transcendent moments, and frustrations in the "world" were all indeed components of my journey though unacknowledged at the time.

    I believe I have gained much from my lived experiences of different religious traditions. During the years I spent at St. Gregory Palamas Monastery, I not only became acquainted with the psychologically astute writings of the ascetic desert fathers, attempting to put the teachings into practice, but also found in Orthodox Christian monastic life the supporting conditions to deepen my relationship with God. The verse that always resonated with me was Deuteronomy 6:5 from the Old Testament, which is spoken by Jesus in all three synoptic gospels in response to being asked what the greatest commandment was: "You shall love the Lord your God with all your heart, with all your soul, and with all your might." When hearing these lines read as I did quite often during the eight years I spent at this

Greek Orthodox monastery, ardor always welled up within me. And when I stood in my cell, clandestinely clad in a *tallis*, I repeated this verse in Hebrew—and the effect was even more potent. For uttering it re-connected me with my Jewish roots which I had come to realize were the undergirding of my present life. Though I eventually distanced myself from a theistic spiritual path, for ten years I wholeheartedly directed love and devotion to the Unborn, the Unconditioned, a transcendent power I could not conceive in my rational mind. During this time I truly yearned for communion with Divinity. And by my ongoing engagement in mystical and spiritual practices, I gradually developed an intimate—albeit tenuous—relationship with God through Jesus Christ. I embraced a devotional aspect to spirituality that I had resisted when I was with Ananda Marga. At that time, I couldn't feel total devotion, I couldn't surrender myself to a human being—even an exceptional one—but in the years I spent in Christian monasteries and for several months afterward, I was able to surrender my "self," or as much of it as I was capable of doing, to the Ultimate.

As a result of such a "detour" I have gained greater respect for, and have recognized the value of, all religions in which dedicated practitioners give their full effort to living a life characterized by non-harming of others and attempting to be a better, kinder, more loving human being. My lived experience of different religious and monastic traditions has also resulted in a greater appreciation for various forms of sacred space, whether a church, a monastery, a meditation temple, or a synagogue. Part of my journey has been informed by a search for—and a dwelling in—a sanctified space conducive for allowing the heart-mind to dive deep within and soar upward into the sacred silence, the lingering air of meditative prayer expressed by countless spiritual seekers of the past.

Through the course of following the path upon which my heart was leading me, on several occasions I felt prompted to make a major change to another religious and/or monastic tradition without actually having been to a monastery of that tradition. Each time I relied on the instinct that arose from deep within me, a guide that I trusted. I received no outside counsel since I had no one to turn to. It was my solo decision. I encourage others who may find themselves in a situation, particularly regarding a spiritual direction, that if they become aware of a deeply felt instinct that their present situation is not working or if they feel that it has served its purpose but is no longer the right environment or teachings, they should listen to their inner voice. But, of course, one needs to be at least fairly sure of its trustworthiness. Many of us change over time and so do our spiritual needs. Our understanding of what we are seeking may alter or become more fine-tuned with age and experience. From my experience, I can honestly say, "don't be afraid to make a change."

Having re-viewed my spiritual journey as I sought to describe it on these pages, I am brimming over with gratitude particularly to those who made it possible for me to enter monastic life. Firstly, I am grateful to His Holiness the Dalai Lama and the late Lama Zopa Rinpoche for opening up the door to monastic life. It was while practicing in the Tibetan tradition that I first felt the strong call to renounce lay life and devote myself completely to following the Buddhist path as a monastic. I recall how inspired I was by the Western monastics I had met, and the teachings that so moved me to make this commitment, that I effortlessly gave up my hard-earned academic career and my life in

NYC—both which might have been envied. I know it was my karma that led me to do this and I also believe it is my karma that has recently led me back to the Tibetan teachings on compassion and generating *bodhicitta*, the mind of enlightenment. The causes and conditions have evidently ripened for me to take this step as a Theravada monk of the earliest Buddhist tradition.

I also give appreciative thanks to Ajahn Sucitto and Ajahn Sumedho, who ushered me into Theravada Thai Forest monastic life as a *samanera* and bhikkhu, respectively. That I was among the last to have Ajahn Sumedho as my preceptor adds to my gratitude. I do not overlook the abbots in the Christian monasteries who also showed such warmth and kindness, welcoming a recent convert into the fold. Lastly, I am grateful that at the age of 69, Bhante Ariyadhammika gave me the opportunity—very rare especially at a Western or international monastery—to join for the second time the ancient community of bhikkhus.

Reflecting on the five different names I have received during the course of my monastic journey, I see a progression, apparent only in hindsight. Marking my entrance into monastic life as a Tibetan *getsul* (novice monk), His Holiness the Dalai Lama conferred on me the rather uncommon name, Lamten (holder of the Path). I later received the name, Chandako (one with zeal [for the Dhamma/Teachings]) when ordained as a Theravada *samanera* (novice) and continuing with this name as a bhikkhu. Thus, I needed zeal in order to properly "hold" the Teachings of the Path—a great responsibility. My prolonged detour into Christian monastic life provided me with two names closely associated with early Christian monasticism. As a Benedictine novice, I was Br. Cassian, named after the influential fifth-century composer of a set of instructions for monks living in communities (rather than as hermits). And as a monk in the Greek Orthodox tradition, I became Fr. Savas. My patron saint, also living in the fifth century, was the builder of a network of monasteries in the Judean desert, one of which, Mar Saba, I had the opportunity to visit. The compulsion that drew me to leave Amaravati Monastery in order to continue as a Benedictine (and later Greek Orthodox) monastic was, in part, a quest to live among a closely-knit brotherhood of monks who endeavored to support one another in the spiritual life. My dedication to the life of a monk was, I believe, fortified by the two inspiring saints after whom I was named. Finally, my re-ordination as a bhikkhu has refocused my attention on my initial name. For it is only with knowledge—true experiential knowledge—of the Buddha's Dispensation that I can progress along the Path, determining to "hold" the Teachings in my mind-stream for my benefit and for that of others. I have thus come to see coherency in the seemingly incoherent monastic journey I have travelled.

I do not try to imagine what enlightenment is like because it is impossible to do so with my current deluded mind. Engaging in such an activity is only another hindrance. My realistic goal-in-progress, to be realized every day and throughout the day, is developing profound awareness of the impermanence, suffering, and non-self of everything I encounter in the "outside" world and also the one "inside." Nothing short of *yathabhutam*, the Pali term for seeing things as they truly are. My practical every day goal is to chip away at the hindrances, working on an increasingly more subtle level, and by doing so fully live my goal-in-progress.

My spiritual path seems to have been circular in that I have "returned" to Buddhism, where, with only an inchoate understanding of it, I began my journey nearly a half century ago in Ithaca, New York. But I have come to see it more like a spiral, recalling the Orthodox Christian idea of *epektasis*, "perpetual progress," whereby one forever stretches out towards God in an unending ascent. While I am not ascending toward God per se, my journey seems to be a perpetual "ascent" towards enlightenment. Yet I maintain the hope that I may one day, maybe in a far-off eon, actually reach the goal.

Once back on U.S. soil, I had initially thought that my spiritual journey had stalled. But it has unexpectedly been recharged by my re-encounter with the Tibetan Mahayana teachings and practices on developing profound compassion to complement my continued study and practice of the early Buddhist teachings. The words of the prayer we recited every day during the monastic training program in Dharamsala take on an even greater power and meaning for me now:

> To the Buddha I dedicate this body and life
> And in devotion I will walk the Buddha's Path of Awakening
> For me there is no other refuge, the Buddha is my excellent refuge,
> By the utterance of this truth, may I grow in the Master's way,
> By my devotion to the Buddha, and the blessings of this practice, —
> By its power, may all obstacles be overcome.

These words resonate differently now than they did more than fifteen years ago. For the profound experiences I had during the years I embraced Christianity and later Judaism have made me aware of the crucial need for self-surrendering devotion and faith not in a God-like Buddha but rather in the transcendent ideal of Buddhahood and my commitment to attain it in order to help relieve the existential suffering of all sentient beings as well as my own. May my ardor and perseverance not slip on the obstacles I will continue to face along the Buddha's Path of Awakening. By the power of my aspiration, may I not lose heart and give up but rather continue with unabated determination to achieve my goal. Amen.

www.ingramcontent.com/pod-product-compliance
Lightning Source LLC
LaVergne TN
LVHW011943060526
838201LV00061B/4195